Rhinegold Study Guides

A Student's Guide to A2 Music

for the **Edexcel** Specification
2002–2005

by

Paul Terry and David Bowman

R·

Rhinegold Publishing Ltd
241 Shaftesbury Avenue
London WC2H 8TF
Telephone: 020 7333 1721
www.rhinegold.co.uk

Rhinegold Study Guides
(series editor: Paul Terry)

A Student's Guide to GCSE Music for the AQA Specification
A Student's Guide to GCSE Music for the Edexcel Specification
A Student's Guide to GCSE Music for the OCR Specification

A Student's Guide to AS Music for the AQA Specification
A Student's Guide to AS Music for the Edexcel Specification
A Student's Guide to AS Music for the OCR Specification

A Student's Guide to A2 Music for the AQA Specification
A Student's Guide to A2 Music for the Edexcel Specification
A Student's Guide to A2 Music for the OCR Specification

A Student's Guide to AS/A2 Music Technology

Rhinegold Publishing also publishes Music Teacher, Classical Music, Opera Now, Piano, Early Music Today, The Singer, British and International Music Yearbook, Music Education Yearbook, British Performing Arts Yearbook, Rhinegold Dictionary of Music in Sound.

First published 2001 in Great Britain by
Rhinegold Publishing Limited
241 Shaftesbury Avenue
London WC2H 8TF
Tel: 020 7333 1721

© Rhinegold Publishing Limited 2001, reprinted 2002

All rights reserved. No part of this publication may be reproduced,
stored in a retrieval system, or transmitted in any form or by any means
electronic, mechanical, photocopying, recording or otherwise,
without the prior permission of Rhinegold Publishing Ltd.

This title is excluded from any licence issued by the Copyright Licensing Agency,
or other Reproduction Rights Organisation.

Rhinegold Publishing Limited has used its best efforts in preparing this guide.
It does not assume, and hereby disclaims any liability to any party
for loss or damage caused by errors or omissions in the Guide
whether such errors or omissions result
from negligence, accident or other cause.

You should always check the current requirements of the examination, since these may change.
Copies of the Edexcel Specification may be obtained from Edexcel Examinations at
Edexcel Publications, Adamsway, Mansfield, Notts. NG18 4FN
Telephone 01623 467467, Facsimile 01623 450481, Email publications@linneydirect.com
See also the Edexcel website at http://www.edexcel.org.uk/

A Student's Guide to A2 Music for the Edexcel Specification (2002–2005)
British Library Cataloguing in Publication Data.
A catalogue record for this book is available from the British Library.

ISBN 0-946890-95-1

Printed in Great Britain by Perfectaprint (UK) Ltd

*La musique exprime ce qui ne peut être dit
et sur quoi il est impossible de rester silencieux.*

*Music expresses that which can not be said
and on which it is impossible to be silent.*

Victor Hugo (1864)

Contents

Introduction		*page* 5
Performing and composing		7
Specialist option A: Composition portfolio		12
Specialist option B: Recital		23
Analysing music		25
Music for large ensemble	(2002 and 2003)	32
	(2004 and 2005)	41
20th-century art music	(2002 and 2003)	49
	(2004 and 2005)	58
Music for small ensemble	(2002 and 2003)	64
	(2004 and 2005)	72
Keyboard music	(2002 and 2003)	80
	(2004 and 2005)	88
Sacred vocal music	(2002 and 2003)	95
	(2004 and 2005)	102
Secular vocal music	(2002 and 2003)	111
	(2004 and 2005)	120
Music for film and television	(2002 and 2003)	127
	(2004 and 2005)	134
Popular music and jazz	(2002 and 2003)	139
	(2004 and 2005)	150
World music	(2002 and 2003)	159
	(2004 and 2005)	162

The authors

Paul Terry was director of music at the City of London Freemen's School for 15 years. He currently works as a music editor, engraver and publisher. He has been a music examiner for more than 20 years and has worked as a consultant to various examination boards. Paul has served as a member of the Secondary Examinations Council and its successor the Schools Examinations and Assessment Council. He was chief examiner for the Oxford and Cambridge Schools Examinations Board (now part of OCR) and he was a chief examiner for London Examinations (now part of Edexcel).

Paul Terry's publications include two books on aural for A-level music, and three *Student Guides to AS Music*, all written in collaboration with David Bowman (see below). He is series editor of, and a frequent contributor to, the *Study Area* section of *Music Teacher* magazine. He is also co-author with William Lloyd of *Music in Sequence, a complete guide to MIDI sequencing* (1991), *Classics in Sequence* (1992) and *Rock in Sequence* (1996), and also *Rehearse, Direct and Play: A Student's Guide to Group Music-Making* (1993), all published by Musonix/Music Sales.

David Bowman was for 20 years director of music at Ampleforth College where he still teaches. He was a chief examiner for the University of London Schools Examination Board (now Edexcel) from 1982 to 1998. He now spends more time with his family, horses and dogs.

David Bowman's publications include the *London Anthology of Music* (University of London Schools Examinations Board, 1986), *Sound Matters* (co-authored with Bruce Cole, Schott, 1989), *Aural Matters* (co-authored with Paul Terry, Schott, 1993), *Aural Matters in Practice* (co-authored with Paul Terry, Schott, 1994), *Analysis Matters* (Rhinegold, Volume 1 1997, Volume 2 1998), three *Student Guides to AS Music* (co-authored with Paul Terry, Rhinegold 2000 and 2001) and numerous analytical articles for *Music Teacher*. He is a contributor to the *Collins Classical Music Encyclopedia* (2000) edited by Stanley Sadie and author of the *Rhinegold Dictionary of Music in Sound*.

Acknowledgements

The authors would like to thank Dr Hugh Benham, chief examiner in music to Edexcel, for his expert advice so freely offered throughout the preparation of this book. Nevertheless if any errors have been made it is only right to state that these are the responsibility of the authors. We would also like to thank Dr Lucien Jenkins of Rhinegold Publishing for so much help and encouragement in the preparation of this latest addition to the series of Rhinegold Study Guides.

Introduction

This book is intended to assist students preparing for the Edexcel A2 Music examination. Like other *Rhinegold Study Guides* it is intended to supplement, but not supplant, the work of teachers.

The full Advanced GCE in Music is made up of six units, three AS and three A2. This book deals only with the latter.

We have included many suggestions and tips which we hope will help you do well in performing and composing, but the main emphasis is on preparation for the paper in *Analysing music*. As part of this unit you will be extending your knowledge of **one** of the areas of study that you covered for AS *and* you will also be working on **one new** area of study.

The basic information for each of the areas of study is given in **A Student's Guide to AS Music for the Edexcel Specification** and we have not repeated those details here, so you will need to refer to the AS guide during your A2 studies.

A Student's Guide to AS Music for the Edexcel Specification (2001–2004) by Paul Terry and David Bowman. *Rhinegold Publishing Ltd.* ISBN: 0-946890-90-0.

In this book each of the chapters dealing with an area of study concentrates on the topics of 'continuity and change' and 'special focus' works that are prescribed for study in the A2 exam. The questions during the course of these chapters will help you check your understanding of the context, style and technical features of the music – they are not intended to be representative of actual exam questions. If you have difficulty with these, you will generally find the right answers by rereading the preceding pages. The sample questions in these chapters are more demanding and these should be worked under examination conditions. For examples of the questions that are likely to be encountered in the exam, you should be guided by the specimen papers and (when they become available) past papers published by Edexcel.

A glossary of technical terms is given at the end of the AS guide. If you need further help with terminology you encounter during the course, we recommend you consult **The Rhinegold Dictionary of Music in Sound**. This comprehensive resource not only gives detailed explanations of a wide range of musical concepts, but it also illustrates them using a large number of examples on a set of accompanying CDs.

The Rhinegold Dictionary of Music in Sound by David Bowman. *Rhinegold Publishing Ltd.* ISBN: 0-946890-87-0.

Planning is the secret of success. Initial ideas for composing are best formulated early in the course and plans for performing need to get under way as soon as possible. Preparation for the *Analysing music* unit needs to be completed in time to allow for revision and the working of complete papers in the weeks before the actual exam.

Remember that it will help enormously if you can perceive the many varied connections between the music you hear, the music you play and the music you compose. Understanding the context and structure of music will not only enhance your enjoyment when listening, but will also inform your performing and illuminate your composing. Composing, performing, listening and understanding are all related aspects of the study of music, and this integration of activities is fundamental to the Advanced GCE in Music.

Warning. Photocopying any part of this book without permission is illegal.

A2 Music

There are three units: *Performing and composing*, *Specialist options* and *Analysing music*. The first two of these each account for 30% of the total A2 mark, while the third is weighted at 40%.

Performing and composing

There are two parts to the *Performing and composing* unit, both of which build on work you undertook for AS music:

+ an assessment of your performing during the course. For this you will need to keep a log of the pieces you have performed and then choose the best four for assessment (you must include at least one solo piece and at least one ensemble item). The work will be assessed by your teacher and the mark moderated by Edexcel (for moderation purposes a recording of one **solo** piece of performing during the course is required).

+ a timed test in compositional techniques, marked by an Edexcel examiner. For this part you will work in greater depth on **one** of the compositional techniques you studied for AS

Specialist options

You must choose one of two different pathways through this unit, both of which are marked by an Edexcel examiner:

+ **either** you will have to write two compositions (together lasting at least six minutes) each based on a different topic from a given list; one of these must be on the same topic you chose for AS

+ **or** you will have to perform a 20-minute recital of music, which will be recorded for assessment purposes.

Analysing music

For the *Analysing music* unit there are two separate assessments, both marked by an Edexcel examiner:

+ a listening paper, consisting of three questions on music on a CD that you can play as many times as you wish within the 45 minutes allowed for the test; the music will be selected from a wide variety of styles

+ a two-hour written paper based on questions about **two** areas of study you have prepared from the *New Anthology of Music*, an unmarked copy of which you may use for reference in the exam.

The *New Anthology of Music* is published by Peters Edition Ltd, ISBN: 1-901507-03-3 (CDs, ISBN: 1-901507-04-1), and is available from Edexcel publications (see page 2) or all good music retailers.

The details of the specification are correct at the time of going to press, but you and your teachers should always check current requirements for the examination with Edexcel as these may change.

Key Skills

Key Skills are becoming increasingly important for success at work, entry into higher education and for making the most of everyday life. A2 Music offers a number of opportunities for you to develop your knowledge and understanding in five of the six Key Skills: Communication, Information Technology, Working with Others, Improving own Learning and Performance, and Problem Solving. You are therefore recommended to discuss with your teachers the ways in which the work you undertake for A2 Music might also be used as evidence for your acquisition and development of skills for these Key Skills units at Level 3.

Warning. Photocopying any part of this book without permission is illegal.

Performing and composing

1. Performing during the course

This section accounts for 50% of the marks for the *Performing and composing* unit. Like the similar component in AS Music it offers an excellent opportunity for you to receive credit for the performing you do during the course. This needs careful planning and record-keeping, and you need to meet all of the following requirements:

- you must submit four *different* pieces for assessment; these must not include any items that you offered for AS Music nor, if you are opting for performing as your *Specialist option*, any piece that you present in your recital
- at least one of the four pieces must be a solo
- at least one of the four pieces must be an ensemble item
- performances must be completed in time for your submission to reach the examiner by 15 May in the exam year
- one solo item must be recorded for moderation purposes
- your teacher must have been present for at least three of the four performances.

To be sure of meeting all these requirements it is going to be essential to make your plans at the start of the A2 course and to discuss with your teacher the practicalities of the last two points above. Remember that there may be little time to arrange performances at the start of the summer term in the exam year.

You can include a performance in which you were the director or conductor of an ensemble, but you may submit only one such piece. In this part of the exam you are allowed to include performances that encompass improvisation if you wish.

The combined length of the four pieces you submit must be at least 7–8 minutes, but there is no maximum time limit. The difficulty of the music is taken into account in assessment and is expected to equate with grade 6 standard (your teacher will help explain what this means if you do not take graded exams). The mark scheme allows credit if the music is of a higher standard. Although the highest marks are not available if the pieces are below grade 6 in level of difficulty, you will probably get a much better mark if you choose music that is well within your capabilities rather than pieces that are so hard that they will cause you to struggle and perhaps even break down in performance. When choosing pieces remember that, while accuracy is expected, the majority of the marks at this level are awarded for your **interpretation** of the music.

The performances can be given in class to your fellow students, or they may include events such as lunchtime concerts, rock gigs, music festivals or concert tours – but remember that your teacher must be present for at least three of the performances you submit. You may include playing on any instrument or singing, but marks are awarded for quality and not variety, so there is no advantage in including music on instruments that you don't play well.

> **Warning.** Photocopying any part of this book without permission is illegal.

There must be an audience at the performances, even if it is only a couple of people, and for that reason you are not allowed to include performances given at music exams or auditions in which there is no audience in the normal sense of the word. However you can include exam and audition pieces if you perform them on some more open occasion.

Ensemble performances can be of many different kinds – piano duets, wind trios, string quartets, jazz bands, rock groups, choirs or orchestras. However a piece in which you are the one dominant performer throughout does not count as an ensemble. Thus in a piece for flute with piano accompaniment the flautist cannot submit the work as an ensemble item, although the accompanying pianist can. When choosing ensemble performances to include on your list, remember that the work will need to be assessed – this may be difficult if it is a piece in which you have played a very minor role in a large ensemble.

Some advice on solo performing is given later in this guide, as part of the section on the recital. A useful handbook which will give you many ideas for getting the best out of ensemble performing of all kinds is:

Music Sales Ltd, Newmarket Road,
Bury St Edmunds, Suffolk IP33 3YB.
Telephone: 01284 702600;
fax: 01284 768301
http://www.musicroom.com/

Rehearse, Direct and Play by William Lloyd and Paul Terry. *Musonix Publishing*, 1993. ISBN: 0-9517214-3-7.
Available from Music Sales Ltd. (Order No. MX 30053, £4.95)

Keeping a performance diary

You will need to keep your own diary of performances, which should include the following information:

- the precise title of the work you performed and the movement(s) performed if it was not complete

- the name of the composer

- a note of whether it was a solo or ensemble item

- the nature of the occasion (such as a lunchtime recital, a rock concert, an arts festival, etc)

- the role in which you participated (such as flute in wind trio, second trumpet in county youth orchestra of 80 players, bass guitar in rock group, one of 12 altos in choir of 60, etc)

- the date and whether it was an internal event at your centre or an external event that occurred elsewhere.

Remember that you will need a recording of one of the solo items which you submit, and a photocopy of your part in the piece.

By early May in your exam year you will have to select the four best pieces from your diary, in accordance with the requirements listed on the previous page, and transfer the details to a log form provided by Edexcel. When you do this be careful not to include the same piece more than once, and do not include any pieces that you offered for assessment in your AS Music examination or that your perform in your recital (if you have chosen this as your *Specialist option* for A2 Music).

Warning. Photocopying any part of this book without permission is illegal.

2. Compositional techniques

This section accounts for the remaining 50% of the marks for the *Performing and composing* unit.

You have to continue and extend your study of the same techniques topic that you chose for AS Music. You will be required to sit a timed exam paper in which you will have to complete an exercise in your chosen technique. During the exam you will be allowed access to a musical instrument and/or music-technology equipment (but not to any written notes or other reference materials).

The exercise to be undertaken will be related to the coursework you did for AS Music, but it will be more demanding, not only because it must be completed as a timed test but also because you will be required to supply more music in your answer.

The table below shows the choice of topics. Remember that you must choose just **one** technique, and it must be one of those that you chose for AS. The table also summarises how the requirements at A2 differ from those you undertook for AS Music.

Compositional technique	AS coursework	A2 exam
A1 Baroque counterpoint Complete an upper part to a given figured bass	12–16 bars	18–24 bars
A2 Minimalism Complete a given opening to make a piece lasting about one minute	For keyboard	For three melody instruments
B1 Bach chorale Add three lower parts to a chorale	Harmonise the cadences only	Harmonise the whole passage
B2 32-bar popular song Realise the middle-eight and turnaround	Add a bass part from given chord symbols	Add chord symbols and a bass part
C1 Renaissance counterpoint Add a part to two given parts	8–10 bars	12–16 bars
C2 Serialism Extend a given opening	For solo instrument, about 12 bars in length	For two instruments, about 20 bars in length
D1 Extended instrumental techniques Develop one of two given openings to make a one-minute piece which exploits: vocal contrast, prepared piano, woodwind chords, glissandi or vocalising through the instrument	Exploit one of the listed techniques in your piece	Exploit two of the listed techniques in your piece
D2 Electro-acoustic music Record a given ostinato, then add material to make a piece lasting about one minute which exploits: envelope shaping, filtering, pitch shifting, sampled sounds, reversing or looping.	Add one track and employ one of the listed processes in your piece	Add one or two tracks and employ two of the listed processes in your piece

In the case of electro-acoustic music you are required to submit a recording as well as some form of notation (not necessarily a score). You will be allowed time to set up the equipment and to record the given ostinato outside the timed part of the examination.

> **Warning.** Photocopying any part of this book without permission is illegal.

We have given some general guidance on the various options below. Your teacher will explain to you the specific techniques required, since these are very detailed and vary greatly between options, but in all cases it is important to listen to (and study, and preferably perform) examples of the music concerned. In addition, aim to practise working plenty of examples and, most important of all, try to learn from any mistakes you might make in those workings.

Baroque counterpoint

Useful books on this topic include **Bach: Chorale Harmonization and Instrumental Counterpoint** by Malcolm Boyd, published by *Kahn and Averill*, ISBN: 1-871082-72-2, and **A Practical Approach to Eighteenth-century Counterpoint** by Robert Gauldin, published by *Waveland Press* (USA), ISBN: 0-88133-853-2.

You will be required to complete an upper part to fit with a given figured bass in the style of Corelli, Handel or their contemporaries. The passage will be 18–24 bars in length. It is likely that the music will include modulations and you may be expected to find opportunities to use imitation and develop the given melodic material. In addition to the harmony you encountered when studying for AS music (first and second inversions, 7ths, 9–8 and 4–3 suspensions and accidentals) the passage may contain the following figuring: $^6_5$, $^4_3$, $^4_2$ and 7–6. Remember that stylistically appropriate melodic decoration is important, that leading notes and 7ths must be correctly treated, and that you must check for consecutives. It will be useful to study (and perhaps play) some of Bach's two-part inventions, Corelli's violin sonatas and Handel's flute sonatas.

Minimalism

You will be required to complete a given opening to make a piece for three melody instruments lasting one minute. Be prepared to use both treble and bass clefs. If you use a MIDI workstation for the task remember that you must nevertheless write for acoustic instruments, taking into account their ranges, characteristics and practicalities in performance. As the required length is only one minute it will not be practical for ideas to unfold slowly, as often happens in this style. Try to study some of the early works of the 'New York minimalists' listed on page 19. Note how, when motifs are shifted out of phase with one another (as occurs in *NAM 12*) new patterns arise from the resulting combination, and notice the free use of unprepared dissonance in this style of music.

Bach chorales

Useful books for this topic include **Bach: Chorale Harmonization and Instrumental Counterpoint** by Malcolm Boyd, published by *Kahn and Averill*, ISBN: 1-871082-72-2 and the examples of Bach's own harmonisations in **Bach: 371 Harmonized Chorales**, edited by Riemenschneider, published by *Schirmer / Music Sales*.

You will be required to add three lower parts to a given chorale melody, in the style of Bach. Revise your AS work for this topic, since the correct harmonisation of cadences is essential to the style. Much of the rest of the harmony can often be established by working progressively backwards from the cadences. Examiners will be looking for strong bass lines, good spacing of parts, the use of quaver passing notes and suspensions. Check your work thoroughly for inappropriate use of second inversions and forbidden consecutives.

32-bar popular song

A useful general resource for this topic is **Songwriting: a complete guide to the craft** by Stephen Citron, *Hodder and Stoughton*, ISBN: 0-340-48872-7. Citron's recent study of **Stephen Sondheim and Andrew Lloyd Webber: The New Musical** is published by *Oxford University Press* (USA) ISBN: 0-19-509601-0. Most useful of all is to make a study of the harmony in some of the many AABA forms in albums of songs by Cole Porter, Irving Berlin, Jerome Kern, George Gershwin, Richard Rodgers, and in collections of jazz and pop standards.

You will be required to complete an AABA popular-song structure by writing a chord sequence **and** bass part for the 'middle eight' (the B section). Your chords should contrast with the given harmony of the A section and should introduce one or more passing modulations to keys such as IV, ii, iii or vi (more remote keys may be appropriate in some styles). You should end with a turnaround that prepares for the return of the A section in the tonic key. The bass part should include passing notes and appropriate licks and fills. The examiners are likely to be more impressed with a strong and stylish use of a wide harmonic vocabulary (including secondary dominants and other chromatic chords) rather than memorised stock chord progressions that are poorly suited to the context.

You will be required to add a part to two given parts, in a late-16th century style. The passage will be 12–16 bars in length and may be either sacred or secular vocal polyphony. You need to remember that control of dissonance is a key feature (including 4ths with the bass), and that the sharpened leading-note will be required in most cadences. Remember to spend time trying to find natural points for imitative entries. Aim for correct underlay of the text, with stressed syllables usually falling on accented beats.

You will be provided with a note row, from which you must construct a piece for two instruments of about 20 bars in length. In addition to using the four basic versions of the row (which you should identify with the letters O, I, R and RI above the staves) you should look out for the opportunity to exploit patterns such as hexachords and trichords in the given material, and to use more advanced techniques such as rotation. Examiners will look for a musical result with melodic shape, idiomatic instrumental writing and a sense of style (note that at A2 the given material may determine the style, such as a specific dance or a jazz style).

As at AS you will be required to develop one of two given openings to make a one-minute piece, but at A2 your composition will have to use **two** of the techniques listed on page 9. You can employ both techniques in a work for a solo performer, or you could write for two or more performers and use the techniques in different parts. Whichever you choose, you must identify in the score which techniques you have employed. Your piece must be performable and you should also give a full explanation in the score of how the techniques are to be realised. The examiners will be looking to see how well your use of the techniques integrates with the musical intentions of the piece, so you should avoid writing music which is merely a study or experiment in the use of technical effects.

As at AS you will be required to record a given ostinato which you must loop or repeat to produce the basis of a one-minute piece. To this you must add one or two tracks which feature **two** of the processes listed on page 9. Your added material could be derived from the given ostinato, or it may be entirely new. It can be either electronic or acoustic, but if you use any pre-existing samples you must identify these and credit their source. The examiners will be looking for a good sense of balance, a clear stereo image and full use of the audible frequency range, as well as appropriate organisation of your musical ideas. For this topic your work should be submitted as a recording, but you should also include written documentation (a computer-printed score, graphic notation, track diagram, table or flow chart) that includes a description of the processes you have used.

What the examiners look for

Whichever topic you choose, examiners will award marks for:

- a clear and accurate presentation of your score (or recording)
- an outcome that is creative, musical and which responds to the demands of the question
- an awareness of style and a fluent use of technical procedures
- a coherent and controlled use of structure in your work

Renaissance counterpoint

A useful reference book for this topic is **Modal Counterpoint, Renaissance Style** by Peter Schubert. *Oxford University Press.* ISBN: 0-19-510912-0.

Serialism

Useful books for this topic include **Serial Composition and Atonality** by George Perle. *University of California Press*, ISBN: 0-520-22921-5, and **Serial Composition** by Reginald Smith Brindle, *Oxford University Press*, ISBN: 0-19-311906-4.

Extended instrumental techniques

Useful works to study for this topic include *NAM 10, 11* and *40*. See also *Stripsody* by Cathy Berberian, an excerpt of which can be found in *Sound Matters* (Bowman and Cole), and *Eight Songs for A Mad King* by Peter Maxwell Davies. The latter includes a wide range of extended techniques for all its performers.

Electro-acoustic music

> Warning. Photocopying any part of this book without permission is illegal.

Specialist option A: Composition portfolio

You must choose one of two different pathways through the unit entitled *Specialist option*, depending on whether you want to focus on composing or performing. Turn to page 23 for the latter.

For Pathway A you have to write **two compositions**, based on two different topics from the following list. One of your topics must be **the same one that you chose for unit 2 in AS Music**.

- Variations
- Romantic miniatures
- Neo-classicism
- Post-modernism
- The popular song
- Club dance and hip hop
- Fusions
- Film and television
- Music theatre

The score should be appropriate to the style of the music. It may be fully notated, a lead-sheet, a track sheet or an annotated diagram.

The two compositions together must last at least six minutes. You have to present both works as scores **and** in recorded format. You will also have to submit a short written description of each piece. Your work must reach the examiner by **15 May** in the exam year.

Planning

Start planning your compositions early in the course, as you will need plenty of time to develop initial ideas, make preliminary sketches and try these out in performance before you even start on the final scores and recordings.

You will first need to decide on the resources you are going to use. Be realistic in what you have time to achieve. While it may be tempting to write for an orchestra, band or large choir, this will require a lot of work and it may prove impossible to get the necessary resources together when needed. It is usually better to write for people who will be available to work with you during the whole composing process, such as the other students in your group or people with whom you regularly rehearse and perform.

You could write for just a solo instrument, especially if it is a harmony instrument such as the piano or guitar, but at this level it is good to be a little more ambitious, and two or three players will give you much more flexibilty and textural variety. Consider combinations such as piano duet (either two pianos, or two players on one piano), piano with solo instrument or voice, acoustic guitar and flute, as well as trios or quartets of various kinds.

As we recommended in the AS Guide, start by discussing with your performers how the characteristics of their instruments and/or voices can best be exploited. Try to identify the skills (and weaknesses) of each performer so that you can use their individual strengths in your composing. Discuss what sort of things are easy and what are difficult for each instrument or voice, and try some improvising both separately and together.

Warning. Photocopying any part of this book without permission is illegal.

Research

Begin by investigating some of the existing music in your chosen topic area. You may find examples in the music you play as well as in the *New Anthology*, but you will also need to investigate what can be found in libraries and in music and recordings that you may be allowed to borrow from your teacher or music department. Aim to make a **detailed** study of several examples that differ in style, mood and resources, and make notes on:

- **Melody** – is there a melody line? If so, what makes it distinctive or memorable? What role does rhythm, particularly rests and repeated notes, play in its construction? Does it have a point of climax? Is the melody regularly phrased? Is it developed? Is it formed from smaller motifs and are these developed separately? How is the melodic material distributed around the various performing resources? Is there any contrapuntal interest?

- **Accompaniment** – is there a distinct accompaniment or do all the parts have equal melodic interest? Does the accompaniment possess musical interest of its own? Is there rhythmic variety in the accompaniment? Does it have a strong bass line? What role does the accompaniment have when there is less interest in the main melody? What role is played by repeated notes and rests in the accompaniment?

- **Structure** – how is the music given shape? How much repetition is there? Is it varied repetition? How much contrast? Do areas of contrast sound as if they are part of the same piece? Why? Are changes of key used to provide areas of contrast? How are these established? Are there distinct sections in the piece? If so, how are they linked? How does the piece begin? How does it end?

- **Texture** – how are different textures used to provide variety? How are the voices and/or instruments exploited? How do changes in texture contribute to climaxes in the music? What use is made of different tone colours within various textures?

In addition, make a note of any useful **techniques** that relate to your chosen topic and try to identify any potential problem areas that you could encounter in your own composition. You will soon begin to accumulate a store of information that will be enormously helpful in planning your own work.

While it is possible to start a composition at bar 1 and gradually work through to the end, you will find your task easier if you first plan out the structure and main events, leaving the detail to be sketched in later. This also makes it easy, if you get stuck, to leave the current section and try out some ideas for later in the piece.

Musical style

Compositions may be in any style that is appropriate to the topic you choose, but you will want to show the best you can do, so it is probably best to opt for a format that will allow you to use a variety of textures and techniques. If you adopt a style that is exceptionally repetitive or very slow-moving it may be advisable to write a relatively long work so that you can achieve some variety and a sense of development in your composing.

Whichever topic you choose, note that you are **not** expected to write in the style of a specific composer. For instance, if you decide to compose a romantic miniature you are not required to write in the style of Chopin or Schumann – you might decide on a modern interpretation of this genre. Similarly, variations are not expected to be realised in the style of Bach or Mozart – you may want to write jazz variations or an electro-acoustic piece in a modern crossover style that uses a ground bass formed from a tape loop.

The topics simply provide you with broad guidelines, which you should interpret imaginatively, and we have suggested some ideas to help you with this later in the chapter. However your two compositions should be in different styles – you should not, for example, write two similar songs for a musical and submit one as a popular song and the other as music theatre.

Information technology

You may find it useful to use a MIDI workstation to develop your compositions, but unless your work is intended only for electronic realisation (as may be the case with club dance and some types of film music) reread the advice on pages 13–14 of the AS Guide, paying particular attention to the notes about computer-generated scores. Don't become so engrossed with the technology that you neglect the composition, and remember that music technology will not give you feedback on the practicality (or enjoyability) of your music that you can expect from live performers.

Developing the brief

Painters often begin with a number of preliminary pencil or charcoal sketches, sometimes followed by some drafts in watercolour, before starting work on the final canvas. A similar procedure can work well for composing. Improvising, either alone or in a group, can be a good start. Each student could contribute a variation to a given theme, or all could arrange a given passage for the ensemble each intends to use in their own compositions.

More specific exercises may involve your trying several alternative sketches for key features of your piece – such as different layouts for the opening, a central climax, or a complex contrapuntal section. You may want to experiment with different voicings in the scoring, or provide alternative treatments for a passage that is technically difficult. Once drafted in rough, ideas for short sections can be tested at the piano or MIDI workstation, and then trialled in performance workshop sessions. Record these for later playback and analysis, noting if some sections seem to flag, fail to cohere, are unplayable, or do not achieve the effect you desire.

Reread pages 16–17 of the AS Guide, noting the following points:

+ Aim to **balance unity and diversity** in your work. Too much repetition will lead to a lack of variety, but too much new material will prevent the piece hanging together. Use your research to suggest ways in which ideas can be transformed, adapted and developed, so there is a sense of moving forward during the work and a sense of completion when it ends. Pay particular attention to ends of phrases and sections, where the music can easily lose its impetus. Explore your musical ideas in depth, exploiting the potential of individual motifs, not just manipulating complete tunes, and experiment with unusual changes of key and more complex types of structure. Watch out carefully for unwanted predictability, such as too many four-bar phrases in succession or rondo/chorus structures in which it is all too obvious where the theme will come round yet again.

- Remember that **variety of texture is essential** for success. All parts should be musically interesting and ideally all should play a leading role at some point in the piece. Use instruments or voices in different parts of their ranges, and remember that rests are more valuable than notes in providing changes in texture. Check that you have contrasts in dynamics and articulation, and ensure that accompanying parts are rhythmically interesting. Remember that long melodies can often be split into shorter motifs that can be assigned to different parts within the texture, and that a counter-melody or some short contrapuntal motifs can add interest to the repetition of a section. Plan points of tension and areas of relaxation carefully, using changes in texture, dynamics and articulation to heighten their contrast.

- Plan your schedule to allow time for testing in performance and subsequent refinement of ideas, before embarking on the final recording and neat copy of the score. Unsatisfactory sections may need to be replaced, and the work as a whole polished. Sometimes a work can get totally stuck, and if this happens you may need time to start afresh on something new.

Presentation

Reread pages 14–15 of the AS Guide and use the composition checklist on page 15 to ensure that you haven't missed anything. If you submit a lead-sheet or chord chart instead of a score, note that it must contain **all** significant cues and performing directions. Similarly, track sheets must include **full** details of the processing you used. For each of the two compositions you will have to submit a score (which may be a lead-sheet or track list if appropriate to the musical style), a recording and a structured commentary which will require answers to the following questions:

- How does your composition relate to the chosen topic?
- What musical resources have you used?
- What is the form or structure of the piece?
- What improvements were made in the process of composition?

Use the commentary to make your intentions clear to the examiner. It is not necessary to explain how you discovered the dominant 7th, or how you mislaid your computer disk and had to start again. Nor should you write a programme note about the piece. However you should draw the examiner's attention to any points about the piece that you feel are important and identify any material you have used that is not original (such as lyrics, samples, or someone else's theme on which you have written variations).

Composition topics

Variations

Listed below are just a few of the more accessible works that use variation form. Aim to make a *thorough* study of about five works, selected from different periods.

Variations for solo instruments

Bach's *Passacaglia in C minor* for organ, *Goldberg* variations and Chaconne from the *Partita in D minor* for unaccompanied violin. Mozart's Piano sonata in A, K331 (first movement) – his complete piano variations are also available. Haydn's *Variations in F minor*, Beethoven's *33 Variations on a Waltz by Diabelli* and Schubert's *Impromptu in B♭* (Op. 142 No. 3). Chopin's *Variations brillantes* (Op. 12), Mendelssohn's *Variations sérieuses* (Op. 54) and Brahms' *Variations and Fugue on a theme by Handel* (Op. 24). Ives' *Variations on 'America'* and Webern's *Variations* (Op. 27). Also look out for CDs of 19th-century virtuoso piano music, such as **The Earl Wild Collection** (*Vanguard* OVC 4033) which includes a number of works based on variation technique.

> Excerpts from Bach's Chaconne in D minor, Brahms' *Variations on a Theme of Handel* and other works in variation form can be found in *The Rhinegold Dictionary of Music in Sound*. The third movement of Webern's Variations appears in *Sound Matters* (Bowman and Cole).

Variations for small ensembles

Pachelbel's *Kanon* (a canon over a ground bass), Purcell's *Chacony in G minor* (for strings) and various ground-bass arias (see *left*). Mozart's Duo for Violin and Viola in B♭, K.424 (last movement), his piano trios in G, K.496 (last movement) and K.564 (second movement) and Clarinet Quintet, K.581 (last movement). Haydn's *Emperor* quartet (second movement). Beethoven's *Harp* quartet (last movement) and his Piano trio in B♭, Op. 11 (third movement). Schubert's *Death and the Maiden* quartet (second movement) and *Trout* quintet (fourth movement). Mendelssohn's *Variations concertantes* for cello and piano. Stravinsky's Octet (second movement).

> Ground-bass arias by Purcell can be found in *NAM 36*, *Aural Matters* (Bowman and Terry, *Sound Matters* (Bowman and Cole) and *The Rhinegold Dictionary of Music in Sound* (A75).
>
> The slow movement (theme and variations) of Haydn's String Quartet in B♭, Op.9 No.5, can be found in *Sound Matters* (Bowman and Cole). Excerpts from the variations in Haydn's *Emperor* quartet can be found in *The Rhinegold Dictionary of Music in Sound*.

Orchestral variations

The second movements of Haydn's symphonies Nos. 94 (*Surprise*) and 103 (*Drumroll*). Mozart's piano concertos in B♭ (second movement) K.450, and in G (third movement) K.453. Brahms' *Variations on a theme by J Haydn* (also for piano duet) and the last movement of his symphony No. 4 in E minor (a passacaglia). Tchaikovsky's *Variations on a Rococco Theme* (for cello and orchestra). Reger's *Variations and Fugue on a Theme of Mozart* (based on K.331 above). Richard Strauss's *Don Quixote*. Elgar's *Enigma* variations. Schoenberg's *Variations for Orchestra*. Dohnányi's *Variations on a Nursery Tune* (for piano and orchestra). Vaughan Williams' *Five Variants of Dives and Lazarus*. Britten's *A Young Person's Guide to the Orchestra* (subtitled *Variations and Fugue on a Theme of Purcell*). Walton's *Variations on a Theme of Hindemith*. Lloyd Webber's *Variations* (compare with Rachmaninov's *Rhapsody on a Theme of Paganini*).

When you study (and hopefully perform) some of these pieces, note how the theme is constructed and harmonised, as well as how the entire work is structured. Many sets of variations build up tension by using increasingly complex figuration as they proceed. Some provide contrast with a slow and/or minor-key variation before an exciting finale (which may be less clearly asssociated with the theme). Some end with a short coda which refreshingly refers back to the theme in its original form.

> **Warning.** Photocopying any part of this book without permission is illegal.

Notice how most themes are simple and based on strong chord patterns – these usually offer the greatest potential for exploitation in the ensuing variations. Make detailed notes on the types of variation used and the differing moods that these can create. The methods employed may include any of the following (often two or more of these techniques will be used simultaneously):

- elaborating the melody with many types of decoration
- redistributing the notes of the melody between different hands (in piano music) or between different instruments
- changing the harmony and/or tonality
- altering the rhythm, metre or tempo (or a combination of these)
- fragmenting the theme
- developing a new theme from the fragments
- reusing the harmony but creating a new melody above it
- treating the theme contrapuntally by using imitation or adding a counter-melody.

If you decide to adopt a theme-and-variations structure, consider whether you want to write your own theme, or use an existing one. Composition will be more straightfoward if the theme has a clear melodic outline and strong harmonic structure. You could instead use a freer variation structure (such as a fantasia on a theme) or a tighter one (such as a ground bass or chaconne), although the latter can be a much harder format within which to work.

Double themes and variations were frequently used by Haydn. For example, in the slow movement of his *Drumroll* symphony a theme in C minor is followed by one in C major, and this pair of themes is then varied in each of the following sections. Explore ways in which you can vary the often predictable variation plan. The slow movement of Stravinsky's Octet repeats the first variation as a sort of rondo after some of the later variations, and ends with a repeat of the theme, giving the form $A-A^1-A^2-A^1-A^3-A^4-A^1-A$.

Aim to include a range of variation techniques, not just different embellishments of the melody line, and if you are working in a tonal idiom, plan how you will achieve variety of key – it is all too easy for sets of variations to get stuck in one key with little or no modulation. Beethoven avoided this as early as 1802 in his *Six Variations* (Op. 34). The theme is in F major and the variations fall in thirds through D, B♭, G, E♭, C minor and back to F major.

Decide whether your variations are going to proceed in discrete sections or if you are going to link them into a through-composed format, like the free variations on a double theme which form the foundation of Richard Strauss's tone poem, *Don Quixote*. This work is of a type known as 'character variations' – each variation portrays one of the fantastical adventures of the hapless old knight. Similarly, each of Elgar's *Enigma* variations portrays the character of one of the composer's friends. Perhaps there might be an idea here for a set of variations characterising your own friends or emotions, or perhaps reflecting various favourite places you have visited.

Finally, remember that variation technique pervades many types of music – it is fundamental in serial music, jazz improvisation, the Indian *rāg* and in the simultaneous variation of gamelan music.

Warning. Photocopying any part of this book without permission is illegal.

Romantic miniatures

A 'romantic miniature' could be a song, a dance form such as a waltz or short ballet movement, an entirely abstract piece (eg a prelude, intermezzo or impromptu) or a 'character piece' that aims to suggest a specific idea, such as a mood, person or place. You could write a piece in the form of a study for your instrument, but studies often concentrate on just one technique, which may make it difficult for you to show a range of skills in composing.

NAM 23 consists of three miniatures from Kinderscenen by Schumann. See also NAM 24 (Debussy) and NAM 39 (Fauré). Romantic miniatures in the Rhinegold Dictionary of Music in Sound include works by Chopin, Mendelssohn's Venetian Gondola Song, an excerpt from Liszt's La Lugubre Gondola I, a waltz from Grieg's New Lyric Pieces, the Trepak from Tchaikovsky's The Nutcracker and extracts from Préludes by Debussy and from Saint-Saëns' Carnival of the Animals.

Romantic miniatures can be found in many instrumental teaching books and in collections of graded exam pieces. Some of the well-known collections for piano include Schubert's *Moments musicaux*, Mendelssohn's *Songs without Words*, Chopin's preludes, nocturnes, waltzes and mazurkas, Grieg's *Lyric Pieces* and *Poetic Tone Pictures*, and the various cycles of short piano pieces by Schumann, such as *Papillons*, *Carnaval*, the *Davidsbündler* dances, the *Album for the Young* and *Kinderscenen*. In addition, there are many attractive works in this genre by minor composers such as Burgmüller, Fibich, Gurlitt, Karganoff, John Field and others.

The character piece proved enduringly popular, so there are many examples from later 19th-century composers such as Tchaikovsky, Borodin, Cui, Dvořák and Smetana. Remember that you are not necessarily expected to compose in a romantic style. Debussy's *Préludes*, Kabalevsky's *24 Pieces for Children*, or Bartók's shorter piano pieces (such as those in *For Children* and *Mikrokosmos*) will reveal how 20th-century composers re-interpreted this genre.

If you are writing for solo instrument with piano or small ensemble, look out for some of the popular arrangements and encore pieces such as Elgar's *Salut d'amour*, *Chanson de matin* and *Chanson de nuit*, Raff's *Cavatina*, Massanet's *Méditation* from *Thaïs*, Monti's *Czardas* and Dvořák's *Humoresque*. If you want to work on a more ambitious scale, look at movements from Grieg's *Holberg* and *Peer Gynt* suites, Dag Wiren's *Serenade for Strings*, movements from Saint-Saëns' *Carnival of the Animals* and the individual dances in Tchaikovsky's ballet scores, such as the 'characteristic dances' from *The Nutcracker*. Singers should remember that German *Lieder* and 19th-century French *chansons* are essentially types of romantic miniature, as are such popular art songs as Tchaikovsky's 'None but the lonely heart' and Dvořák's 'Songs my mother taught me'.

From this wealth of material you should be able to deduce that the romantic miniature is short, focused on a single musical idea and usually memorably melodic, all ingredients that make for easy listening. Note the forms used, which are often quite basic (binary, rounded binary or ternary) perhaps with a short introduction and coda. It may be difficult to sustain your own piece for three minutes or more with such simple forms, so look carefully at what happens in longer works. You could, if necessary, write a matching pair of movements, perhaps both based on the same theme.

Notice that while some works in this genre have abstract titles, such as prelude or 'album leaf', others specify the style of the piece (march, waltz, song without words) and still others (such as those in *NAM 23*) suggest very specific images. You can use whatever is appropriate to your own work, but try to make the title relevant to the musical content.

Warning. Photocopying any part of this book without permission is illegal.

Although melody is important, you should notice that harmony is often quite luxurient. Try to analyse why. You should spot that chromatic chords such as secondary dominants and diminished 7ths are often used, and tertiary modulations (shifts to a key a 3rd away, such as G to E♭) are employed to give an exotic effect. Notice how dissonances are created by lingering on non-harmonic notes and by using long appoggiaturas, often with resolutions that are so brief that they seem almost to be an after-thought.

Neo-classicism

Three movements from Stravinsky's *Pulcinella* suite are printed in *NAM 7* – try to listen to the rest of the suite or the original ballet score. Stravinsky arranged some of these movements for violin and piano in his *Suite Italienne* (also available for cello and piano) – this version would be particularly useful for study. Other well-known neo-classical works by Stravinsky include *The Soldier's Tale*, the concerto for piano and winds, Symphony in C, *Oedipus Rex* (modelled on the baroque oratorio) and *The Rake's Progress*.

The *Bransle Simple* from Stravinksy's neo-classic ballet *Agon*, is included in *Sound Matters* (Bowman and Cole) No.42.

Works by other composers include Prokofiev's *Classical* symphony (try to hear at least the third movement, which is a modern gavotte), Hindemith's *Ludus Tonalis* for piano, and Satie's *Sonatine bureau-cratique* (a satiric paraphrase of a classical piece by Clementi). The clear textures of neo-classicism can be found in the work of a number of other early 20th-century composers, including Bartók (Dance suite for orchestra), Poulenc (see *NAM 19*) and Shostakovich (*NAM 25*).

The *Rhinegold Dictionary of Music in Sound* includes an extract from Ravel's *Le Tombeau de Couperin* (C33) – compare it with the extract of a Forlane by Couperin (C32) in the same publication.

Your own piece could take the form of a sonatina, a contrapuntal form such as a trio sonata or fugue, or perhaps some linked dance movements, using pre-1800 dance forms interpreted in a bitonal idiom. While it is possible to base your work on existing music, this technique was quite rare among the neo-classicists – the only other work by Stravinsky which does so is *The Fairy's Kiss*, in which he reworked compositions by Tchaikovsky.

Post-modernism

A good starting point for research is the early work of the 'New York minimalists': *In C* (Terry Riley), *Music in Similar Motion*, *Music in Fifths* and *Another Look at Harmony* (Philip Glass), *Phase Patterns* and *Drumming* (Steve Reich). An excerpt from Reich's *Clapping Music* is included in the *Rhinegold Dictionary of Music in Sound* (C89) and his *New York Counterpoint* is in *NAM* (No. 12).

Other post-modernist music in the *Rhinegold Dictionary of Music in Sound* includes extracts from the music of Giles Swayne (C91), Sylvie Bodorová (C96) and James MacMillan (C97).

Look out for larger-scale works such as Stockhausen's *Stimmung*, and *Harmonium* (1981) and *Harmonielehre* (1985), both by John Adams. Certain post-modernist pieces became immensely popular in the closing years of the 20th century, particularly Henryk Górecki's third symphony, *Short Ride in a Fast Machine* by John Adams, and the works of Arvo Pärt and John Tavener (both influenced by the mystical style of Eastern Orthodox church music). Tavener's *The Lamb* is in *NAM* (No. 32) and an excerpt from his much earlier *Ultimos Ritos* can be found in the old London Anthology, No. 119. Look out also for his cello concerto (called *The Protecting Veil*) and *Song for Athene*.

Because musical change tends to occur over a long time span in minimalist music, you will need to consider how you can show a range of skills if you choose this style – it may be necessary to write

Warning. Photocopying any part of this book without permission is illegal.

a piece rather longer than the minimum requirement. In addition to art music (choral works, instrumental pieces, etc.) you could choose other formats in which a contemporary musical style is appropriate – educational pieces that might incorporate parts for children, music intended for a sound installation (eg music for a science exhibition or a virtual-reality experience) or a suite of music for a computer-games program (splash-screen music, mood music to underline fear, safety, excitement and aggression, location music for different levels of the game, and so forth). If you are tempted by this last category, remember the need for consistency (a 'brand image') across separate items, be sure to include some more extended pieces as well as shorter looped tracks, try to avoid items that are purely sound effects, and concentrate **on the music** as CD-ROMs, artwork or videos are not required. However you can submit your work on tape, CD or minidisk, accompanying it with explanatory diagrams or a flow chart.

The popular song

You could write a song with accompaniment for piano or guitar, or a more elaborate setting that includes backing vocals, rock group, jazz band or even orchestral parts. Any style is acceptable (including folk, jazz, soul, reggae, as well as contemporary styles) but remember that you will need to show a good range of skills within a single composition, so try to avoid types of music in which there is much repetition and little variety. Your song will be expected to feature a vocal line (the lyrics of which will not be assessed). You are permitted to submit your work as a lead-sheet, but the accompaniment must be fully worked out on the recording. Aim for a strong bass line, and remember that you will be expected to show imagination in your choice of chords and modulations, and in the musical detail you assign to backing instruments. Aim for an interesting structure, perhaps with varied treatment of verses and choruses, a middle section in a more remote key, and additional sections such as an intro, an instrumental bridge and a coda. Consider how these might be unified through the use of a hook line or common chord pattern. Pay attention to stylish licks and fills, and aim for some variety when writing drum patterns.

There are many songs for you to study in the popular music and jazz section of the *New Anthology*, and in the jazz and pop section of *Sound Matters* (Bowman and Cole). However most pop music is published in easy arrangements for voice and piano/guitar, and this format does not form a good model for study as too much important detail is missing. Instead look out for the detailed transcriptions that are published in the *Rock Scores* series by Music Sales and in the *Off the Record* series from IMP, as well as collections such as *Beatles: The Complete Scores* (Music Sales).

There are also detailed scores of 17 classic hits from the 1950s to the 1990s, with hints on sequencing, in *Rock in Sequence* (Lloyd and Terry), published by Music Sales.

Club dance and hip hop

At first sight this topic may appear rather confusing: hip hop developed in 1970s New York as a cultural movement of the urban ghetto, in which music (and specifically rap) is only one element. Club dance music, on the other hand, can encompass a broad range of music that may include anything from 'golden oldy' tracks by Abba and Queen, through house, techno, trance, garage, jungle and Nu-NRG to eclectic mixes by that night's DJ. In Britain, hip hop became popular in the early 1980s, quickly being adopted by the strong club scene. This commercial, dance-orientated style (which has been disparagingly called trip-hop) tends to avoid the violent subject matter and frank language sometimes found in rap itself.

However the intention here is to give you the opportunity to submit modern dance music and not to limit you to one particular style. It is likely that your work will include tightly sequenced rhythms, carefully set at the appropriate speed (bpm) for the intended dance style, and it may well include samples of pre-recorded material. You may choose to include a vocal part, either sung or rapped, or you may prefer to write a purely instrumental dance track.

Research will need to be mainly by ear from existing recordings, since this type of music is not normally notated, although magazines and web sites on hip hop may be useful. You may wish to produce a score of your own piece but this is not necessarily expected – a good-quality recording plus a fully annotated track diagram showing the processes used will be fine. Note that it is essential to identify all samples used in your recording.

Your composition should show variety in its use of textures and drum patterns, so you should be sure to adopt a style in which this is possible. Work at this level should be ambitious in structure, with a variety of well-balanced tracks and an imaginative use of sampled sounds, perhaps modified by various effects processes, in order to achieve a rich mix of stylish material.

Fusions

Here again there is the opportunity to work in any one of a huge range of styles, the essential requirement being that the music draws on different cultural traditions, combining elements from both to produce a distinctive style of its own. Originally the term fusion was applied to the rock-influenced jazz style adopted by Miles Davis in the late 1960s, and taken up by groups such as Weather Report. Other types of fusion popular at this time included folk-rock, the latin-based rock of Carlos Santana, the art-rock interpretations of classical music by Emerson, Lake and Palmer, and the vocal jazz arrangements of Bach performed by the Swingle Singers.

Recent decades have witnessed a still greater range of fusion styles, including bhangra, salsa and celtic rock. Indeed, many multicultural pop styles can be seen as a type of fusion, arising from the influence of western pop music on local cultural traditions. In addition there has been further exploration of the ground between pop- and art-music styles in the work of cross-over artists such as Steve Martland and John Casken. It might also be useful to explore some earlier examples of the use of popular styles in art music, such as Debussy's *Golliwogg's Cakewalk*, Satie's *Parade*, Walton's *Façade*, Stravinsky's *Ragtime* for 11 instruments and the use of popular idioms in the music of Maxwell Davies.

Casken's *Piper's Linn* and Martland's *The World is in Heaven* appear in *Sound Matters* (Bowman and Cole). Martland's *Principia* and folk-rock from Steeleye Span can be found in *Aural Matters* (Bowman and Terry). Both these books also include examples of world music that may be useful for this topic. *The Rhinegold Dictionary of Music in Sound* includes excerpts from Debussy's *Golliwogg's Cakewalk* and the *Popular Song* from Walton's *Façade*.

Your work may be in any appropriate form, but it should exploit the idea of fusion and draw on appropriate elements from the different styles and idioms involved.

Film and television

The *New Anthology* provides one of the most useful sources of research material for this topic. There are also a number of books and websites about film music composition. Themes from many famous films are available as sheet music, but such publications are usually simplified arrangements for piano, and thus omit many important details, and they seldom include more than the main title theme so they are unlikely to be very helpful. However it would be useful to look out for scores and CDs of the following works, which are all based on film music: Prokofiev's *Suite from Lieutenant Kijé*, Walton's *Henry V Suite*, Copland's *Our Town Suite* and Vaughan Williams' Symphony No. 7 (based on his music for the film *Scott of the Antartic*).

Your own music could be for an existing film or video, an imaginary one, or perhaps one that is being made by other students at your school or college. You may submit your work as a recording dubbed on video if you wish, but this is not required – a clear account of the image that the music is intended to underscore is sufficient.

The subject could be historical (possibly giving the opportunity for some pastiche of an old musical style), a travelogue such as a video of a school foreign trip (perhaps including local musical styles to give a sense of location to the various scenes), a cartoon, a sports sequence or an extended commercial. Try to choose a topic with some dramatic content as this is likely to give you the opportunity for some interesting and vivid contrasts in your music.

It is acceptable to submit several short extracts for this topic – perhaps a title theme, a piece of illustrative music, various link passages (eg bridges that are designed to change mood) and a sequence for the final credits. Try to maintain a consistent style in such a submission and, if appropriate, link the sections thematically. Aim to convey a clear sense of mood, paying attention to the way music is used in the visual media to heighten and release emotional tension, as well as to create atmosphere. This will need careful attention to scoring.

Music theatre

For exam purposes this topic covers any type of music that involves a staged element in its presentation and so includes opera, operetta, ballet, musicals, and rock opera, as well as the type of small-scale, semi-staged work in which the instrumentalists frequently take a dramatic role and which is often specifically described as music theatre. This last category includes works such as Stravinsky's *The Soldier's Tale*, Schoenberg's *Pierrot Lunaire* (which is often staged), Britten's church parables, such as *Curlew River*, and Peter Maxwell Davies' *Eight Songs for a Mad King* and *Vesalii icones*.

One of the songs from Pierrot Lunaire is in NAM (No. 40) and an extract from another is in The Rhinegold Dictionary of Sound. An excerpt from Vesalii Icones can be found in Sound Matters (Bowman and Cole).

Your own composition could be a short section of a musical or other music-theatre work, perhaps including a vocal introduction, a solo or duet, and ending with a dance number or a finale in which you could combine several voices and a chorus. It is not essential to score the accompaniment for full orchestra – you could confine yourself to a piano reduction (as used in rehearsals) or you could write for just a small ensemble of accompanying instruments. You could instead choose to write purely instrumental music designed for a dramatic work, such as an overture, music for a contemporary dance production, or incidental music for a play.

Choose a subject that will give you the opportunity to show a dramatic quality in your music, and a sense of theatre. A slow, dreamy ballad might be part of the submission, but it would be best to include some points of tension and conflict as well.

Specialist option B: Recital

If you choose pathway B for the specialist option, you will have to perform a solo recital instead of submitting the composition folio described on pages 12–15.

Requirements

You will need to plan a program that lasts at least 20 minutes. The minimum size of audience is two (your teacher and one other person) but you may feel that performing to such a small group seems more like an exam than a recital. Some people find that a class concert presented to a group of friends and fellow students is more natural, and provides a good focus for the preparatory work involved, but the occasion can be on any scale, including a lunch-time or evening concert at your school or college, or a gig at a public venue. Note, though, the requirements that your teacher must be present and that the recital must be recorded, so you need to discuss the proposed occasion with your teacher.

Any music that you play which is intended to be accompanied must be performed with accompaniment. This can be provided by a keyboard instrument, a group of other performers, or by a tape or electronic backing. It is important that you should feature clearly in a solo capacity in any ensemble pieces you choose to include, such as jazz improvisations or rock numbers. Remember that the examiners need to hear and assess only your part, and not the playing of other musicians.

If you are at all unsure if a particular piece would be regarded as a solo, check with your A level teacher, since Edexcel provides guidance on this matter.

You can include just selected movements from longer works if you wish, and if there are long sections in which only the accompaniment plays (as may occur in a concerto) these can be curtailed. But in other respects the music must be complete – you should not omit sections that you find too difficult.

You may use more than one instrument in your recital. For example trumpeters may wish to include a piece for cornet or flugelhorn, or perhaps a baroque piece for trumpet in D. Similarly a recorder player may wish to include works for both descant and treble instruments, and percussionists should certainly plan to show their skills on a range of both pitched and unpitched instruments.

Note that there are no marks for diversity. For example, if you are primarily a singer who can also manage a bit of piano playing, there is nothing to be gained by including an easy piano piece – it would be better to concentrate on achieving a high standard in your vocal repertoire. If you do play a second instrument to the same standard as your main study, the music for that instrument should be chosen with regard to achieving a coherent overall program.

Difficulty level

The technical difficulty of the music you choose also needs careful consideration. Easy pieces played musically are much more likely to be successful than difficult pieces marred by hesitations and breakdowns. In order to be able to achieve the highest marks the pieces need to be of grade 6 standard or higher (if you do not take graded exams your teacher will help explain what this means). If the majority of works are at grade 7 standard (or higher) your mark will be scaled up accordingly. There is no need to struggle to reach

Warning. Photocopying any part of this book without permission is illegal.

a high difficulty level (and risk a potential disaster if it proves too hard) since you will be given credit for what you can do with the music you offer, but you should be capable of presenting a recital in which all of the pieces are at least of grade 5 standard if you choose this option. If the pieces are below grade 6 in standard, or if the recital is less than 20 minutes in length, your mark will be scaled down.

Whatever your technical standard it is better to choose music that you can perform with confidence than to attempt a difficult work which stretches your technique to its limit. Works that are too demanding will leave no leeway for the inevitable nervousness that *will* arise under the conditions of a live assessment. The anxiety and tension they generate will be communicated to the listener, and will inevitably impede your musical interpretation.

Choice of music

The minimum 20 minutes length for the recital can include time for applause and any brief spoken introductions you choose to make. Audiences greatly appreciate the latter – it provides a moment of human contact rather than just seeing you sneak on and off without apparent awareness of others in the room. However keep to a short announcement of the work and perhaps a word or two about your reaction to the piece – such as why you enjoy performing it. Avoid a lecture about its date and form, and try to be positive – if you sound miserable and scared, your audience will be, too.

Choose pieces that you enjoy playing and that allow you to show a range of skills. Note that you must not include any items you offered for AS Music, or that you performed during the course as part of the *Performing and composing* unit. A surprising number of pieces, whether single-movement classical works or pop songs, are only about three minutes in length, so make sure that you have enough repertoire to last at least 20 minutes.

A programme with some variety is likely to serve you best. Your audience (and that includes your examiner) are likely to be more impressed by items which vary in style, mood and speed than a succession of all-too-similar slow movements. Try to start with something that grabs the attention, but that is not necessarily too difficult, such as a baroque allegro, or a lively electric-guitar solo. Alternate slow pieces with more lively items, and try to end with something destined to get the audience still wanting more – a humorous modern work or a hard-rock number.

Also remember to pace yourself carefully. Don't start with the most challenging work – if it goes wrong, your nerves may be shattered for the following items. Plan some items for the middle where you can relax a bit, such as an expressive slow movement or a lazy blues. This is especially important if you are a wind player or singer as you will need the opportunity to recover your breath and/or lip. Note that the recital can consist of a single long work, such as a concerto or song cycle, since this will by its very nature include the necessary variety for both performer and audience.

Preparation, performance and assessment

Reread the advice on pages 10–11 of the AS Guide, noting the importance of performing the complete programme in advance to someone who can give you some dispassionate feedback. Adequate rehearsal with the accompanist (if applicable) is vital, and a run-through in the final venue is essential.

You are required to provide programme notes on a form supplied by Edexcel. Mention the characteristics of each piece and how you intend to convey them, and also give reasons for your choice and order of items. After the event you can, if you wish, add a comment about the extent to which your intentions were realised in the recital. Note that the examiner will require photocopies of your solo part(s) as well as a recording of the event and programme notes.

Warning. Photocopying any part of this book without permission is illegal.

Analysing music

There are two parts to this unit:

+ a 45-minute listening test that accounts for just under 40% of the marks for this unit

+ a two-hour written paper that accounts for just over 60% of the marks for this unit.

1. Listening test

The test is presented on CD and you will be given your own copy of this CD which you are allowed to play as many times as you wish in the 45 minutes allowed. Each extract is recorded only once, so you will need to be familiar with the controls of your CD player in order to locate and repeat individual tracks efficiently; you will also need to pace yourself carefully so that you have time to answer all three questions in the test.

1. You will hear **three** different passages of music for which no notation is given. For each passage you will have to give a context for the music by answering questions on matters such as its style (eg baroque, minimalist, jazz, etc), its genre (eg anthem, opera, 12-bar blues, etc) and any prominent elements (eg atonality, irregular metre, etc). You will be asked to suggest a date of composition and to name a person (composer or performer) likely to be associated with the music. — **Context**

2. You will hear **two** excerpts of music for which no notation is given. You will have to answer questions on the similarities and differences between the two excerpts in matters such as instrumentation, shared material, technique, style and so forth. The two extracts may be from different parts of the same piece or they may be from two different pieces by the same composer or band, that are related in style. Note that there may well be more differences than similarities, and that you may also be asked to identify the type(s) of music, and how they are related. — **Comparison**

3. You will hear **one** excerpt of music for which a two-stave skeleton score will be provided. There will be three questions on pitch and rhythm, of which you must answer two: — **General test of aural perception**

    (a) three short rhythms or melodies will be printed, and you must locate where in the score each of these is heard
    (b) you will be asked to notate the rhythm of a specific short passage heard on the CD
    (c) you will be asked to notate the pitches of a specific short melody heard on the CD (the rhythm will be given).

    In addition you will have to answer two further questions:

    (d) you will have to identify four specific keys, key relationships, chords or chord progressions in the music
    (e) you will have to write a short commentary on important features of the music that you can hear in the recording (and that are not obvious from the score or covered in the preceding questions) and place the extract in context.

Warning. Photocopying any part of this book without permission is illegal.

I, II, IV, V (root position or first inversion)
III and VI (root position only)
VII in first inversion
V^7 in root position or any inversion
Ic, II^{7}b, diminished 7th
augmented 6th, Neapolitan 6th.

Bass part played by bassoon.
Opening phrase repeated octave higher.
Second section develops the opening motif.
Ascending chromatic scale in third section, followed by oboe and flute in dialogue.
Dominant pedal prepares for the recap.
Flute imitates clarinet near the end.
Homophonic texture in the coda.

The following books, all of which come with CDs, contain many short extracts of music that are useful for listening practice:

Aural Matters (Bowman and Terry). *Schott and Co Ltd*. ISBN: 0-946535-22-1.

Aural Matters in Practice (Bowman and Terry). *Schott and Co Ltd*. ISBN: 0-946535-23-X.

Sound Matters (Bowman and Cole). *Schott and Co. Ltd*. ISBN: 0-946535-14-0.

The Rhinegold Dictionary of Music in Sound (Bowman). *Rhinegold Publishing*. ISBN: 0-946890-87-0. This also includes a chapter on 'Style, genre and historical context' that will help you identify these concepts with the aid of many recorded examples.

In 3(d) questions on tonality will require you to identify specific keys, and they may involve recognising the following simple key relationships: dominant, subdominant, relative minor/major, and tonic major/minor (eg a change from C major to C minor, or vice versa). Questions on chords may involve identifying any of the chords listed left. Questions on chord progressions might include recognising the standard types of cadence, the circle of 5ths, and patterns such as V–I, I–V, IV–I, I–IV and V–VI.

In question 3(e) you will be asked to mention significant features of the music that are not immediately obvious from the skeleton score and that have not been identified in the other questions on this extract. You can answer in note form or continuous prose. You are likely to get one mark for each accurate point, so if eight marks are available you should aim to make eight points about the music. If you refer to specific events in the music you should give their location. For instance you should write 'imitation between flute and clarinet near the end' – not just the single word 'imitation'. An example of a successful type of answer is shown *left*.

If you include a general point about the impact of the music, make sure it is justified with evidence. For instance, you might state that 'a jolly mood is created by the major tonality, frequent cadences and lively articulation'. Just saying that it sounds happy, without giving reasons, will not be rewarded with a mark.

None of the music extracts in the listening test are linked to any particular area of study, so you are likely to encounter music which will be unfamiliar. In order to gain confidence in answering questions on identification it will be essential to listen to a wide range of music and to practise recognising its main features.

Beware of jumping to conclusions too quickly. For example the presence of a harpsichord in orchestral music might seem an obvious clue that the music is baroque – but if the orchestra also includes horns then the extract might actually be early classical, perhaps from the period 1750–80, when the harpsichord was still in common use. You need to listen for further evidence – if the phrase lengths run mainly in clear four-bar periods and the textures often consist of a melody with subordinate accompaniment, early classical would seem likely. But if the texture is more contrapuntal, and the parts are formed from short motifs that are spun out into long melodic lines, then late baroque might seem more probable.

Similarly, remember that although church music might be sung by an unaccompanied choir, not all unaccompanied choral music is church music – it could be a madrigal or an excerpt from an opera, for instance. Get into the habit of tuning into a radio station such as Classic FM and trying to identify what you hear.

Your teacher will help you with practice materials (some are listed *left*), and you could also make your own listening tests by devising questions on a short extract from a piece that you play and could perform for the rest of the group to use as an aural test. You can also develop your own skills in dictation by writing down the rhythm and pitch of short melodic fragments you know by heart, and then checking the results by playing them on an instrument.

2. Written paper

For this part of the unit you must prepare **two** of the areas of study shown *right*. One of these **must be an area of study that you offered for AS Music**. For A2 you will extend your earlier work by:

a) studying a prescribed 'special focus' work (or works) from the area of study, **and**

b) investigating a topic of continuity and change that relates to the area of study as a whole.

Music for large ensemble
20th-century art music
Music for small ensemble
Keyboard music
Sacred vocal music
Secular vocal music
Music for film and television
Popular music and jazz
World music

Your other area of study must be one that you did **not** offer for AS Music. For this area of study you are required only to prepare a prescribed 'special focus' work (or works). You do not have to learn about the other works in the area of study.

The music for each of these areas of study is provided in the *New Anthology of Music* (referred to as *NAM* in the rest of this book) with recordings on a companion set of four CDs. You are expected to use an **unmarked** copy of the anthology in the exam.

In the examination you will have to answer five questions, four from Section A and one from Section B. The questions are arranged as follows:

Section A

There will be three questions on each of the 'special focus' works. You must answer **two** on the prescribed work(s) from the Area of Study that you also offered for AS Music **and two** on the prescribed work(s) from the new Area of Study that you chose for A2 Music.

Section B

There will be two questions on each Area of Study. You must choose to answer **one**, which must be on the Area of Study that you started for AS Music and have extended for A2.

There is no division of works into list A and list B, as there is for AS Music. For A2 you need to study all of the works that relate to the prescribed topic of continuity and change. However remember that you only study **one** such topic – the one set for the Area of Study that you began at AS and that will appear in Section B of the paper. For the other Area of Study, the one that you start specially for A2, the only requirement is to study the prescribed 'special focus' work(s).

Check that you are studying the right works

There is one set of prescribed works and topics for candidates taking A2 in summer 2002 or summer 2003, and a different set for those taking the exam in summer 2004 or summer 2005. In the rest of this guide we have indicated what you are expected to study with symbols such as those shown *right*.

| Special Focus Work for 2002 and 2003 |
| Topic for examination in 2004 and 2005 |

It will be obvious that the structure of this paper is quite complex, so be sure to double-check that you are studying the correct works (one for each area of study) and the right topic (just one, for the area of study you started at AS) for your own examination year.

| Warning. Photocopying any part of this book without permission is illegal. |

Preparation

Reread pages 21–23 of the AS Guide, noting the importance of focusing your studies on the music itself, not on peripheral matters such as learning biographies of composers or quotations of what other people have said about the pieces.

It is important that you have a clear understanding of technical terms relating to the music you study. Terminology is not an end in itself – it is merely a convenient way of explaining to other musicians precisely what you mean in as few words as possible. But remember that if you use technical terms incorrectly it will confuse rather than elucidate. We haven't included a glossary of terms in this guide, but you should refer to the glossary in the AS Guide if you encounter any term about which you are unsure. The most important thing is to be certain you know how the term relates to the sounds you hear – if you need further help, look up the word in the *Rhinegold Dictionary of Music in Sound*, play the example(s) on its associated CDs and check the notation in its set of scores.

For A2 it becomes increasingly necessary to listen to an extensive range of music, not only to prepare for the listening test but also to help you amplify your answers in the written paper. Try to make use of the holidays for this enjoyable task, remembering to listen for pleasure as well as for understanding.

The rest of this Guide consists of chapters on each Area of Study. These cover the information you are likely to need to know for the exam and sometimes include suggestions for additional listening and reading. During the course of each chapter there are a number of questions headed 'Private study' that are designed to help you check your understanding – these are not necessarily the type of question that you will encounter in the exam and in most cases the answers should be clear by carefully rereading the preceding paragraphs or the related section in the AS Guide. However at the end of each main section you will find a set of 'Sample questions' to give you some exam practice, particularly in your final weeks of revision. Some notes on how to revise effectively are given on pages 24–25 of the AS Guide.

> Remember that your revision plan needs to include rereading the introductory information on your Areas of Study given in the AS Guide, as well as a thorough reappraisal of your AS notes for the Area of Study that you are carrying through from AS to A2.

Exam technique

In Section A you will have to answer four questions – two on each of your 'special focus' works. Each of these four questions attracts 10 marks (out of a total of 60) and your answer can be written in continuous prose, or note form, or as a set of bullet points. A good rule of thumb is to reckon that there will be one mark for each valid point that you make. A 'valid point' is one that helps answer the question directly. Just stating a fact about the music will not gain a mark if it is irrelevant.

Support your points by making frequent references to the music, usually by means of bar numbers (eg 'a modulation to the dominant is confirmed by a perfect cadence in bars 13–14'). Be precise, adding the name of the part and/or the beat number(s) if necessary to avoid ambiguity. A widely understood method is to use small suffix numerals for beat numbers: for example, bar 4^3 means bar 4, beat 3. Be aware that giving detailed and relevant references to substantial points in this way can often gain you extra marks.

> **Warning.** Photocopying any part of this book without permission is illegal.

Make sure you answer the correct number of questions (four in Section A and one in Section B). Pace yourself carefully so that you are not rushed towards the end of the paper and that you have a few minutes to check your answers at the end of the exam. Choose your questions with care. Don't just dive in as soon as you happen to recognise the general gist of a question – first consider if you have enough knowledge to provide a really full answer.

For each of the four questions in Section A you are going to need to make 10 valid points in under 20 minutes. Although you have to answer only one question in Section B, it attracts 20 marks and must be written in continuous prose, as a short essay. It would therefore be wise to allow yourself 40 minutes to complete this question.

Essay writing

Developing a good clear style in writing prose will not only help your exam technique but will also prove useful in later life if you are required to write reports, evaluations or proposals. This takes practice, so it is important that you write essay answers (including some timed examples) during the course, as you work your way through your chosen specified topic.

The assessment will include your skill in written communication (which can gain you extra credit if it is good, and not just lose you marks if it is weak). If this is an area you find difficult, remember that one of the most useful tips listed below is to keep to short sentences. Make a point and then follow it up with an example (see the first essay on the next page). It will also help to make a brief plan of the essay, so you get an overview of all the points you wish to make, and can then arrange them in a logical order. Having to change tack in mid-essay in order to go back to some point you had previously forgotten can make your reasoning difficult to follow.

Nine tips for a good essay

- Make sure that you understand the requirements of the question.
- Plan the structure by making a note of the main areas to cover. It can be useful to devote one paragraph to each of these areas.
- Begin by immediately addressing the question – don't waste time trying to 'set the scene' with background information.
- Keep to the point. If you run out of ideas, it is better to examine the score carefully to see what you may have missed rather than to start introducing irrelevant facts.
- Try to support each one of your arguments with evidence from the music itself, given in the form of references to specific bar numbers.
- Avoid repetition. You don't get extra marks for making the same point twice, even if you clothe it in different language.
- You should normally stick to factual information – if a personal opinion is required remember that it (like all your arguments) should be supported by reference to specific examples in *NAM*.
- Avoid long sentences whenever possible.
- Aim for handwriting that is legible and unambiguous.

Many of the Section B questions require you to make a specific evaluation of the works you have studied – such questions often begin 'Compare and contrast ...' or 'To what extent does ... '. The examiners will be looking for a balanced argument in your answer: 'In these respects there are similarities ... but in these respects there are differences ...' Check that all your points relate to the question posed, since there is no credit for irrelevant information.

The ticks in these two examples show the type of points that are likely to be given credit, but they do not represent an official markscheme. In practice, the examiners will have agreed on a detailed markscheme for each question after an initial evaluation of a large number of answers.

As you can see from the example below, it is possible to cover a large number of points in a short essay if you are concise and stay focused on the question. When you look at this, and the essay on the next page, **remember that there is no one way of tackling a question – these are merely examples of different styles and neither represents a mythical 'right answer'.**

13a. *Compare the structures of the Sarabandes by Bach and Debussy*

Bach's Sarabande is in binary form,✓ typical of most baroque dances. The two sections are defined by their tonality.✓ The first ends in the dominant at bar 12.✓ The second is longer✓ and modulates more widely✓ before returning to the tonic at bar 29.✓ At this point there is a modified restatement of the opening material.✓ This is known as rounded✓ binary form.

The movement is based on a continuous development of the opening material.✓ For example, the sequence beginning in bar 5✓ is derived from the motif in bar 1✓ and the second section begins with a transposition of bars 1-2.✓

● Debussy's Sarabande is also in two sections of unequal length,✓ separated by a double bar-line in bar 22, although the sections are not repeated.✓ It also returns to the opening material in the second section (at bars 42).✓ But whereas Bach's Sarabande is monothematic, Debussy uses a variety of independent themes.✓ There are two in the first section (bars 1 and 9),✓ the first of which is repeated at bar 15.✓ He uses a new theme for the second section (bar 23)✓ and another new theme at bar 50.✓ Unlike Bach, he ends the movement with a coda, starting at bar 63.✓

● While Bach uses tonality to define the sections of his form, Debussy's melodies are modal and his harmonies are complex, using key more as a means of colour than as a way to define structure.✓

This is a first-rate answer which directly addresses the question by means of a valid point in every sentence. The structure is clear: the first half is devoted to Bach's Sarabande, the second to Debussy's, and comparisons are clarified in constructions such as 'Debussy's Sarabande also ...', 'But whereas Bach ...', and 'Unlike Bach ...'.

The short sentences are unambiguous and almost every point is backed-up with references to specific bar numbers in the music. The use of technical language is secure, and the concluding paragraph is perceptive, showing an understanding that it is tonality which defines structure in Bach's Sarabande, but not in Debussy's.

Now, can you see why the following answer is less successful than the first? It is the same length, but relevant points appear far less frequently and there are no references to specific bars in the music.

> 13a. **Compare the structures of the Sarabandes by Bach and Debussy**
>
> The sarabande is one of the dances of the Baroque suite. Bach's partita, which is really a suite, was published in 1728 and is in D major. Debussy's sarabande was written in 1894 and is a more modern version of the old dance.
>
> Both works are lovely pieces, but Bach's music sounds more lively because it is often played on the harpsichord while Debussy's music is more dreamy because it is played on the piano.
>
> Debussy uses thicker chords than Bach, to make his piece more interesting, and he uses more themes ✓ with several laid back tunes that pop up as the piece goes on.
>
> Not everyone appreciated Debussy's music. Someone said 'he doesn't like the piano much'. That seems an unfair criticism.
>
> Bach uses binary form ✓ but Debussy doesn't. He uses some other form. Another difference is that Debussy uses several different themes in his Sarabande. It is hard to work out the form because he doesn't write in clear keys for different sections like Bach ✓ does, but it looks like he has two sections and the second is longer, like Bach's. ✓
>
> Debussy wrote a lot of other pieces, with titles like 'La Mer' and 'The Girl with the Flaxen Hair'. These were all composed after Bach had died so they are romantic pieces.
>
> Neither sarabande would be very good music for dancing to, because they are both too slow.

There is nothing inaccurate in the first two paragraphs, but neither tells us anything about structure. The first is 'scene setting' narrative while the second consists mainly of subjective opinion.

Not until the third paragraph is there an attempt to tackle the question. The slang terms in the colloquial expression 'laid back tunes that pop up as the piece goes on' are not appropriate to this style of writing – it would be better to support the good first point by giving some examples (by bar number) from the score. The fourth paragraph throws in a memorised but unattributed quotation (it is actually from Debussy's piano teacher) which doesn't contribute to answering this question about structure.

The fifth paragraph is much more successful, with several valid observations (although the point about Debussy using more themes has already been made). The sixth introduces some irrelevant information, while the conclusion is unrelated to the question and misses the point that neither Sarabande was written for dancing.

Of course in reality most answers tend to fall between these two extremes, but hopefully these made-up examples will help you to develop your own written style in a clear and focused way.

Note that it is not necessary to copy out the question at the start. Some people find it helps to keep the wording in focus, but just writing the question number is sufficient.

Warning. Photocopying any part of this book without permission is illegal.

For examination in summer 2002 and 2003

Music for large ensemble

The first part of this chapter deals with the special focus work and topic set for examination in summer 2002 and 2003. If you are taking the exam in summer 2004 or 2005 turn to page 41.

Debussy, Prélude à L'Après-midi d'un faune

Special Focus Work for 2002 and 2003
NAM 5 — CD1 Track 5
Concertgebouw Orchestra
Conducted by Bernard Haitink

Before starting on this section you should work through (or revise) the information about the context and structure of this music given on pages 35–36 of the AS Guide. Make sure that you understand all of the terminology used on those pages.

Content and style

In an interview he granted in 1891 Mallarmé, who wrote the poem that inspired Debussy's *Prélude*, said that hitherto poets childishly believed that by writing the names of precious stones they would be making precious stones. He said this was impossible, for poetry consisted in creation:

> we must delve into our souls for ... gleams of such perfect purity, so perfectly sung and illuminated, that they will truly be the jewels of man. When we do this we have symbol, we have creation, and the word 'poetry' has its full meaning.

Here Mallarmé is proclaiming the central creed of the French symbolist poets of the late-19th century. We know that he was also speaking for his friend, Debussy, in whose music he saw the ultimate expression of symbolist aspirations.

Ces nymphes, je les veux perpétuer.
Si clair,
Leur incarnat léger, qu'il voltige dans l'air
Assoupi de sommeils touffus.
Aimai-je un rêve?

I desire to perpetuate these nymphs.
So bright
their light rosiness that it flutters in air
drowsy with tufted slumbers.
Was it a dream I loved?

Mallarmé believed that nothing lay beyond reality, but that the poet could create ideal versions of real things that would live on through poetry. This is what he means in the first line of his poem (see *left*). There are several layers of symbolism in his reference to nymphs. They are mythological incarnations of semi-divine spirits, they are maidens associated with rivers and woods, and poetically they symbolise the absolute beauty of young women. Mallarmé begins to create his own unreal but immortal vision of them in his second sentence, with its voluptuous alliteration.

It is perhaps because Debussy was as much influenced by contemporary poetry as by other composers that his music is so original. He took one of the most typical of romantic genres, the tone poem, and within it created musical symbols that reflect the verbal symbols of Mallarmé. After the first performance of the *Prélude* Mallarmé said it 'goes further into the nostalgia and the light with finesse, malaise and richness', later adding: 'This music prolongs the emotion of my poem, and sets its scene more vividly than colour.'

How did Debussy, in the opinion of Mallarmé, achieve more than was possible in words or paint? In the end it is obvious that words cannot explain the magic of Debussy's pantheistic vision, but we can observe some stylistic elements that contribute to it. But first we ought to be clear about Debussy's aims. These can be summed up in the composer's own words:

> The music of this prelude is a very free illustration of the poem ... it does not claim to be a synthesis of it. Rather there are successive tableaux through which pass the desires and dreams of the faun in

Warning. Photocopying any part of this book without permission is illegal.

the heat of the afternoon. Then, tired of chasing … the nymphs … he succumbs to intoxicating sleep in which he can finally realise his dreams of possession by Nature.

Let us consider how Debussy achieves this. The unaccompanied flute at the beginning represents the panpipes played by the faun. The drowsy heat of an antique afternoon, timeless and still, is expressed through:

- complex rhythms that lack any sense of time-bound metre
- a melodic line whose chromaticism negates any sense of tonality engendered by the prominent C♯s at the start of each bar
- a swing between C♯ and G♮, notes that form an ambiguous tritone
- a continuation (bars 3–4) that contains all but one of the pitches of the dorian mode on C♯ (the pitch heard at the start of the first three bars), yet ends inconclusively on A♯ (the sixth degree of the mode).

This A♯ is part of the woodwind chord that confirms the dorian mode on C♯ by forming the tonic triad plus added 6th (see *right*). But a melodic fragment on the horn leads, not to a resolution of this sensuous discord, but to B♭^{7}, a chord related to the first by two common pitches: A♯ (= B♭) and G♯ (= A♭). Although notated as V^7 of E♭ major it is drained of any dominant function by its context, for, after total silence, the added-6th chord returns on divided and muted strings and is followed once more by B♭^{7} decorated with fragmentary horn motifs (bars 7–10).

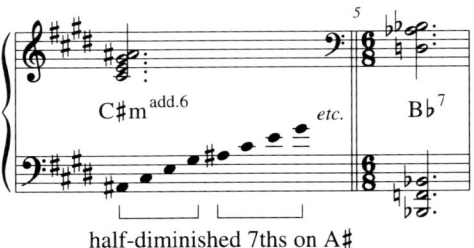
half-diminished 7ths on A♯

When the flute melody returns in bar 11 it is harmonised with a major 7th on D, a chord that is related to B♭^{7} only by a single common note (D). It is these successions (not progressions) of unrelated discords that prompted the composer Boulez to suggest that the *Prélude à L'Après-midi d'un faune* was 'the beginning of modern music'. A tonal progression suggests purposeful motion from and towards a defined goal (the tonic). Debussy's succession of chords is simply a series of harmonic colours suspended out of time.

It has often been observed that, while Debussy acknowledged his debt to Wagner, his music sounds utterly different. We can observe similarities and differences between the styles of the two composers in microcosm by comparing the first chord of Debussy's *Prélude* with the first chord of *Tristan und Isolde* (*NAM 4*). Debussy's harp glissando in bar 4 forms the chord shown in the above example – A♯–C♯–E–G♯. This is known as a half-diminished 7th, and Wagner notates his famous 'Tristan chord' as a half-diminished 7th at the climax of his Prelude (bar 83, see *right*). So Debussy's first chord in the Prélude (bar 4), which at first seemed to be a modal C♯ minor triad with added 6th (oboes and clarinets), can also be heard as an inversion of the first chord in Wagner's *Tristan und Isolde* – the tonally unstable 'Tristan chord'. But the context and effect of the two composer's half-diminished 7ths is quite different. Where Wagner's harmony yearns restlessly for resolution, Debussy's harmony moves through a succession of static chords used purely for harmonic colour. It is clearly impossible to analyse all of Debussy's harmonies in such depth, but wherever you cut into the music you will almost always find similarly ambiguous colouristic chords.

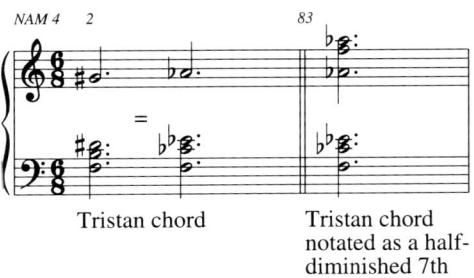

Whereas a diminished-7th chord is formed from a diminished triad surmounted by a diminished 7th above the root, the half-diminished 7th chord is made up of a diminished triad surmounted by a *minor* 7th above the root. For example:

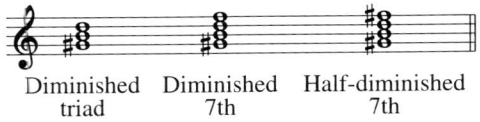

Form

The structure of the *Prélude* is as deliberately ambiguous as the melodies and harmonies, so there are many different analytical accounts of the work. But one thing upon most commentators agree is that the perfect cadence in bars 54–55 marks the beginning of a new section (and forms a moment where the harmony is functional and not merely colouristic). They all also agree that Debussy avoids the sort of motivic manipulation that had been such a feature of the central Germanic tradition for two centuries (evident in works as diverse as *NAM 1, 2* and *4*). Instead Debussy varies his melodies by such means as:

Bars	Form	Bars	Subsections
1–54	A	1–30	A^1
		31–36	Transition
		37–54	A^2
55–78	B		
79–93	A	Recap of A^1 only	
94–110	Coda		

- reharmonisation (compare bars 11–12 with bars 94–95)
- the addition of new arabesque-like figures (compare bars 21–22 with bars 26–27)
- alterations to significant intervals (in bars 31 and 34 the melodic range is compressed from an augmented to a diminished 4th)
- rhythmic augmentation (bars 86–89).

Debussy's constant blurring of structural cadences makes analysis a little difficult, but a ternary form (with coda) can be discerned.

Section A

A^1 (bars 1–30) amounts to a set of variations on the opening flute arabesque and the fragmentary horn motifs that follow it.

In the exact repeat of the first four bars of the flute melody (bars 11–14) we glimpse the tonic key of E major for the first time (V^{13}–I in beats 3–4 of bar 13) but, as the oboe extends the quaver melody, tonality is again obscured until we reach the 'dominant 7th' of F♯ minor in bars 19–20.

In bar 21 the 'dominant 7th' turns out to be nothing of the sort, for it simply sinks voluptuously on to a chord of E^6 as the flute begins to unwind a two-bar variant of the original arabesque.

Over V^9 of E major (bar 23) then V^9 of A major (bar 26) two more variants of the arabesque are heard, the second extended to reach a perfect cadence in the dominant (V^{13}–I in bars 29–30).

The transition (bars 31–36) begins with another variant of the arabesque (clarinet, bar 31) and continues with a whole-tone figure (bar 32, echoed by flute in the next bar). How is this three-bar unit (bars 31–33) treated in the next three bars (bars 34–36)?

A^2 (bars 37–54) introduces a new theme that passes from oboe to violins to flute and so on. It also refers to fragments of A^1, such as the repeated three-note crotchet figure of bars 48–50, which is an augmentation of the three-note quaver figure of bars 18–20. It is differentiated from A^1 by the largely pentatonic melody and by the fact that it moves away from sharp keys to progressively flatter keys until it reaches dominant preparation for D♭ major (bars 51–54).

Section B

B (bars 55–78) is clearly differentiated from all of Section A by:

- key (D♭ major is about as far from E major as it's possible to get)
- metre (simple triple time is much clearer despite syncopation)
- diatonic melody (bars 55–58 and 63–78), as opposed to the chromatic, modal, whole-tone and pentatonic melodies in A
- orchestration (sumptuous octave doubling in both wind and strings, as opposed to the soloistic textures of A).

The recapitulation (which is of A¹ only) and coda occur in bars 79–100 and are characterised by:

Section A (recapitulation)

- a rhythmically augmented variant of the original flute melody (bars 79–83)
- a return to E major (and this time the first two bars of the flute melody are accompanied by an unambiguous chord of E major in first inversion)
- a scherzando variant of the flute melody, harmonised in C major (bars 83–85)
- a transposed version of the augmented flute melody (E♭ major in bars 86–89)
- a repeat of the scherzando variant (bars 90–93)
- a coda (bars 94–110) in which the original flute arabesque returns on two flutes (bars 94–95) then solo flute and solo cello (*un peu en dehors* at bar 100 means 'standing out somewhat'). Here, despite modal and chromatic inflexions and a return to the opening half-diminished 7th at the start of bars 108 and 109, the tonic key of E major is never in doubt.

Private study

1. Why do you think that Boulez regarded the *Prélude à L'Après-midi d'un faune* as the beginning of modern music?
2. Why could *NAM 5* be described as a tone poem?
3. Explain the difference between functional and non-functional (or colouristic) harmony, and give an example of each type from page 118 of the *New Anthology*.
4. Why is the tonality ambiguous in the first 20 bars of *NAM 5*?

Sample questions

In the exam there will be three questions on this work, from which you must choose to answer **two**.

(a) Show how bars 79–93 relate to the music of the first 30 bars.

(b) To what extent is it true to say that Debussy frequently suggests particular keys in *NAM 5*, but never settles in any of them?

(c) Why is the style of *NAM 5* often described as impressionist?

Continuity and change in instrumental writing

Topic for examination in 2002 and 2003

You do not need to study this topic unless *Music for large ensemble* is the Area of Study that you undertook for AS Music and which you are now extending for A2.

The notes in this section will also be useful for those taking the topic set in 2004 and 2005, *Continuity and change in texture*.

Before starting work on this topic you need a thorough understanding of the material on *Music for large ensemble* in the AS Guide (pages 26–39). Remember that for A2 the topic draws on works from across the **entire** Area of Study, not just those in one of the two lists, A or B.

The historian Albert Schweitzer said of the *Brandenburg* concertos that here 'we are on the very borderline between chamber and orchestral music'. This remark is particularly true of *NAM 1* since the two *flauti d'echo* specified by Bach are almost certainly intended to be treble recorders. In passages such as bars 35–50 they hold the

Bach

NAM 1   CD1 Track 1
Northern Sinfonia of England
Directed by George Malcolm

most important line in the contrapuntal web. If a large string orchestra were used the recorder duet in this passage would be seriously challenged whenever the upper strings were playing. In fact it is quite possible to perform the concerto with a ripieno of single strings. The precise size of the ensemble would have been determined by the musical establishment at Cöthen, where Bach had access to half a dozen professional chamber musicians and a small string band. The leader, Joseph Spiess, must have been a formidable performer judging by the virtuoso solo in bars 187–208.

The solo violin dominates the texture in much of the movement, even stealing the recorder's parallel 6ths (eg bars 65–67) in the double-stopping of bars 217–229. Only in the trio-sonata texture of bars 165–184 is the spotlight firmly on the recorders. Although the ripieno violins are more independent of the solo parts than in comparable concertos by Vivaldi, their ranges are narrower than the solo violin. Their top note (D above the stave) requires the use of the third position while the soloist needs to have mastered the sixth position. The viola part is rarely independent: for much of the time it acts as a harmonic filler, and for the rest it is either doubled or hidden in the middle of complex counterpoint. The largely functional bass part is written for cello and violone (the latter meaning a double bass in most early 18th-century music). Since, in the most literal sense, this concerto is chamber music the continuo part would almost certainly have been realised on a harpsichord (there is little evidence to suggest that Bach had access to the other plucked instruments that were so popular in contemporary Italian ensembles).

The most notable feature of Bach's instrumentation is the linear writing, something that is characteristic of baroque orchestration generally. Thus the solo violin is employed continuously from bar 37 to bar 165 and, although the recorders are given breathing spaces, they too spin-out their melodic material in long sections.

Haydn

NAM 2   CD1 Track 2
Academy of Ancient Music
Directed by Christopher Hogwood

Even the *Lamentatione* symphony is still on the borderline between chamber and orchestral music. When this work was composed Haydn had at his disposal at Eszterháza only about four violins, a couple of violas, one cello, one double bass (not mentioned in the *NAM* score, but obviously essential), and a harpsichord (*cembalo* in the score). To this small ensemble a few wind instruments were added as occasion demanded.

In his later symphonies, written for large-scale public concerts rather than for private entertainment at court, Haydn was able to use a much fuller wind section than he had available in 1767. In many of his *London* symphonies written after 1790 he was able to use eight woodwind instruments (with bassoons often in the high tenor register rather than always doubling the bass), two horns and two trumpets (plus timpani) – with a much larger string section to balance. However at the time even works on this scale were arranged for trio. As suggested *right*, NAM 2 could be played by two violins and cello (or piano) – and this would be an excellent way to get to know the music.

The bare textures of this symphony are in striking contrast to the dense counterpoint of Bach's concerto, written nearly 50 years earlier. Haydn's wind instruments are given little independence. The oboes are yoked to the violins, the bassoon doubles the string bass and the horns provide sustained notes until bar 99. Horns were a new addition to the orchestra in the classical period, but the natural horns of the day did not possess valves and could play only a limited number of notes, so they were commonly used to sustain and the harmony and give weight to the texture, as they are here. The violas fare little better: for most of the movement they simply double the bass part. Much of the music is in only two or three parts, represented by the violins and the bass, and it is not impossible to imagine a performance by only three instruments.

One could with some justification say that Haydn's *Lamentatione* is a great symphony *despite* its primitive instrumental writing while *Harold in Italy* is a great symphony *because* of its brilliant instrumental writing. By 1834, partly due to Berlioz's insatiable demands, the orchestra had been greatly expanded (in this piece he demands at least 61 strings). Only a few of the extra instruments he specified figure in the third movement, the most notable being:

✦ a piccolo (sounding an octave above printed pitch)

✦ a cor anglais (sounding a 5th below printed pitch)

✦ four instead of two horns (by using natural horns crooked in C, F and E Berlioz is able to cover a wide range of pitches without the players having to resort to hand stopping)

✦ a harp (an instrument that was introduced into the romantic orchestra by French composers such as Berlioz).

Berlioz

NAM 3 CD1 Track 3
London Symphony Orchestra
Conducted by Colin Davis

Berlioz is famed for his skill in orchestration and his book on the subject (*Grand traité d'instrumentation et d'orchestration modernes*, 1843) became a standard source of reference. In *Harold*, Berlioz's instrumental writing is largely determined by his programmatic intentions. At the start the sustained woodwind chord evokes the sound of bagpipe drones while divided violas begin the saltarello. The biting timbre of a shawm is imitated by piccolo and oboe in octaves. The accompaniment to the cor anglais (an instrument often used to suggest pastoral scenes) is notable for a texture in which pizzicato violins and cellos surround bowed broken chords played by divided violas (bars 34–48). Like the violas, the double basses have become independent. In bars 71–95 their delicate pizzicato provides the bass part and thus allows the cellos to play rustling semiquavers that enliven the otherwise static string parts.

No wonder Paganini refused to play the viola solo in this hybrid symphony-cum-concerto. Despite not going above the fifth position in this movement the part lies awkwardly for the instrument (Bach's violin fireworks are much easier), its octaves are doubled by other strings and it is relegated to accompaniment in the figuration of bars 99–110. Even when allowed to play the *idée fixe* unmolested (from bar 167) its thunder is stolen by a stratospheric flute augmentation and the continued saltarello rhythms of the violas.

In *NAM 4* we have a return to counterpoint, but a type of counterpoint quite unlike that of Bach. Where Bach's contrapuntal strands are distinguished by the pure tone colour of a single type of instrument, Wagner often doubles his melodies to give a much richer texture. In bars 81–82, for instance, three leitmotifs are contrapuntally combined, the first on flutes, oboes, clarinets and English horn, the second on horns, bass clarinet, violas and cellos, and the third on a trumpet. The texture is further thickened for dramatic effect by the violins' rushing chromatic scales, by the timpani pedal note, and by trombone chords (with the bass trombone strengthened by independent double basses). Yet only two bars later the texture thins to a monophonic exchange of the first two motifs (violins, then violas and cellos in bars 84–85). This is followed by the third motif on flutes, first oboe and clarinet with homophonic accompaniment. These contrasting textures highlight

Wagner

NAM 4 CD1 Track 4
Vienna Philharmonic Orchestra
Conducted by Georg Solti

another aspect of Wagner's instrumental writing – the 'unending melody' explained in the AS Guide. Typically the melodic line winds its way through the orchestra so its tone colour is constantly changing. In the relatively thin texture of bars 84–100 it is easy to hear the main melodic line as it passes between string and woodwind instruments without break (though it often shifts abruptly from one register to another). A more subtle example of unending melody can be heard in bars 17–32 where the tone colours change within the string section (cellos, violins on the G string, cellos again, and finally violin and cello octaves).

The most remarkable difference in the individual instrumental parts is the supreme importance of Wagner's cello section compared with its subservient status in *Harold* (in other works Berlioz could be much more original in his cello writing). From the start of *NAM 4* they are centre stage, the first extended melody begins on cellos (bars 17–22) and at bars 57– 58 (and elsewhere) they reach D, a 9th above middle C (notice that most of the cello part is written in the tenor clef). Since most of his melodic lines derive from the three leitmotifs heard in the first 24 bars it is not surprising that the wind parts are not particularly idiomatic. And only as the greatest climax approaches does the string writing become idiomatic (rushing violin scales and viola tremolo in bars 77–82).

Debussy

NAM 5   CD1 Track 5
Concertgebouw Orchestra
Conducted by Bernard Haitink

We have already seen that Debussy was influenced by Wagnerian harmony, but only in the central section of the *Prélude* (bars 55–74) does his scoring betray Wagnerian influence. Elsewhere his instrumental writing is often soloistic and thus more akin to Berlioz's practice. This is most clearly evident at the start, with its opening for unaccompanied flute followed by fragmentary horn motifs. Here are just a few examples of Debussy's instrumental wizardry – you should be able to find many more for yourself.

In bars 4–5 the harp glissando lights up the wind chord which then resolves on to the dark muted (*sourdine*) colour of an unrelated chord played on divided strings and second harp. Note that the double basses, playing the root of the chord, are not muted. A similar difference in the treatment of the double basses and upper strings is apparent from bar 11, but here the gentle rustling noise is achieved by the use of tremolo bowing above the fingerboard (*sur la touche*). The whole texture in this passage is engineered so that the sensuous timbre of the low solo flute can achieve maximum effect (notice that only two double basses play in bars 11–17). Given that the upper strings are still muted, Debussy directs that the normal bowing position (*position nat.*) between fingerboard and bridge should be resumed for the crescendo starting in bar 17.

The change of timbre and mood when a solo clarinet takes over the arabesques at bar 30 is accompanied by a change from muted strings to muted horns in the accompaniment. Meanwhile the strings quickly remove their mutes (*ôtez vite les sourdines*). Notice the cello part in bars 31 and 34, and the quicksilver changes of timbre between harp acciaccatura chords, loud pizzicato chords and soft bowed chords in bars 32–33 and 35–36.

Compare the melody and accompaniment of bars 55–58 and 75–78 and you will immediately hear the difference between a Wagnerian-influenced texture and pure Debussy. The latter is as contrapuntal as Wagner's texture on page 81 of *NAM* (both have three melodic strands), but Debussy's parts are solo, and instead of brass chords we hear a single double bass pedal note.

The instrumental writing in bars 106–110 is among the most magical ever written. The strings are divided into ten parts with two solo violins at the top and four muted horns in mid texture. Against this E-major triad, played ***ppp***, harp octaves add both sharpened and flattened versions of the leading note. Then the opening bar of the work is recalled, harmonised as a series of unrelated triads played by muted horns and violins. Finally the tonic and dominant are sounded on antique cymbals (tiny discs of metal struck edge to edge and sounding two octaves higher than printed). The pure sound of harp harmonics (indicated by little circles) rise in 3rds to reach the dominant as all dissonance melts away into an almost inaudible chord of E major spread over more than five and a half octaves.

Tippett

> NAM 6   CD1 Track 6
> Academy of St Martin-in-the-Fields
> Conducted by Neville Marriner

Compared with his continental contemporaries Tippett was conservative in his approach to instrumentation in the Concerto for Double String Orchestra. In part this reflects the medium (strings only) and the resonances of older musical styles which permeate the work, but even compared with earlier composers he seems a little unadventurous. In only three bars does he require double stopping, nowhere does he use solo strings or extreme registers, and special performance techniques are limited to a few short-lived and isolated pizzicato bass parts and a passage beginning at bar 113 marked *sul tasto poco a poco Naturale* (bowed over the fingerboard then gradually reverting to the normal bowing position). Compare these brief passages with Debussy's use of mutes, his bowed and fingered tremolo, his multiple divisi textures, his varied use of pizzicato effects and his combination of *sur la touche* with tremolo.

This concerto was written for the South London Orchestra, and first performed by them at Morley College in Lambeth on 21st April 1940. This group had been formed under Tippett's direction to provide performance opportunities for unemployed professional musicians, particularly those who had worked in cinema orchestras in the days of the silent film. Such players would have been proficient in a wide range of string techniques, but Tippett is willing to sacrifice special instrumental effects in order to concentrate on the two elements that most characterise this concerto – counterpoint and syncopation. In both respects his melodic lines are similar to Bach's contrapuntal strands. For example, compare the complex hemiolaic syncopation in bars 231–234 of *NAM 1* with similar rhythms in bar 15 of *NAM 6*. Compare, too, Bach's leaping violin melody in bars 244–249 with a similarly athletic violin melody in bars 80–86 of *NAM 6*. However in one particularly important respect Tippett's string writing is closer to that of Haydn in *Sturm und Drang* mode than it is to Bach in contrapuntal mode. Like Haydn, Tippett more often than not doubles his melodies at the octave above and/or at the octave below. Compare the first eight bars of the two works and you will discover that both are in lean two-part counterpoint doubled at the octave and both are characterised by galvanising syncopation.

Private study

1. Why can Bach's style of instrumentation in *NAM 1* be described as linear? Was this typical, or unusual, in the baroque period?

2. Why is Haydn able to use a greater number of pitches in the horn parts of *NAM 2* from bar 100 onwards?

3. In *NAM 3*, what is the **sounding** interval between (i) oboe and piccolo in bars 4–31, and (ii) cor anglais and oboe in bars 48^6–61? How does the scoring of the solo for bassoon and cor anglais in bars 129^6–135 differ from the first two examples?

4. Write out the music on page 83 of the *New Anthology* on two staves, using only treble and bass clefs and notating all parts at their correct sounding pitch.

5. In the violin parts of *NAM 5*, what is the difference between the tremolo in bar 11 and the tremolo in bar 94?

Sample questions

In the exam there will be two questions on this topic, from which you must choose to answer **one**.

(a) Explain in detail why the instrumentation of bars 94–110 of Debussy's *Prélude à L'Après-midi d'un faune* is so effective.

TIP: Read the notes on *NAM 3* below before tackling this question.

(b) How does the instrumentation of *NAM 3* help create its mood?

(c) Discuss and account for the differences in woodwind and brass writing between *NAM 2* and *NAM 4*.

Music for large ensemble

For examination in summer 2004 and 2005

This part of the chapter deals with the special focus work and topic set for examination in summer 2004 and 2005. If you are taking the exam in summer 2002 or 2003 turn to page 32.

Berlioz, Harold in Italy (III: Sérénade)

Before starting on this section you should work through (or revise) the information about the context and structure of this music given on pages 31–32 of the AS Guide. Make sure that you understand all of the terminology used on those pages.

Special Focus Work for 2004 and 2005
NAM 3   CD1 Track 3
London Symphony Orchestra
Conducted by Colin Davis

Berlioz was born in what was then a remote valley in the French Alps where his only musical experiences were local folk song and the music of minor composers arranged for whatever instruments lay to hand. He was taught by his father, a local doctor who wished Hector to follow in his footsteps. From the age of 12 Berlioz learned to play the flute and guitar, but, unlike most aspiring composers, he never learned the piano. These facts go some way to explain his remarkably original musical style. At the same age he fell hopelessly in love with Estelle Duboeuf: he was 12, she 18. It was an unrequited love that, for Berlioz, lasted a lifetime. This was the beginning of his passionately romantic attitude to life and music.

Background and style

At the age of 17 he left for Paris to study medicine, but he hated the dissecting room and so, at the late age of 22, he enrolled at the Paris Conservatoire, France's leading college of music. There he rebelled against the academicism of his teachers, but learned much about German music, and became an ardent admirer of Beethoven, especially the romantic Beethoven of the *Pastoral* symphony. In 1830, at the age of 26, Berlioz wrote his *Symphonie fantastique*, a milestone in romantic music and a demonstration of his wholly original orchestral style. In the same year he composed a cantata in a deliberately antiquated style that he knew would please his reactionary teachers. For this he was awarded the *Prix de Rome* – a valuable prize which required residence abroad in order to pursue further musical studies.

A few months later he left for Rome, where he was to experience at first hand the Italy of Byron's romantic poetry. While in Italy Berlioz walked in the Abruzzi mountains where, as he wrote in his *Mémoirs*, he delighted in 'the rustic tunes of the *pifferari* [with] the traditional tambourine beating time to improvised saltarellos'. After his return to Paris, Paganini, the greatest virtuoso violinist of the 19th century, commissioned Berlioz to write a piece for viola and orchestra. The result was *Harold en Italie*, composed in the summer of 1834 and a work he described as a 'Symphony in four movements with an obbligato viola part'.

The final part of Byron's *Childe Harolde's Pilgrimage*, which centres on the poet's impressions of his adopted home, Italy, was published in 1818. The word 'Childe' in the title is a medieval usage, meaning a young nobleman, not a child in the modern sense. Byron's poetry was hugely popular throughout Europe and exerted a great influence on the romantic movement, for which he became something of an icon following his death at the age of 36, en route to fight for a group of Greek revolutionaries.

As in the *Symphonie fantastique* the four movements are linked by an *idée fixe* played by the soloist in an Adagio at the start of the first movement (the complete melody is played by the soloist in bars 72–95 of *NAM 3*). But, unlike his first symphony, this theme remains largely unchanged and represents not himself but Byron's hero as a detached observer in picturesque Italian settings. Also unlike the

Warning. Photocopying any part of this book without permission is illegal.

Symphonie fantastique there is no definite programme, just descriptive titles (as in Beethoven's *Pastoral* symphony) around which the audience is free to create their own more specific images. It may even be questioned if Berlioz actually read *Childe Harold's Pilgrimage* very thoroughly, since his descriptive titles do not match the poem at all convincingly. The commentator Donald Tovey wryly noted that 'no definite elements of Byron's poem have penetrated the impregnable fortress of Berlioz's encyclopaedic inattention'.

> The most famous orchestral version of a saltarello is the brilliantly fast finale of the *Italian* symphony by Mendelssohn, whom Berlioz had met in Rome in 1830 – at the very time Mendelssohn had begun working on the symphony. The slow movement of his symphony illustrates a pilgrim's march through the Abruzzi mountains – and so does the slow movement of *Harold*!

The movement begins (bars 1–31) with what is doubtless a version of the saltarello mentioned in his *Mémoirs*. By the early 19th century this Italian folk dance was cultivated in Rome and the surrounding countryside, including the Abruzzo. The dance was (and still is) characterised by wild hopping steps to music in fast compound time. Whether or not Berlioz had a specific saltarello in mind his melody is typical of many primitive folk melodies in its use of:

- repeated melodic cells of narrow compass. Here there are two principal motifs. The first initially appears in bar 4, the second in bar 7. As in many folk dances they are varied by such means as inversion (eg bar 10), sequence (bars 14–17) and pitch changes (eg bar 23, where the rhythm and weak-beat accent of bar 21 is retained but two of the three pitches are altered)

- tonic and dominant pedals that imitate bagpipe drones (oboe, clarinets and bassoons)

- a very limited range of chords above the drones: just I and V^7 are used (even when a touch of subdominant harmony is heard in bars 15–19 the chords are V^7 and I of F major).

> At the head of the movement Berlioz wrote *Sérénade d'un Montagnard des Abbruzes à sa maîtresse*. The translation given in *NAM 3* would be more accurately rendered as 'Serenade of a mountain-dweller of Abruzzi to his mistress', since *Montagnard* does not mean mountaineer (the latter are too busy climbing to sing serenades!) and the modern spelling of the region is Abruzzi.

The melody of the serenade proper (first heard on the cor anglais in bars 34–61) is quite unlike the classically balanced melodies that Berlioz's teachers would have approved at the Paris Conservatoire. The syncopation in its third and fourth bars throws the pastorale rhythm off-balance and its four phrases fall into an asymmetrical pattern of 7+7+4+7 bars. The first of these (phrase 'a') concludes with a most peculiar version of an imperfect cadence ending on the sharpened dominant in bar 40:

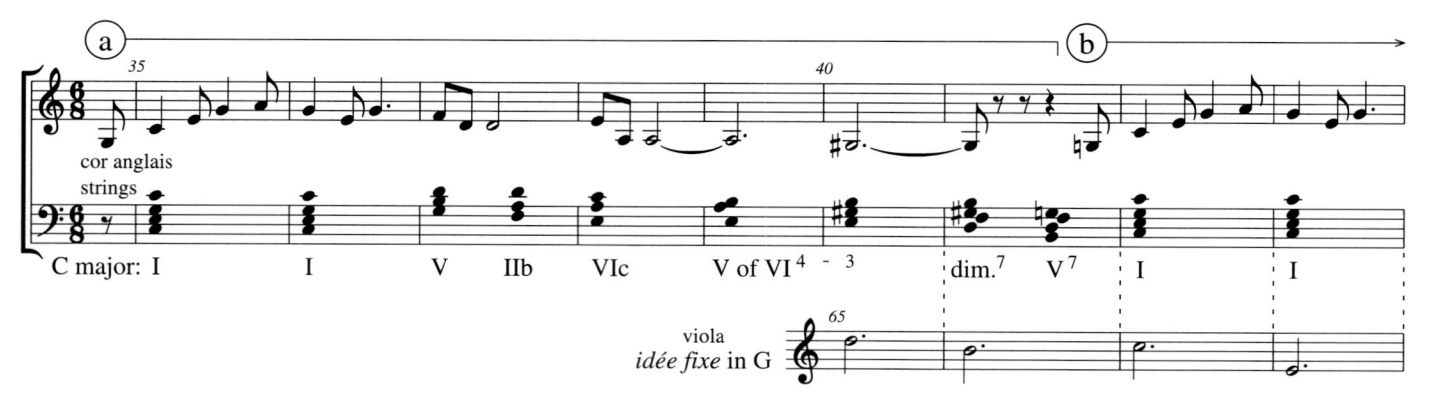

The harmony is equally eccentric. Bar 38 is harmonised with VIc, and this is followed by versions of the dominant of chord VI – first a suspended 4th resolving to the dominant of VI (a chord known as a secondary dominant), followed by a diminished 7th. It's odd enough to end the phrase on such an unstable chromatic discord, but it's even odder to then begin the next phrase ('b') with V^7 of the tonic key as though nothing unusual had happened.

Would Berlioz have written more conventional harmony had he been able to compose at the piano? Whatever the answer we should just be grateful that he was capable of such harmonic eccentricity, because without it a very important element of his original style would have been lost.

The clarinet figuration that supports the third phrase in bars 48–52 could come from a serenade by Mozart, but the melody is disrupted by another G♯ and its apparent F-major tonality is negated by the perfect cadence in D minor supplied by accompanimental instruments. Berlioz reserves his oddest phrase for the end of the serenade melody (bars 53–61). Bars 53–54 sound as though they are in G minor (VIb–Vb–I), but the modified sequence of bars 55–56 suggests – then denies – the distant key of A♭ major. After such chromaticism and tonal ambiguity Berlioz has to repeat dominant and tonic harmony in order to re-establish the home key of C major and end on an imperfect cadence ($V^7b–I–V^7b–I–V^7$ in bars 57–59).

The second part of this central section (bars 59–99) overlaps the last note of the first part. All four phrases of the melody are now heard in various guises as countermelodies to the *idée fixe* which enters in bar 65, linking and overlapping the repetition of phrases 'a' and 'b', as shown previously. Berlioz strikingly chooses to present the first seven bars of this cantus firmus in the key of G major but harmonised in C major. It as if the onlooking Harold, represented by the *idée fixe*, takes a few moments to adjust to the scene before him, which only really comes into focus from bar 72, when the whole *idée fixe* is presented by the viola (doubled in octaves by upper strings) in the 'correct' key of C major (bars 72–95).

Berlioz's *idée fixe* seems to portray Harold more as a dreamy onlooker than as the passionate rebel depicted by Byron. Part of the reason for this may be that the theme was not actually composed for *Harold in Italy* at all – it comes from *Rob Roy*, an overture Berlioz wrote in 1831 but then discarded.

The easiest way to follow Berlioz's harmonisation from bar 72 is to read the harp part.

While phrases 'a' and 'b' are repeated without alteration, the four bars of the third phrase (first heard on cor anglais and oboe in bars 48–52) are varied as follows:

✦ in bars 73–75 the first two bars are played in a transposed version on clarinets and horns
✦ in bars 75–79 a decorated version of the whole phrase is heard on cor anglais and oboe – both beginning and end are modified to fit the cantus firmus
✦ in bars 79–81 the cadence is echoed by overlapping clarinet/horn, piccolo/flute and bassoon entries
✦ in bars 80–84 the whole phrase is repeated unchanged (apart from the addition of an accompanimental horn part) and the cadence is echoed by bassoons
✦ in bars 85–91 woodwind instruments subject the phrase (and its echo) to fragmentation and variation.

The whole of the final phrase (first heard in bars 53–61) is then presented in a version that is modified to fit the end of the cantus firmus. The Lombardic rhythms of bars 57–58 are extended and echoed as the music moves decisively to an imperfect cadence in the key of D minor (bars 98–99).

The ternary form of the central section is then completed by a restatement of the four phrases of the serenade melody. This starts with phrases 'a' (horns) and 'b' (woodwind) in the delightfully 'wrong' key of D minor, reinforced by a resounding perfect cadence

Bars	Form		
1–31	A	Saltarello	
32–135	B	Serenade:	32–59 B
			59–99 B'
			99–122 B
			122–135 Coda
136–208	A	Saltarello	

in bars 110–111. The third and fourth phrases are repeated without change (apart from the first note) in bars 111–122. Meanwhile the viola supplies decorative figuration and countermelodies.

A coda in bars 122–135 consists of a restatement of bars 59–72 without the *idée fixe*, with minimal tonic and dominant harmony in phrase 'b', with semiquaver decorations of the falling 3rd and falling 6th figures, and with a definitive perfect cadence in C major at the end. The central section is thus a ternary structure (with coda) nested inside the ternary form of the complete movement. The latter ends with:

- a restatement of the saltarello (bars 136–166 = bars 1–31)
- a complete restatement of the *idée fixe* (played by flute with harp harmonics in bars 167–190) contrapuntally combined with fragments of the middle two phrases of the serenade melody (with many sequential repetitions of the cadence first heard in bar 52), all accompanied by saltarello rhythms on divided violas
- repetition and augmentation of the cadence (bars 191–193)
- fragments of the saltarello rhythms fading away to a bare 5th on the tonic (bars 194–202)
- an unaccompanied performance of the first two bars of the serenade extended down the tonic triad to reach the lowest note of the viola (bars 202–206)
- detached, muted tonic triads (bars 206–208).

The whole movement differs from simple ternary form in that the return of the first section is extended by a final summation in which all three basic ingredients of the movement – the saltarello, parts of the serenade melody and the *idée fixe* – are combined.

Private study

1. What is the significance of the title *Harold in Italy*?

2. Why is this work not regarded as a concerto?

3. What is meant by the term 'cantus firmus' in the description on page 43?

4. (i) What is a saltarello? What are its musical characteristics?
   (ii) Why do bars 1–31 sound like a folk dance?

5. Look up the term 'romantic' in a good dictionary of music and then list the features of *NAM 3* which show it to be music of the romantic period rather than baroque or classical.

Sample questions

In the exam there will be three questions on this work, from which you must choose to answer **two**.

(a) Compare and contrast bars 48–59 with bars 73–99.

(b) Comment on the role played by the *idée fixe* in this movement.

(c) A leading music reference book of 1837 claimed that Berlioz's 'melodies are deprived of metre and rhythm, and his harmony [is] a bizarre assemblage of sounds'. Does the music of *NAM 3* warrant this harsh judgement?

Continuity and change in texture

Topic for examination in 2004 and 2005

You do not need to study this topic unless *Music for large ensemble* is the Area of Study that you undertook for AS Music and which you are now extending for A2.

Before starting work on this topic you need a thorough understanding of the material on *Music for large ensemble* in the AS Guide (pages 26–39). Remember that for A2 the topic draws on works from across the **entire** Area of Study, not just those in one of the two lists, A or B.

Because texture is so closely related to instrumentation, you are strongly recommended to work through the section on 'Continuity and change in instrumental writing' (the topic prescribed for 2002 and 2003) starting from page 35. The notes that follow are largely confined to additional matters which amplify that material.

Bach

NAM 1   CD1 Track 1
Northern Sinfonia of England
Directed by George Malcolm

The first movement of *NAM 1* is in ritornello form. What chiefly distinguishes it from ritornello movements by other late baroque composers is what Albert Schweitzer described as Bach's 'interpenetration of soli and tutti sections' compared with the clearly differentiated sections in the fast movements of composers such as Vivaldi. This is evident in the first few bars. Instead of a substantial tutti the movement begins with solo recorders accompanied by an alternation of tutti four-part detached chords (bars 1–3 and 7–9) with a thin-textured homophonic continuo accompaniment (bars 4–6 and 10–12). When ripieno violins are allowed a more melodic role in bars 14–22 they simply act as reinforcements of the continuous melody of the solo violin. Even in the fullest texture at the end of the ritornello (bars 79–83) Bach's scoring allows the solo recorders to be heard in this marvellously syncopated passage.

The reverse process is evident in the three solo episodes. In bars 83–113, for instance, the violin solo is punctuated by tutti chords that come from the beginning of the ritornello (bars 89–91, 103–105 and 111–113). Even more remarkable in this first episode is the way Bach introduces the first substantial and independent ripieno violin parts in bars 129–132. There is an amazing variety of textures in the second solo episode (bars 157–208):

+ in bars 157–165 the two-part counterpoint of the recorders is punctuated by tutti chords

+ in bars 165–185 a concertante cello part joins the recorders' counterpoint to form a texture that is no different from that of contrapuntal movements in contemporary trio sonatas

+ interpenetration of solo and tutti material is again evident when ripieno violins take over the soloistic figures of the recorders, while the recorders themselves are relegated to the role of accompanists (bars 193–197)

+ in the accompaniment of bars 205–208 tutti strings and solo recorders are equal partners, the former proposing a two-note on-beat figure that is echoed by the off-beat figure of the latter

+ in the last solo episode (bars 235–322) ripieno violins are cast as soloists in their close imitations of the violin solo (bars 235–240), and in bars 263–270 all instruments (except the violone) share in the contrapuntal texture, the cello imitating the solo violin and recorders imitating ripieno violins.

It is this soli-tutti interpenetration that not only allows a kaleidoscopic range of textures, but also enables structural integration of a type that was never again to be achieved in the baroque concerto.

Haydn

NAM 2   CD1 Track 2
Academy of Ancient Music
Directed by Christopher Hogwood

Partly because of Haydn's use of a metrical version of a plainsong melody as a cantus firmus the textures in this symphony are much more clearly differentiated than they are in Bach's concerto. Four principal types of texture can be discerned:

- two-part counterpoint in bars 1–8 (with a few sustained tonic and dominant horn notes), 13–16, 45–52, 80–87 (again with a couple of sustained horn notes) and 92–95
- chordal textures in bars 9–12, 53–56 and 88–91
- a cantus firmus (oboe and second violins) with homophonic accompaniment (including decorative broken-chord figuration for strings) in bars 17–38 and 100–121 (the latter passage with horn doubling the oboe and second violin cantus firmus)
- tutti unison textures and tutti chords at important cadences (bars 43–44 and 126–133, the latter with independent wind parts).

There are a number of more subtle textures in which wind instruments achieve more independence, but by and large most textures are characterised by the dominance of the strings and the subservience of the wind. These textures are typical only of Haydn's early period. In his later symphonies enlarged wind sections achieved both integration with and independence from the strings.

Berlioz

NAM 3   CD1 Track 3
London Symphony Orchestra
Conducted by Colin Davis

Although Berlioz is famed as the most progressive orchestrator of the mid-19th century, the bucolic nature of this representation of the Abruzzi mountains and its inhabitants means that his textures here are less subtle than in much of his other music. The saltarello (bars 1–31 and 136–166) is a fusion of three textural elements:

- a folksy melody in octaves (upper woodwind)
- a drone (lower woodwind)
- divided viola chords incessantly alternating between two typical saltarello rhythms.

In the serenade proper (bars 32–135) there is a wide variety of textures, but they change abruptly. In the exposition, for instance, the cor-anglais melody of bars 34–48 is accompanied by pizzicato chords and bowed broken chords throughout. Suddenly the texture changes in bars 48–52 to three main strands:

- the melody in octaves on double-reed instruments
- clarinet broken chords (Mozartian, but the ultimate source for both composers is the music of the village band)
- a functional bass and harmonic filling provided by two bassoons.

With the advent of the next phrase (bars 53–59) textural change is just as abrupt. Here the melody is spread over two octaves on double-reed instruments and the accompanying strings also play in octaves while clarinet and horn provide harmonic filling. The effect, as was no doubt Berlioz's intention, is peculiarly primitive.

In the middle section (bars 59–99) the serenade melody (or at least fragments of it) is contrapuntally combined with the *idée fixe*, supported by homophonic strings and harp chords. The textures that follow the end of the cantus firmus were described earlier.

The most inventive orchestral textures are heard in bars 166–208, where stratospheric flute and harp sail serenely above a combination of fragments from the serenade melody and the saltarello ostinato. Most remarkable of all is the reduction of the texture to just two parts with telling silences (bars 194–201), the entirely unaccompanied soloist, and the final muted chords. Notice that, having played continuously for 67 bars, Berlioz leaves the orchestral violas out of these chords so that the C string of the soloist is just audible against the second cellos.

Wagner

NAM 4   CD1 Track 4
Vienna Philharmonic Orchestra
Conducted by Georg Solti

The opening bars of *Tristan and Isolde* contrast unaccompanied cellos with four-part wind chords (the latter particularly biting because of the preponderance of double-reed instruments). The texture of bars 10–15 is notable for antiphonal exchanges characterised by shifts in register (compare bars 10–11 with bars 12–13, and bar 14 with bar 15). The interrupted cadence (bars 16–17) looks homophonic, but in reality there is enormous contrapuntal tension between the violins' melody and the horn/oboe part, which, moving while the violins are stationary, falls tellingly to the tonic at the same time as the violins leap to their long-held and extremely dissonant appoggiatura (B♮).

Once 'unending melody' begins to unfold in the cellos (entering in bar 17 as the violin appoggiatura resolves) the texture is seamless until bar 36. At this point Wagner returns to antiphonal exchanges, this time between clearly differentiated and spacially dissociated strings and wind (the full impact of which can only be experienced in a live performance). When 'unending melody' begins again in bar 45 seamless counterpoint continues all the way through to the climax in bar 83. The score looks forbidding, but if you listen carefully you will notice that nearly every contrapuntal strand is doubled, sometimes over several octaves, and rarely are there more than four elements to Wagner's complex polyphonic web. In this operatic version of the prelude antiphonal exchanges (bars 84–100) give way to more thinly scored versions of the opening phrases over ominous timpani rolls (bars 100–106), then to unaccompanied octaves as the curtain rises.

Debussy

NAM 5   CD1 Track 5
Concertgebouw Orchestra
Conducted by Bernard Haitink

The chief textural difference between this *Prélude* and Berlioz's *Sérénade* is the subtlety with which Debussy slides from one texture to another with few discontinuities compared with Berlioz's deliberately abrupt textural changes. As the monophonic flute melody comes to rest on A♯ the note changes to oboe timbre and a four-part woodwind chord. The first horn enters, not with the woodwind chord, but immediately after it, then blossoms into a telling melodic fragment as both harmony and texture changes from mid-register woodwind to low-register muted strings. In bars 8–11 fragmentary two-part counterpoint melts into five-part string chords as the flute solo returns, and this melody itself changes timbre when the oboe takes over in bar 14. Many other examples of orchestral textures in this work are discussed in the notes starting on pages 32 and 38.

Warning. Photocopying any part of this book without permission is illegal.

Tippett

NAM 6   CD1 Track 6
Academy of St Martin-in-the-Fields
Conducted by Neville Marriner

This neo-classical concerto harks back to the textures of the concerto grosso. But it differs from its baroque forebear in several important respects. Firstly, both of Tippett's string orchestras are tutti ensembles so there is no timbral contrast between them (unlike the contrasting ripieno and concertino of *NAM 1*). This means that antiphonal exchanges such as that in bars 8–12 only fully impact on the listener when spacial separation is apparent. Secondly, there is a preponderance of two-part counterpoint (eg bars 1–4) relieved by monophony (eg bar 37) with few homophonic passages (the chordal accompaniment to the cello/bass semitones in bars 99–106 is exceptional). Equally exceptional is the decorated pedal that alone accompanies the scherzando melody in bars 21–29 and the arpeggiated accompaniment that follows it (bars 30–32).

Only rarely does the texture expand and become more complex. In bars 179–183, for instance, parallel root-position triads (violins I and II in the first orchestra and violin II in the second orchestra) are accompanied by arpeggio figures and both are counterpointed against the second main theme in the second orchestra (violin I and viola in octaves). But this texture immediately gives way to bare octaves (bar 184) and brief homophony (bar 185). The whole effect is governed by the infectious syncopated melodies that leap athletically from start to finish.

Private study

1. How does the relationship of concertino and ripieno textures in *NAM 1* differ from that of most other baroque concertos?

2. Describe how the cantus firmus relates to its accompaniment in the exposition of *NAM 2*.

3. Describe how the *idée fixe* relates to the surrounding texture in *NAM 3*, and compare Berlioz's handling of this device with Haydn's use of a cantus firmus in *NAM 2*.

4. Berlioz described *Tristan und Isolde* as 'a sort of chromatic moan' and in 1863 the French composer Auber described Wagner's music as being like 'Berlioz without the melody'. On the evidence of *NAM 4*, do you think such criticisms are justified?

5. To what extent are the textures of *NAM 6* similar to those found in *NAM 1*?

Sample questions

In the exam there will be two questions on this topic, from which you must choose to answer **one**.

(a) To what extent is it true that the textures in *NAM 2* are much more clearly differentiated than those in *NAM 1*?

(b) Wagner was frequently accused by his contemporaries of using thick, unvarying textures and of neglecting the importance of melody in his music. Is such criticism justified?

(c) How well does Tippett succeed in obtaining variety of texture in *NAM 6*, despite writing entirely for string instruments?

20th-century art music

> For examination in summer 2002 and 2003

The first part of this chapter deals with the special focus work and topic set for examination in summer 2002 and 2003. If you are taking the exam in summer 2004 or 2005 turn to page 58.

Cage, Sonatas and Interludes (Sonatas I–III)

> **Special Focus Work for 2002 and 2003**
>
> *NAM 10* CD1 Tracks 12–14
> Joanna MacGregor (piano)

Before starting on this section you should work through (or revise) the information about the context and structure of this music given on pages 48–50 of the AS Guide. Make sure that you understand all of the terminology used on those pages.

In 1935 the young John Cage (then 23) began a two-year study of composition and counterpoint with Schoenberg, who had moved to California the previous year. Although Cage did not specifically study serial technique in these lessons, his early works reveal something of the influence of Schoenberg's rigorous approach to composing and show an interest in devising new ways to organise music without depending on tonality for structure. In particular, Cage experimented with short melodic cells that could be extracted from note rows, using elements that derive from serialism (such as rule-based techniques to control repetition within a predominantly contrapuntal style), but in a very free and expressive way.

> For a relatively early (non-serial) work by Schoenberg, see *NAM 40*. For a serial work by Webern, see *NAM 8*.

However it is rhythm that emerges as the predominant element in many of these early works. Perhaps this was because Schoenberg declared that Cage lacked a feeling for harmony, although it is more likely that it was a natural outcome of Cage's employment, from 1937 onwards, as musical director for various contemporary dance groups who were interested in exploring percussion-based music.

Another important influence on Cage was the Californian avant-garde composer, Henry Cowell (1897–1965), whose classes in world music Cage attended in 1934. Cowell pioneered the use of new piano techniques, such as chord clusters (groups of adjacent notes, sometimes played with the whole forearm on the keyboard) and strumming the strings with the fingers. Cage developed a similar interest in exploiting new timbres in his own percussion music. *Imaginery Landscape No. 2* (1942), for example, includes parts for tin cans, a metal wastepaper bin and electric buzzers. Another work of 1942, *Credo In Us* (written for Merce Cunningham, one of the key figures in the creation of modern dance) includes a part for radio (tuned to whatever happens to be on) or gramophone (set to play an arbitrary recording of classical music), introducing the idea of random sound sources which interact with Cage's own music.

> John Cage was not only one of the most influential composers of the 20th century, but he was also one of the century's great musical intellects. In a lecture given in the late 1930s, entitled 'The Future of Music: Credo', he anticipated the age of the synthesiser by nearly 50 years: 'I believe that the use of noise to make music will continue and increase until we reach a music produced through the aid of electrical music instruments which will make available for musical purposes any and all sounds that can be heard'.

The prepared piano

Cage's interest in both dance and new musical materials led directly to his invention of the prepared piano. In 1940 the dancer Syvilla Fort asked John Cage to provide music for a new dance with an African theme. The intended venue had insufficient room for the usual percussion group and Cage himself explained his solution:

> I couldn't use percussion instruments for Syvilla's dance, though, suggesting Africa, they would have been suitable; they would have left too little room for her to perform. I was obliged to write a piano

> **Warning.** Photocopying any part of this book without permission is illegal.

piece. I spent a day or so conscientiously trying to find an African twelve-tone row. I had no luck. I decided that what was wrong was not me but the piano. I decided to change it. Besides studying with Weiss and Schoenberg, I had also studied with Henry Cowell. I had often heard him play a grand piano, changing its sound by plucking and muting the strings with fingers and hands.

Cage originally wrote this account for the foreword to Richard Bunger's book *The Well-Prepared Piano* (1973). A revised version appears in the preface to *Cage's Prepared Piano Music Volume 1* (Peters Edition).

Cage then describes how he experimented with different objects to modify the tone, and how these modified tones could be changed again by depressing the damper (soft) pedal while playing. His description ends with the following significant comments:

> When I first placed objects between piano strings, it was with the desire to possess sounds (to be able to repeat them). But, as the music left my home and went from piano to piano and from pianist to pianist, it became clear that not only are two pianists essentially different from one another, but two pianos are not the same either. Instead of the possibility of repetition, we are faced in life with the unique qualities and characteristics of each occasion.
>
> The prepared piano, impressions I had from the work of artist friends, study of Zen Buddhism, ramblings in fields and forests of mushrooms, all led me to the enjoyment of things as they come, as they happen, rather than as they are possessed or kept or forced to be.

Amores I can be found in the 1986 edition of the *London Anthology of Music*, No. 109.

When Cage moved to New York in 1942 he was unable to take his percussion instruments with him, and turned again to the prepared piano for its potential as a one-man percussion ensemble. It figured prominently in his music over the next few years, starting with *Amores* (1943), his first concert work to include prepared piano. Cage used relatively few preparations at first, and sometimes (as in *Amores*) gave general indications about the aural effects he wanted, rather than the very detailed instructions and measurements seen on page 167 of the *New Anthology*. As indicated in the quote above, Cage found that being so specific could also be misleading, because of the varying string-lengths and construction of different pianos.

Eastern philosophy

Cage wrote the account quoted above more than 30 years after his invention of the prepared piano. During the intervening period he had moved ever closer to a Zen philosophy of inner calm and balance. Part of this belief is an acceptance that everything is subject to change, and that discontentment arises from becoming attached to things (and thoughts) which are impermanent. Letting go of preconceived ideas, likes and dislikes, even the very notion of 'self', can lead to a state in which the mind welcomes change and reacts positively to new ideas and chance events in the world. Cage's interest in Eastern philosophy eventually led him to regard music as 'sounds thrown into silence', like the irregular rocks on a lawn of raked sand that forms the contemplative garden of a Zen temple.

Another important influence came from reading books on the aesthetics of Indian art, particularly *The Dance of Shiva* (1924) by Ananda Coomaraswamy, which expounds the view that art should 'imitate nature in her manner of operation'. Just as so much of the beauty of nature arises from constant change and the result of apparently chance events, so Cage came to incorporate indeterminate elements in his work – thus also fulfilling the Buddhist desire to let go of preconceived ideas and open the mind to the infinite possibilities of the here and now. This was a revolutionary approach to composition, overthrowing many of the rule-based principles on which western music had depended for a millenium, and Cage knew it. As early as 1946 he dismissed harmony as 'the tool of western commercialism' (in an article entitled 'The east in the west') adding, in a lecture of 1948, that it is 'a device to make music impressive, loud, and big, in order to enlarge audiences and increase box-office returns'.

The influence of Indian philosophy is evident as early as *Amores*, which Cage described as 'an attempt to express in combination the erotic and the tranquil, two of the permanent emotions of Indian tradition'. This is a reference to the Hindu theory of *rasa* (see *right*). Five years later Cage developed this idea further in the *Sonatas and Interludes*, in which he set out to reflect all eight mood of *rasa*, and their common tendency towards tranquillity. It is not known how the composer implemented the details of this plan but it seems likely that each movement expresses a single emotion, and that the entire collection of 20 pieces resolves towards the tranquillity of its last four movements. It would be unwise to expect too literal an interpretation of mirth, sorrow, disgust, and so forth – remember that the eastern aesthetic is often more concerned with a detached, ritualised experience that frees the mind to contemplate ideas of the unknown and infinite, rather than the western idea of art, which so often attempts the cathartic experience of taking an observer through a personal re-living of emotional states.

Nevertheless, James Pritchett (see *right*) suggests that the 'supple, seductive lines' of Sonata III are an expression of the erotic, and that Sonata IX (not in the *New Anthology*) inhabits the world of fear. You may be tempted to consider which 'permanent emotions' are expressed in the first two sonatas, but remember that any conclusions you reach will be purely speculative.

Despite the importance of Indian philosophy in Cage's works of the 1940s, the *Sonatas and Interludes* do not reflect the sounds of Indian music. Compare the recording of *NAM 10* with those of *NAM 58* and *NAM 59*, and see if you agree that Cage's sonatas seem closer to the far-eastern sound of gamelan music (the type of music Cage had studied with Cowell in 1934) than that of an Indian *rāg*.

The term sonata has had various meanings at different times in history. Cage uses it not in the familiar sense of a multi-movement work (see *NAM 22* for the first movement of a classical sonata) but in the way it was used by the baroque composer Domenico Scarlatti, who wrote hundreds of single-movement keyboard sonatas. On a superficial level, Cage adopts the binary form of these short works, but 18th-century musical structures use contrasts in tonality to define their sections and this is not an option with the complex, often indeterminate pitches produced by the prepared piano.

Cage had been developing musical structures without recourse to pitch since his percussion works of the late 1930s. His solution was to adopt duration as the main structural element – an idea that possibly arose from his work with dancers. In his *First Construction (in Metal)* of 1939 we see a simple version of the principle that underpins *NAM 10*. The first 16 bars form a unit of five phrases with the bar-lengths 4+3+2+3+4. The entire 256 bars consists of 16 repetitions of this unit, in the order 4+3+2+3+4 (see *right*).

The permanent emotions

The Hindu theory of *rasa* (emotional character) is described in Coomaraswamy's *The Dance of Shiva*. There are four light moods (the heroic, comic, wondrous and erotic) and four dark moods (fury, fear, disgust and sorrow). A ninth *rasa*, tranquillity, exists as a common tendency of the other eight.

A useful source for further reading is *The Music of John Cage* by James Pritchett, in the series 'Music in the Twentieth Century'. Cambridge University Press (1993), ISBN: 0-521-56544-8 (paperback).

Structure

A complete sonata in rounded binary form by Scarlatti can be found in the 1986 edition of the *London Anthology of Music*, No. 28.

```
×4   43234  43234  43234  43234
×3   43234  43234  43234
×2   43234  43234
×3   43234  43234  43234
×4   43234  43234  43234  43234
```

John Cage described this type of structure as 'micro-macrocosmic'. Today we would recognise it as the self-symmetrical formation known in mathematics as a fractal, in which each sub-division is a miniature version of the whole. It is a form found in nature (for example it is the basis of the snowflake and fern) and thus we see that Cage's 'micro-macrocosmic' structure fulfils Coomaraswamy's edict that art should 'imitate nature in her manner of operation'.

The structures in the *Sonatas and Interludes* are more complex than the simple $16^2 = 256$ formula of *First Construction (in Metal)* because Cage uses irregular lengths for his basic units. In the AS Guide we showed how the first sonata is built on a seven-bar unit whose 28 crotchets are arranged in the pattern 4:1:3 + 4:1:3 + 4:2 + 4:2. The whole sonata mimics this pattern by using seven-crotchet units in the multiples 4, 1, 3 (repeated) and 4, 2 (repeated).

The rhythmic structure of Sonata II is more complex, being based on the asymmetric 31-crotchet unit of bars 1–9:

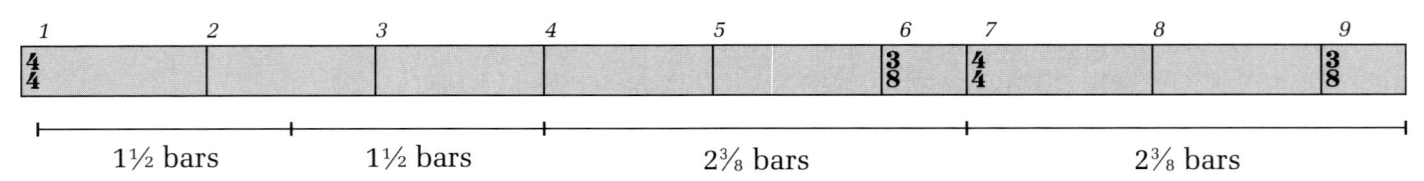

However, again the whole sonata mimics this pattern by using 31-crotchet units in the multiples 1½ (repeated) and 2⅜ (repeated):

Bars 1–9	31 crotchets	= 1 × 31
Bars 10–14	15½ crotchets	= ½ × 31
Bars 15–23	31 crotchets	= 1 × 31
Bars 24–32	31 crotchets	= 1 × 31
Bars 33–37	11½ crotchets	≈ ⅜ × 31

Notice how these sections are delineated by the double barlines in *NAM 10*, and how the final section involves a slight mathematical approximation to fit with the practicalities of clear notation.

Sonata III is based on a unit of 34 crotchets (bars 1–8):

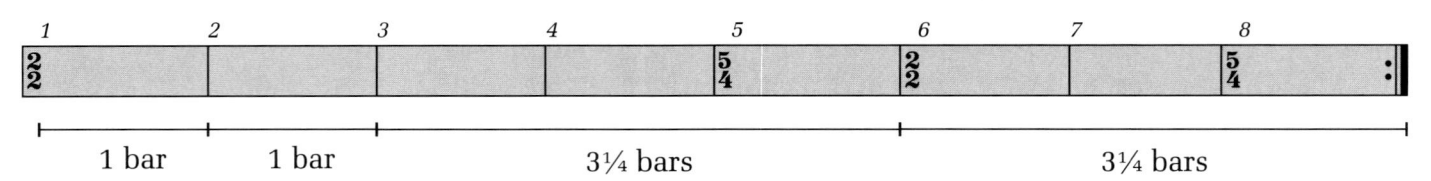

Like the other sonatas, the proportions of this pattern (1:1:3¼:3¼) also provide the proportions of the entire movement:

Bars 1–8	34 crotchets	= 1 × 34
Bars 1–8 repeated	34 crotchets	= 1 × 34
Bars 9–32	110½ crotchets	= 3¼ × 34
Bars 9–32 repeated	110½ crotchets	= 3¼ × 34

This careful attention to proportionality makes its impact in a subconscious way. Aurally more obvious is the fact that, because the two sections of the macrocosmic binary form are repeated, the microcosmic structures of the individual sections also create paired units (this is particularly evident at the start of Sonata I, where bars 3–4 form a varied repeat of bars 1–2). There are many other internal repetitions which strengthen the structure of each sonata:

- In Sonata I, bars 20–21 are subjected to varied repetition in the next two bars. The entire progression of Debussy-like parallel chords creates a decidedly cadential effect that is strengthened by the following tiny coda (in which the right hand of bar 24 is subjected to varied repetition in bars 25–26).

    Don't miss the figures attached to the tops of the treble clefs in this passage (and elsewhere). *8* means play an octave higher and *15* means play a 15th (ie two octaves) higher than written.

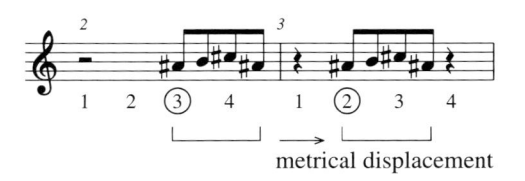

- When the six-beat phrase at the start of Sonata II is answered by the left hand Cage substitutes a crotchet rest for the note in the middle of the pattern. This rest falls on a strong beat and so creates syncopation, an effect which is enhanced by the metrical displacement of the repeated four-quaver motif (see *right*). Such jazz-like rhythms permeate much of this sonata (is it reflecting the *rasa* mirth?). For example, the metrical displacement of the repeated figure in bars 7–8 is essentially the early-jazz device of 'secondary rag', in which a three-beat figure is repeated across the four-fold beat of quadruple time. A cascade of rag-like syncopation follows in the rhythmic repetitions of bars 10–14.

- Repetition is just one of many traditional devices in the third sonata. The first section consists of three statements of the opening right-hand figure, in the second of which the final note is truncated to a crotchet. The initial three demi-semiquavers of this motif are augmented to eight times their value in bar 13. These crotchets are heard in retrograde order in bar 14, extended into bar 15 by means of a sequence. The left-hand of bars 14–15 repeats the ostinato accompaniment first heard in bars 11–12, but in bar 14 (only) it is transposed up a semitone.

The left-hand motif in bar 9 is subtly transformed into a rising chromatic scale in bar 17, truncated to two notes in bar 18, and then greatly extended in bars 19–21. The last F of bar 21 is also the first note of a retrograde repetition of the previous 14 pitches, so the two-note chord in bar 24 is the same chord with which the pattern began in bar 19. A further variant appears in bars 25–26 and versions of the two-note chord (a 4th) are heard until the end of the work. Meanwhile the right hand picks up the chromatic scale figure in bar 22. It begins in octaves with the left hand, but the tied A causes it to lag by a beat, producing minor 9ths in bar 23. This right-hand pattern is inverted in bars 27–28, and is subsequently joined with variants of the motif from bar 2 in the final system of the sonata.

Private study

1. What were the main influences on Cage's early work?
2. In what sense are the movements in *NAM 10* sonatas?
3. Explain how the concept of *rasa* applies to *NAM 10*.
4. What is meant by the expression 'metrical displacement'?
5. Why did Cage describe the structure of works such as these sonatas as 'micro-macrocosmic'?

Sample questions

In the exam there will be three questions on this work, from which you must choose to answer **two**.

(a) Discuss in detail the structure of **one** sonata from *NAM 10*.

(b) To what extent does Cage rely on traditional techniques of melodic development and repetition in *NAM 10*?

(c) In what ways does *NAM 10* reveal Cage's interest in eastern philosophy?

Continuity and change in instrumental and vocal techniques

> Topic for examination in 2002 and 2003

You do not need to study this topic unless *20th-century art music* is the Area of Study that you undertook for AS Music and which you are now extending for A2.

Before starting work on this topic you need a thorough understanding of the material on *20th-century art music* in the AS Guide (pages 40–52). Remember that for A2 the topic draws on works from across the **entire** Area of Study, not just those in one of the two lists, A or B.

Stravinsky

NAM 7 CD1 Tracks 7–9
Academy of St Martin-in-the-Fields
Conducted by Neville Marriner

Stravinsky's early ballets were scored for the very large orchestras that were common in the late-19th and early-20th centuries. For example, *The Rite of Spring* (1913) requires some 150 players. Economic conditions after the first world war often necessitated the use of smaller ensembles – the *Pulcinella* suite requires a chamber orchestra of only 33 players: six woodwind, four brass, 18 orchestral strings (the proportions 4:4:4:3:3 are suggested in the complete score) and string quintet. The small scale of this ensemble allows Stravinsky to exploit solo writing in textures that often resemble those of chamber music – this is particularly evident in the Gavotte and two variations, scored entirely for wind soloists.

The absence of clarinets in *NAM 7*, and the division of the strings into concertino and ripieno groups, lends baroque colour to the score, but in most respects Stravinsky's orchestration, especially his brass writing, is decidedly modern. The most characteristic sound of baroque music, the harpsichord, is entirely absent (it dropped out of use in the late 18th century and was not widely revived until the second half of the 20th century).

In the AS Guide (pages 41–43) we mentioned a number of features in the instrumentation of *NAM 7* that would not be found in an 18th-century score and it is not difficult to identify many others. Compare the second section of the gavotte (starting at bar 11) with the original keyboard version to see how Stravinsky transforms Martini's walking bass into a smooth line of minims for bassoon and his inner pedal on D into an ostinato of sighing horn appoggiaturas (see *left*). Compare the horn writing in *NAM 2* with Stravinsky's horn parts at the start of *Variazione I*. The natural horns of the 18th century had only a few widely-spaced pitches available in the lower register (which Haydn doesn't use at all) whereas the modern valve horn enables Stravinsky to allocate the bass of the entire texture to second horn, despite its scalic outline.

Note that horns in F sound a 5th lower than written when in the treble clef, but a **4th higher** than written when in the bass clef.

Variazione II shows a similarly modern approach to instrumental technique. The first horn is required to take a melodic solo role, in dialogue with the flute, and the virtuoso bassoon passagework presents considerable technical difficulties (despite Stravinsky's consideration in splitting it between the two players) especially in the fingering of the high tenor-clef section.

However it is the *Vivo* which most clearly reveals *Pulcinella* to be a 20th-century ballet score rather than a mere pastiche of baroque music. The trombone is an instrument of ancient pedigree and when it appeared in 18th-century music (which was rare) its solemn tone was used with restraint and usually in the context of grand, priestly ritual. But Stravinsky's trombone solo, with its cheeky glissandi is pure circus music and there is no 18th-century precedent for such heterophonic textures as that in bars 38–45, where solo double bass, trumpet and two flutes simultaneously play different versions of the same melody.

Throughout *NAM 7* Stravinsky follows the convention of his time by giving very detailed performance directions for dynamics and articulation. In the *Vivo* this extends to such specific instructions as *détaché* (detached) and *du talon* ('with the lower part of the bow' – this gives added force to the tone).

Although the saxophone had been invented in about 1840 it was rarely used in art music before 1920. Then, during the jazz age of the 1920s, it became more widely known through its adoption by jazz bands and started to appear in works by composers such as Milhaud, Gershwin, Walton (*Façade*) and Ravel (*Bolero*). A more direct precedent for the scoring of Webern's quartet is a trio for viola, tenor saxophone or heckelphone (a large tenor oboe) and piano, by the German composer Hindemith. This appeared in 1928, the year in which Webern commenced work on Op. 22. Although the saxophone is capable of a much more powerful tone than other woodwind instruments, Webern clearly understood that it is also capable of the subtlety of tone and dynamic needed for good balance in small-scale chamber music such as *NAM 8* – notice how he requires quiet playing both in the lowest register (eg first note of bar 8) and near the top of the range (eg bar 27).

The four instruments mainly play one at a time with little overlap, apart from bars 22–23 where the central climax is delineated by a thicker texture, wider range and louder dynamic level. They also play few notes at a time – mainly just two- and three-note cells – but almost every note is given its own indication of dynamic and articulation. As Schoenberg noted, in music of this concentration and intensity the slightest nuance conveys an almost unbearable significance.

Webern's sparse use of resources in *NAM 8* is very different from Stravinsky's much more traditional orchestration of *NAM 7*. This is largely due to the *pointillist* texture resulting from Webern's use of *Klangfarbenmelodie*. The fragmentary melodies and irregular entries require meticulous counting, and the sudden and frequent wide leaps across different registers need to be executed without losing a sense of line – a point that particularly concerned Webern at the first performance of his Symphony, Op. 21 (1928).

Webern

NAM 8   CD1 Track 10
Jacqueline Ross (violin),
Ruth MacDowell (clarinet),
Jan Steele (saxophone),
Mark Racz (piano)

Shostakovich

NAM 9 — CD1 Track 11
Coull Quartet

Notes that can be produced only on the lowest string:
Cello — from / to
Viola — from / to
Violin — from / to

Cage

NAM 10 — CD1 Tracks 12–14
Joanna MacGregor

Berio

NAM 11 — CD1 Track 15
Cathy Berberian

Warning. Photocopying any part of this book without permission is illegal.

Works for string quartet have been the foundation of the chamber-music repertoire since the mid 18th century. With more than two centuries of tradition behind it, the instrumentation of *NAM 9* is more conventional than other works in this area of study, and is in striking contrast to the scoring of Webern's quartet.

The first movement is given its dark colour by the mainly quiet dynamic level, the low tessitura (all four instruments frequently play on their lowest string – see *left*), the long pedal points, the simple rhythms, the often slow rate of harmonic change, and the extended sections with few or no rests (eg bars 55–85). Shostakovich uses no special effects such as pizzicato or tremolo, nor is there any double- and triple-stopping (as in *NAM 7*) or use of the extreme high register (as in the solo double-bass part of Stravinsky's *Vivo*). There is, though, a deep sense of continuity with tradition in this work – not to earlier 20th-century music, but to the string quartets of composers such as Brahms and Beethoven.

Cage's use of the prepared piano represents a fundamental break with the past of the sort not seen in the work of the conservative Shostakovich. The example of the latter's piano music given in *NAM 25* was composed two or three years **after** *NAM 10*, although you may well feel that it sounds very much earlier in style. Even in comparison with Webern's atonal piano part in *NAM 8*, Cage's prepared piano (details of which are given in the section beginning on page 49 of this book) seems to inhabit a totally new timbral world – one in which the creative process begins not with pitch and rhythm, but with the choice of materials (or mutes, as Cage calls them) for modifying the sound of individual notes.

On page 55 we noted that Stravinsky, like most composers in the early 20th century, provided very explicit performing directions. This is equally true of *NAM 10*, in which Cage's table of preparations sets out to prescribe specific timbres for each prepared note, and it is also the case in *NAM 11*, in which Berio gives full details of the various extended vocal techniques required and how he has notated them. Compare *Sequenza III* (1966) with the much earlier *Pierrot Lunaire* (1912, *NAM 40*). Schoenberg was one of the first composers to use the voice in new ways, but he is far less explicit in how his *Sprechgesang* should be interpreted. However just as performances of *Pierrot* differ radically from one reciter to another, and Cage's sonatas can sound very different on different pianos, despite careful following of the preparation instructions, so performances of Berio's *Sequenza* can vary widely when given by other performers capable of realising the virtuoso vocal techniques required.

As in *NAM 10*, an important aspect of the work is the selection of the raw materials from which it is formed. The text is short and simple, and Berio's setting is concerned not so much with the meaning of its words as their potential to be changed in order, exaggerated, distorted and blurred into other vocal events, such as coughing and laughing, which in turn are transformed into displays of coloratura virtuosity. There are many precedents in light opera and music-hall songs for musical representations of effects such as laughter, but *Sequenza III* inhabits a new, under-explored world on the very border between music and language, with its huge variety of rapidly changing vocal techniques. Berio encourages a dramatic performance by means of cue words (tense, witty, etc) that are unrelated to the poem. He indicates that these may be used by the performer as triggers for bodily and facial gestures but also warns that literal expressions of these emotional states should be avoided – their purpose is to focus the colour and intonation of the voice. In other words *Sequenza III* is not a piece about a dramatic situation – it is itself the drama. It is music theatre.

Reich

NAM 12   CD1 Track 16
Roger Heaton

The 'desire to possess sounds (to be able to repeat them)' that John Cage recognised in his own earlier work is often less strongly felt by post-modernist composers. Many scores of minimalist music are also minimal in their directions for interpretation, leaving such matters largely to the performer. Certainly the directions in the score of *NAM 12* are confined mainly to dynamics and structure, and there are no extended instrumental techniques to explain. Two significant aspects of the work are the use of a single instrumental colour (clarinet tone in the score, but Reich has also approved a saxophone arrangement of the work) and the use of technology (multi-track recording) to enable all 11 parts to be delivered by a single performer. The first of these poses little problem – the wide range of the clarinet (extended by the inclusion of bass clarinets), its distinctively different timbres in low, middle and upper registers, and Reich's control over textural change ensure plenty of variety. The second point, though, raises an interesting dilemma: is spontaneity in performance, particularly with regard to tempo, compromised when playing against a pre-recorded backing tape?

Private study

1. (i) What do you notice when you compare the horn writing in *NAM 7* with Haydn's horn parts in *NAM 2*?
   (ii) What is the main reason for such differences?

2. State what is meant by a heterophonic texture and give an example of such a texture in the *Vivo* of *NAM 7*.

3. Which movement of *NAM 7* is scored only for wind?

4. To what extent does *NAM 10* support John Cage's description of the prepared piano as 'a percussion orchestra under the control of a single player'?

5. Give the meaning of each of the following: *détaché*, *du talon*, *mit Dämpfer*, *una corda*, $\overset{15}{\&}$, *loco*, dental tremolo.

Sample questions

In the exam there will be two questions on this topic, from which you must choose to answer **one**.

(a) How does the orchestration of *NAM 7* reveal that *Pulcinella* is a 20th-century work?

(b) Contrast the use of instruments in the quartets by Webern (*NAM 8*) and Shostakovich (*NAM 9*).

(c) The critic Paul Griffiths has claimed that the works of Berio's *Sequenza* series 'are showpieces, certainly, but the showiness is not an extra'. Is this true of the vocal writing in *NAM 11*?

For examination in summer 2004 and 2005

20th-century art music

This part of the chapter deals with the special focus work and topic set for examination in summer 2004 and 2005. If you are taking the exam in summer 2002 or 2003 turn to page 49.

Special Focus Work for 2004 and 2005

NAM 8 CD1 Track 10
Jacqueline Ross (violin),
Ruth MacDowell (clarinet),
Jan Steele (saxophone),
Mark Racz (piano)

Webern, Quartet Op. 22 (movement 1)

Before starting on this section you should work through (or revise) the information about the context and structure of this music given on pages 43–46 of the AS Guide. Make sure that you understand all of the terminology used on those pages.

In the AS Guide we explained how this concentrated movement uses serial technique within a structure that resembles sonata form, employing rhythms that derive from just three rhythmic cells and mirror canons that derive from a basic note row:

Form	Bars	Details
Introduction	1–5	Mirror canons for pairs of instruments
Exposition	6–15	Cantus firmus on saxophone (consisting of two presentations of the 12-note series) with mirror canons on accompanying instruments
Development	16–27	Mirror canons on all four instruments, reaching a central climax in bars 22–23. The link in bars 24–27 includes a retrograde version of the Introduction
Recapitulation	28–38	The cantus firmus is now presented as a *Klangfarbenmelodie*, shared between violin, clarinet and saxophone. Mirror canons continue on piano
Coda	39–43	Mirror canons matching those of the introduction and the link in bars 24–27

All of this material is based on a note row of 12 pitches which can appear in four orders (prime, inversion, retrograde and retrograde inversion) and transposed to any of 12 pitches. We now need to look at this in more detail. The basic series is called the prime and is first heard on the tenor saxophone starting at bar 6:

P^0 ▶	C♯	E	F	D	D♯	B	B♭	A	G♯	F♯	C	G

Since this is the prime version of the row in untransposed form we have called it P^0. The row can be transposed to any of the other 11 pitches in an octave, and we can use numerals to indicate the amount of upward transposition:

P^0 ▶	C♯	E	F	D	D♯	B	B♭	A	G♯	F♯	C	G	◀ R^0
P^1 ▶	D	F	F♯	D♯	E	C	B	B♭	A	G	C♯	G♯	◀ R^1
P^2 ▶	D♯	F♯	G	E	F	C♯	C	B	B♭	G♯	D	A	◀ R^2

... and so on. The retrograde versions of these transpositions (R^0, R^1, R^2, etc) can be found by reading these rows from right to left.

We can use this technique to construct a matrix of all the possible permutations of the row. In the table that follows prime versions are read from left to right, retrograde versions from right to left. Inversions of the row are read from top to bottom of a column, and retrograde inversions are read from bottom to top of a column:

Warning. Photocopying any part of this book without permission is illegal.

	I^0	I^3	I^4	I^1	I^2	I^{10}	I^9	I^8	I^7	I^5	I^{11}	I^6	
P^0 ▶	C#	E	F	D	D#	B	Bb	A	G#	F#	C	G	
P^9	Bb	C#	D	B	C	G#	G	F#	F	D#	A	E	
P^8	A	C	C#	Bb	B	G	F#	F	E	D	G#	D#	
P^{11} ▶	C	D#	E	C#	D	Bb	A	G#	G	F	B	F#	◀ R^{11}
P^{10} ▶	B	D	D#	C	C#	A	G#	G	F#	E	Bb	F	◀ R^{10}
P^2	D#	F#	G	E	F	C#	C	B	Bb	G#	D	A	
P^3	E	G	G#	F	F#	D	C#	C	B	A	D#	Bb	
P^4 ▶	F	G#	A	F#	G	D#	D	C#	C	Bb	E	B	
P^5	F#	A	Bb	G	G#	E	D#	D	C#	B	F	C	
P^7	G#	B	C	A	Bb	F#	F	E	D#	C#	G	D	
P^1 ▶	D	F	F#	D#	E	C	B	Bb	A	G	C#	G#	
P^6 ▶	G	Bb	B	G#	A	F	E	D#	D	C	F#	C#	
	▲ RI^0										▲ RI^{11}		

Some analyses identify the prime as the series we have preferred to describe as I^5. This is because Webern wrote the second movement of the quartet first, basing it on that version of the row. Since you are studying only the first movement (which never uses I^5) it is more logical to regard the prime as the first 12 notes of the cantus firmus in the exposition, heard in the tenor saxophone from bar 6. If you agree, it may help to avoid ambiguity in your answers to mention that this is what you are treating as the prime version of the row.

The permutations actually used by Webern in this movement (15 out of the possible 48) are shown in bold. When following these remember that notes may be printed enharmonically (eg Eb for D#) and that octave displacements occur all the time – there are few instances of stepwise movement. Also, be aware that notes of the series may occur simultaneously in the piano (eg in bar 12, notes 2 and 3 of I^0 appear as a chord in the right hand and are immediately mirrored by notes 2 and 3 of P^{10} in the left hand).

The complete row is easiest to see in the saxophone cantus firmus. This starts with P^0 (bars 6–10), which ends on G. The note G is also the first note of P^6 which then follows straight on in bars 11–14. The row is always used in its entirety, but its other appearances are split between instruments, and occur in the following order:

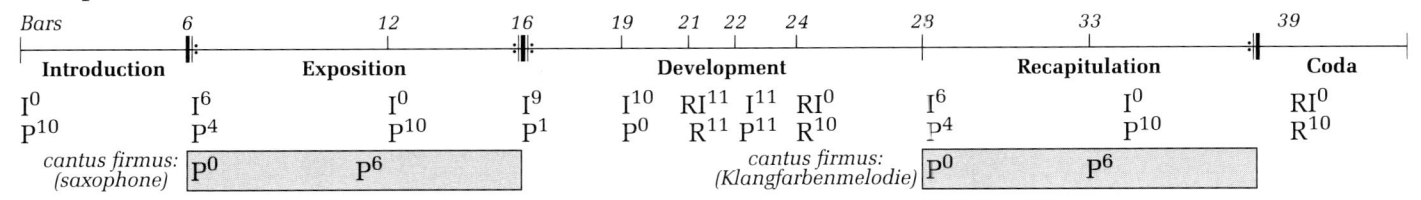

Bars	6	12	16	19	21	22	24	28	33	39
	Introduction	Exposition		Development				Recapitulation		Coda
	I^0	I^6	I^0	I^9	I^{10}	RI^{11} I^{11} RI^0		I^6	I^0	RI^0
	P^{10}	P^4	P^{10}	P^1	P^0	R^{11} P^{11} R^{10}		P^4	P^{10}	R^{10}
	cantus firmus: (saxophone)	P^0	P^6			cantus firmus: (Klangfarbenmelodie)		P^0	P^6	

Webern reserves the loudest dynamics and widest instrumental range for the central climax of the development. We can now also see that he intensifies this section by introducing all four versions (P, I, R and RI) of the eleventh transposition in quick succession, using retrograde versions of the row for the first time at this point.

Notice that the first and last notes of the row are always a tritone apart – the interval of six semitones that divides the 12 semitones of an octave into two. A similar type of symmetry can be seen in the rows that form the mirror canons, these being chosen so that the tritone F#–C usually appears at the same numeric positions in the row (see *right* – I^9 and P^1 also pair in a similar way).

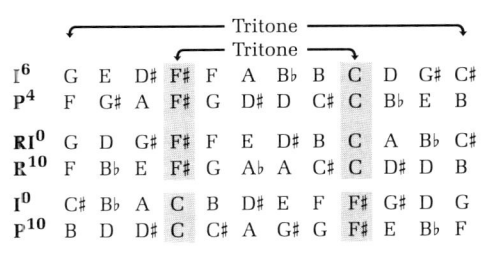

			⎯ Tritone ⎯									
		⎯ Tritone ⎯										
I^6	G	E	D#	F#	F	A	Bb	B	C	D	G#	C#
P^4	F	G#	A	F#	G	D#	D	C#	C	Bb	E	B
RI^0	G	D	G#	F#	F	E	D#	B	C	A	Bb	C#
R^{10}	F	Bb	E	F#	G	Ab	A	C#	C	D#	D	B
I^0	C#	Bb	A	C	B	D#	E	F	F#	G#	D	G
P^{10}	B	D	D#	C	C#	A	G#	G	F#	E	Bb	F

This tritone between C and F♯ permeates the work in other ways. For example, the first two entries of the row (bars 1 and 2) are on D♭ and B – a semitone either side of C – the next two (piano, bar 6) are on G and F – a semitone either side of F♯. And, as mentioned earlier, the prime row of the second movement begins on F♯ and ends on C. But, unusually for such a strictly serial piece, it is the single pitch F♯ that Webern often singles out for special attention. It appears twice in succession in bar 4 (clarinet), as the ninth notes of P^{10} and I^0 almost coincide – although when this passage is heard in retrograde it is (of course!) the note C that is heard twice in succession (bars 25 and 41), and four F♯s (all in the same octave) are heard on four consecutive semiquavers in bar 21, as the climax of the movement approaches.

Private study

TIP: The canonic entries in bars 12–13 are derived from the note rows as follows:

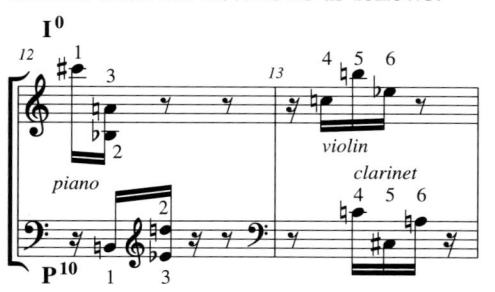

On page 45 of the AS Guide we showed how P^{10} and I^0 are divided between the instruments to form mirror canons in bars 1–5. Draw up a plan to show the distribution of mirror canons in bars 6–15. They start with P^4 and I^6 in bar 6, and are followed by P^{10} and I^0 which start in bar 12. Remember that the saxophone does not take part in the canons in this section.

Sample questions

In the exam there will be three questions on this work, from which you must choose to answer **two**.

(a) Analyse bars 1–15 of *NAM 8*, showing in detail how Webern uses serial technique in this section.

(b) How does Webern create a sense of intense unity in *NAM 8*?

(c) (i) What is meant by the term mirror canon?
 (ii) Discuss Webern's use of mirror canons in *NAM 8*.

Topic for examination in 2004 and 2005

Continuity and change in approaches to tonality

You do not need to study this topic unless *20th-century art music* is the Area of Study that you undertook for AS Music and which you are now extending for A2.

Before starting work on this topic you need a thorough understanding of the material on *20th-century art music* in the AS Guide (pages 40–52). For A2 the topic draws on all the works in the **entire** Area of Study, whether they use conventional tonality or not, and is not limited to just those in one of the two lists A or B.

Tonality

The key-defining nature of V^7–I:

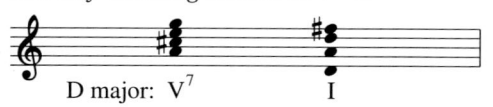

D major: V^7 I

The combination of C♯ and G♮ shows that the key must contain sharps – but no more than two since G is natural. It can only be D major or D minor (B minor is ruled out by the presence of A♮). Chord I is major, so the key is D major.

Scholars debate the precise meaning of the term tonality, but for our purposes it can be said to refer to music based primarily on major and/or minor keys. A key is a hierarchy of notes in which one (the tonic) has special importance as the 'home' note. Similarly, in the tonal system one key (the tonic key) tends to predominate. Keys such as the dominant and relative major are said to be closely related because they share many notes in common with the tonic. Keys are established by cadences, particularly perfect cadences. The progression V^7–I is one of the most common ways to establish the tonality of a passage as the notes used in this pair of chords occur together in only one single key (see *left*).

Tonality gradually developed from the modal system in the years around 1600 and became the foundation of almost all western art music for the next three centuries. One of the reasons for its success is the potential tonality gives for creating longer musical forms, based on the use of different key centres for structural purposes. By the late 19th century many composers were tending to blur the boundaries of simple tonal relationships by modulating to remote keys, using dissonant harmonies designed to delay resolution to the tonic, and employing extensive chromaticism to give colour without defining key. All of these traits can be heard in the preludes by Wagner (1859, *NAM 4*) and Debussy (1894, *NAM 5*). The work of both men led the way for 20th-century composers to explore new systems for the creation of music, in a process that is often known as the breakdown of tonality. This is an inaccurate expression, because tonality has never actually broken down. Much music (particularly pop music) continues to be written in a tonal idiom, and a diatonic, tonal style has once again become popular in much of the post-modernist and minimalist music of recent decades.

The dances in *Pulcinella* are based on the tonal structures of the 18th-century music from which they are arranged. Let's take the binary-form gavotte as an example. It is in D major and its first section modulates to the dominant (A major), confirmed by the definitive perfect cadence in A in bars 9–10. The second section modulates more widely: G major in bars 11–14 then up a tone to A major for the four-bar sequential repetition in bars 15–18. Tonal sequences of this kind are as much a fingerprint of tonal music as the ubiquitous perfect cadences. Another sequence, this time two bars in length, descends stepwise through F♯ minor (bars 19–20), E minor (bars 21–22) and D major (bars 23–24), and the final eight bars are then concerned with re-establishing D major as the tonic, balancing the earlier excursions to various other keys.

Stravinsky

NAM 7 CD1 Tracks 7–9
Academy of St Martin-in-the-Fields
Conducted by Neville Marriner

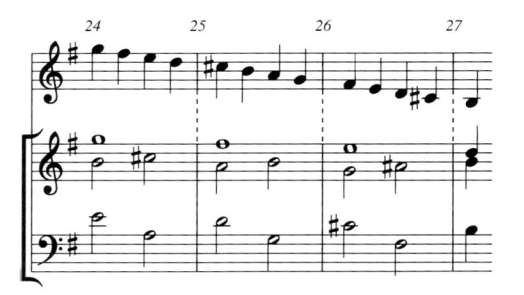

Although Stravinsky doesn't depart from a clear tonal structure in any of the dances, his neo-classical style sometimes undermines it. For instance, bars 24–27 of the *Sinfonia* basically consist of the progression shown on the two lower staves *right* (a cycle of 5ths – yet another fingerprint of the tonal style). But Stravinsky overlays this with a long descending scale for violins (topmost stave) which introduces a string of unprepared diatonic dissonance in a distinctly un-baroque style. Here are more examples of such modernism:

✦ Stravinsky subverts the perfect cadences in bar 31 of the *Sinfonia* by leaving the second violins playing B against the chord of A minor in the rest of the strings (see also the cadence in bar 32)

✦ romantic appoggiaturas for horn clash gently against Martini's two-part counterpoint in bars 11–13 of the gavotte and another scale (this time ascending and in the second oboe) dissonantly cuts through the texture in bars 17–18

✦ in *Variazione I* the brass stick resolutely to a chord of D in bars 43–45, totally ignoring the woodwind's G-major harmony on the first beat of bar 44 (repeated a tone higher four bars later) – and in bar 51 another second-oboe scale (this time descending) clashes merrily with the prevailing G-major harmony of the first oboe, as does the C♯ of the first bassoon in the same bar

Warning. Photocopying any part of this book without permission is illegal.

- some more dissonantly modern cadences appear in the *Vivo*. In the 'perfect cadence' at bar 33 Stravinsky anticipates the tonic (G) in the V^7 chord – and then leaves the leading-note (F♯) lingering on into the tonic chord (see *left*). This device is repeated in sequence four bars later. Careful balancing of parts makes the progression sound recognisably cadential, but the astringent modern twist mocks the most fundamental key-defining device of tonal music, the perfect cadence, by blurring the functions of both dominant 7th and tonic harmony.

Webern

NAM 8 CD1 Track 10
Jacqueline Ross (violin),
Ruth MacDowell (clarinet),
Jan Steele (saxophone),
Mark Racz (piano)

Read pages 43–44 of the AS Guide for the background to serial music. Although written only ten years after *Pulcinella*, the atonal style of *NAM 8* is in total contrast to the tonal idiom of Stravinsky's neo-classical ballet. Unlike tonal music, serialism places equal importance on all 12 pitches of the octave. The consistent use of a note row ensures this equality and also gives unity and structure to the music. But Webern goes far beyond this, superimposing on his serial structure mirror canons around a cantus firmus and even an overall sonata form (although one without the slightest hint of tonality), all used with the utmost economy of means in one of the most concentrated movements in the *New Anthology*.

Shostakovich

NAM 9 CD1 Track 11
Coull Quartet

The opening D–Es–C–H motif (D–E♭–C–B♮) resolves on C and, when heard in isolation, seems to circumscribe a clear tonality of C minor. But tonal ambiguity is produced by the imitative entries of the other parts (all 12 semitones of the octave are used by bar 6) and by the shifting triadic harmony of bars 13–14 (E minor, E major, E♭ major). However the harmonisation of the opening motif in bars 23–25 is a textbook-like affirmation of C minor and from this point onwards the movement remains anchored to that key with long dominant and tonic pedal points. Sometimes Shostakovich prefers major 3rds to minor ones (F♭ in bar 33, E♮ in bar 55 for a quotation from his 5th symphony) and sometimes he prefers no 3rd at all (bars 26 and 50). But neither the chromatic writing nor the short excursion to A minor (starting in bar 86) suggest that this is anything other than a profoundly tonal movement. The overall structure – a chromatically unstable opening which soon resolves into triadic harmony, often with much interplay of major and minor 3rds, is typical of many of the composer's mature works.

Cage

NAM 10 CD1 Tracks 12–14
Joanna MacGregor

Superficially there are features in the sonatas that resemble those of tonal music, such as the triadic-looking chords in Sonata I, or the pedal point in the first eight bars of Sonata III. But listening to CD1 immediately reveals that these are not tonal pieces. Cage's 'mutes' not only change the timbre of the piano but also radically affect its tuning, creating some notes of indeterminate pitch and others in which the relationship between notes is quite different from that of the tempered scales of western music. In any case Cage's focus is not on tonality (his views on harmony were mentioned earlier, on page 51) but on units of duration, rhythm and timbre.

Berio

NAM 11 CD1 Track 15
Cathy Berberian

Indeterminacy of pitch is even more striking in *Sequenza III*. Berio himself directs that the borderline between speaking and singing will often be blurred, and even when precise intervals are notated, their pitch is not absolute. Unlike Webern, Berio does not fight shy of passing references to tonal music (most notably in the minor triadic structure around 3'30" in the score) but in essence *NAM 11* typifies a post-war modernist perspective that tonality was no longer of relevance in music of the day.

This view was not shared by composers such as Terry Riley, whose *In C* (written in 1964, two years before *Sequenza III*) is based on 53 motifs firmly centred around C major. The very title of that work became symbolic of a return to diatonic writing in the work of many minimalist composers of the post-modernist era. Reich's *New York Counterpoint* (1985) is entirely diatonic – every note belongs to the key of B major (heard as A major, since the clarinets sound a tone lower than written). The melodic ostinati are centred on hypnotic alternations of chords IV and V, but their canonic entries cause the chords to overlap and change at different times in different parts:

Reich

NAM 12	CD1 Track 16
Roger Heaton	

For clarity pairs of parts that are a 10th apart have here been printed a third apart.

These melodic parts always use a hexatonic (six-note) scale – the note D♯ occurs only in the pulsating homophonic textures that add a harder edge. Even when these hint at a tonic chord there is always an added diatonic dissonance to cloud the issue, as in the C♯ bass to the B-major harmony which introduces these textures in bar 27.

This is diatonic music, but is it tonal? The continual oscillation of two chords with blurred harmonies and the lack of progression towards the tonic means that the harmony is non-functional – it is colouristic, and there is no contrast of sections by use of modulation. There is continuity with the tonal traditions of the past, but there is change in this 20th-century reinterpretation of tonality.

Private study

1. Explain what you understand is meant by tonality.
2. Look up the expression 'functional harmony' in a good music dictionary and then gives examples of its use in *NAM 7*.
3. What examples would you choose from *NAM 9* to show that Shostakovich often reveals a traditional view of tonality?
4. Is *NAM 12* merely an example of new wine in an old bottle?

Sample questions

In the exam there will be two questions on this topic, from which you must choose to answer **one**.

(a) Was the approach to tonality by 20th-century composers one of evolution or revolution?

(b) To what extent does the use of serialism in atonal music serve a similar purpose to the use of tonality in tonal music?

(c) Comment on changing attitudes to dissonance in the works you have studied.

Warning. Photocopying any part of this book without permission is illegal.

For examination in summer 2002 and 2003

Music for small ensemble

The first part of this chapter deals with the special focus work and topic set for examination in summer 2002 and 2003. If you are taking the exam in summer 2004 or 2005 turn to page 72.

Haydn, Quartet Op. 33, No. 2 (movement 4)

Special Focus Work for 2002 and 2003
NAM 16　　　　　　　CD2 Track 5
The Lindsays

Before starting on this section you should work through (or revise) the information about the context and structure of this music given on pages 58–60 of the AS Guide. Make sure that you understand all of the terminology used on those pages.

Style　After completing his Six Quartets (Op. 33) in 1781 Haydn wrote to potential purchasers that he was offering

> for the price of 6 ducats, a work, consisting of 6 Quartets for 2 violins, viola and violoncello concertante ... written in a new and special style.

What was this 'new and special style'? To answer this question we must first go back to a set of quartets written nine years earlier. Most movements in these six quartets of Op. 20 are serious in style: two are in minor keys, three end with learned fugues, and all of them contain stately minuets and meditative, sometimes tragic, slow movements. There could hardly be a greater contrast between this set and Opus 33. The latter became known as *Gli Scherzi* ('The Jokes') because the minuets are replaced with sprightly scherzos. But the nickname is appropriate to the last movements too. Instead of the solemn fugues or sonata-form finales of Op. 20, four of the Op. 33 quartets end with bubbling prestos, and even the two that end with allegrettos are based on cheerful, tuneful melodies quite unlike those in the last movements of the earlier set. You can see the contrast at its most extreme if you compare the start of the last movement of Op. 20 No. 5 (a double fugue in F minor) ...

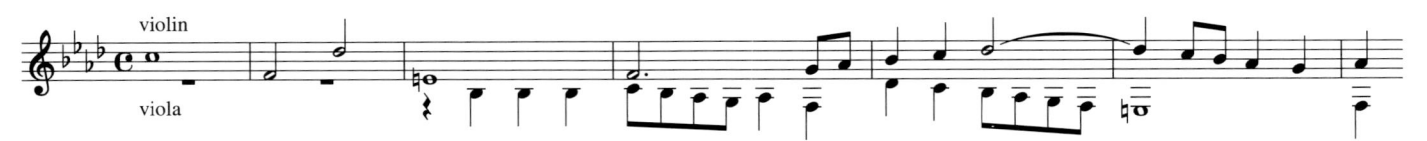

... with the start of the romping finale of Op. 33, No. 2:

What happened to occasion such a change in style? As a servant in the court of Prince Esterházy, Haydn was obliged to compose and conduct whatever the prince required – and that was often operas for his lavish private opera house and marionette theatre. So between 1772 (when Haydn wrote his Op. 20 quartets) and 1781 (when he composed the Op. 33 set) the most famous composer in Europe was so busy writing and directing theatrical music that he

Warning. Photocopying any part of this book without permission is illegal.

had no time to compose quartets, and only managed to write a handful of symphonies. Many of the theatrical works performed at the prince's palace were *opere buffe* (comic operas), a type of opera developed in early 18th-century Italy. The following example, from Pergolesi's comic intermezzo *La Serva Padrona* (1733), is typical of the light-hearted, melodious *opera buffo* style:

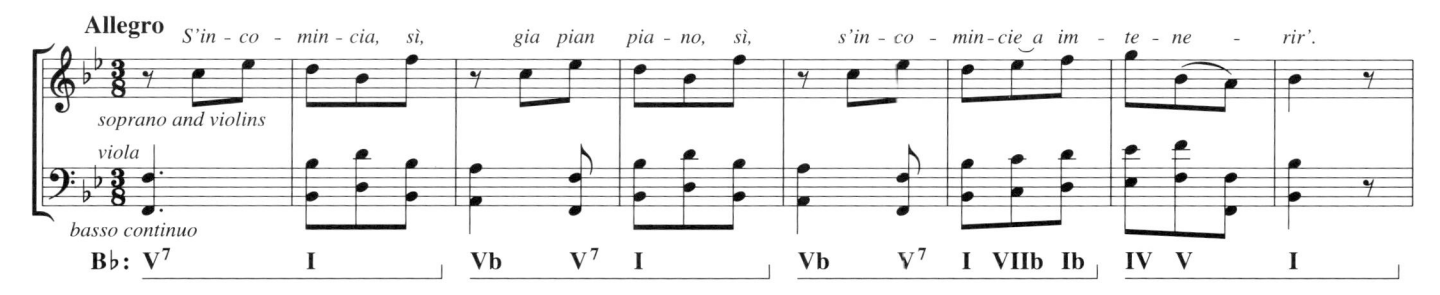

By Haydn's time *La Serva Padrona* had achieved fame throughout Europe. A comparison with the example on the previous page shows that the 'new and special style' of the Op. 33 quartets owes a good deal to the *buffo* style of composers such as Pergolesi, and this is especially true of the finale of the aptly-nicknamed 'Joke Quartet'. Both examples are easily memorable because their melodies contain a good deal of rhythmic repetition, because they fall into four balanced phrases, and because they are harmonised with a simple, homophonic, tonic-and-dominant accompaniment that accentuates the periodic phrasing.

But the differences are as striking as the similarities. Pergolesi uses a thin, two-part texture, depending on continuo instruments to provide harmonic filling, while Haydn relies on three independent solo strings to provide his homophonic accompaniment. Where Pergolesi's music is entirely diatonic, Haydn introduces a touch of the dominant in his second phrase and adds piquancy to the third phrase with a chromatic B♮. Where Pergolesi's bass is continuous, Haydn varies his texture by omitting the cello in bars 3–4 and by varying the length and spacing of his accompanying chords.

The most striking difference, however, becomes apparent when the melodies are examined more closely. Where Pergolesi simply repeats his two-bar phrase then tags on a cadence, Haydn uses three little motifs (x, y and z) which are subtly manipulated to form the rest of the melody. At first hearing bars 3–4 sound like a sequence of the first two bars, but motif y is inverted (y^1), and the four-note motif z changes from a triadic figure to one characterised by a lower auxiliary note (z^1). The last two phrases (bars 5–8) are constructed from transpositions of x, y, z, y^1 and z^1.

Haydn's most radical contribution to *buffo* style is his unification of the whole movement by 'growing' apparently new tunes from these tiny motifs. Look at the melody starting on the last quaver of bar 8, and then complete the blanks in the following account to explain how Haydn develops motifs x, y and z in bars 8^6–12^5.

This section begins with motif .... In bar 9 a chromatic passing note is added to motif .... , which is followed by motif .... The three notes beginning with the last quaver of bar 10 are a melodic inversion of motif .... The second half of bar 11 is an adaptation of motif y, and the phrase ends in bar 12 with motif ....

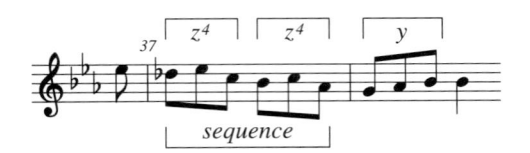

This intensely motivic style continues throughout the movement. In bars 12^6–14^5 motif x is altered by the introduction of a chromatic appoggiatura on B♮ (see *left* and compare it with bar 5) followed by the cadential motif z, which is extended by turning its fourth note into a suspension (B♭) resolving to A (motif z^3).

In bars 14^6–16^5 a new variant of x includes a diatonic appoggiatura (F at the start of bar 15), followed by a modification of z^3, which we have called z^4 – it will later assume much more importance.

Next look at the melody beginning on the last quaver of bar 22. Do you see how Haydn has altered motif x again? Its middle note has been changed to a quaver, and this variant is repeated to form a sequence. In bars 24–26 the repetitions of this version are drawn together to form a sequential rise from D to G.

Motif z^4, which seemed to be no more than a cadential flourish in bar 15, introduces the middle section of the movement (starting with the last note of bar 36). The example *left* shows how an apparently new melody is constructed from the sequential treatment of its first three notes, which are followed by motif y (itself treated in sequence on the repeat in bar 40).

This should not surprise you, for by this stage of the movement the original three motifs and their variants have grown and mutated in a manner that mirrors the complexity of cellular evolution, which is why many writers describe such melodic growth as 'organic'.

Form

On page 59 of the AS Guide we described the form in terms of a rondo structure (ABACABA) followed by a coda. However such an analysis does not unpack the contents of the lengthy coda and, as we mentioned, there are other ways of hearing the structure of the complete movement – remember that both the pessimist and the optimist are right when one says a glass is half empty and the other says it's half full. What follows is an alternative and more detailed account of the movement than that given in the AS Guide.

The movement begins with a rounded binary form structure (bars 1–36) consisting of two themes. The first, which we shall call A (bars 0–8), is defined by the perfect cadence in the tonic key of E♭ major with which it ends. The second, which we shall call B (bars 8–28), remains in E♭ major, but is distinguished from A by:

✦ a slower rate of chord change at the start (V and I in bars 8–12) and generally a more sustained style of accompaniment

✦ prominent appoggiaturas at the ends of the third and fourth two-bar phrases (bars 14 and 16)

✦ a 12-bar dominant pedal with some chromatic colouring (A♮ and G♭, both resolving by step, one to the root and the other to the fifth of chord V). These last 12 bars of B form a dominant preparation for the exact repeat of A in bars 28–36.

The next thematic group, which we shall call C (bars 36–70), is chiefly distinguished from A and B by its exploration of related keys – A♭ major in bars 36–47 and F minor in bars 48–53, and then back to E♭ major for bars 54–70. The harmonic rhythm speeds up after the last pedal resolves to chord I of E♭ major (bar 59). This progression includes a sequential rise from the tonic to the submediant (I–IV–II–V–III–VI in bars 59–61) that creates tension, which is released when VIIb of V (the second chord of bar 63) resolves to another dominant pedal of E♭ major in bars 64–68.

The entire rounded binary structure of the first 36 bars is recapitulated (without repeats) in bars 71–107.

There is a modified recapitulation of C in bars 107–140 (which we shall call C^1). It begins with a more extensive treatment of motif z^4, remains in the tonic key throughout, and ends with yet another another dominant pedal (bars 128–140).

Theme A is repeated in bars 140–148. This could make an excellent end to the whole movement since it finishes with a decisive perfect cadence in E♭ major. Instead Haydn adds a short Adagio that begins with a melodramatic dominant major 9th (bars 148–149) and ends with another perfect cadence in the tonic key. The Presto returns, but now A is chopped up into its constituent two-bar phrases by general pauses (marked G.P.). It ends, of course, with another perfect cadence that could make another satisfactory end to the movement. Instead Haydn plays his last card, a repeat of just the first two bars of the whole movement – which we now realise contained a definitive perfect cadence all the time!

Bars	Form	Key
‖: 0–8	A	E♭ major
8–36	BA	E♭ major :‖
36–70	C	A♭, Fm, E♭
71–79	A	E♭ major
79–99	B	E♭ major
99–107	A	E♭ major
107–140	C^1	E♭ major
140–148	A	E♭ major
148–152	Adagio	E♭ major
152–172	A^1	E♭ major

Private study

1. Can Haydn's claim that Op. 33 was written in a 'new and special style' be justified, or was it merely advertising 'hype'?

2. What is implied by the expression '*buffo* style'?

3. (i) What is meant by harmonic rhythm?
   (ii) Compare the rate of harmonic change in bars 1–8 with the rate of harmonic change in bars 9–28.

4. To what extent are the three lower string parts confined to an accompanimental role in *NAM 16*?

5. (i) From bar 54 onwards the music is essentially in E♭ major. Explain the harmonic functions of the following: (i) E♮ and C♯ in bar 80, (ii) B♮ in bar 84, and (iii) A♮ in bar 103.
   (ii) Why do none of these notes signify a modulation?

6. What does G.P. stand for? Is it really a type of pause?

Sample questions

In the exam there will be three questions on this work, from which you must choose to answer **two**.

(a) To what extent is it true to say that *NAM 16* is built entirely upon the motifs heard in its opening two bars?

(b) How does Haydn maintain interest in this movement when his chords are so simple and his modulations are rare?

(c) Give a detailed account of bars 107–140, explaining how the melodic material in these bars relates to music heard earlier in the movement.

> **Topic for examination in 2002 and 2003**

Continuity and change in writing for strings

You do not need to study this topic unless *Music for small ensemble* is the Area of Study that you undertook for AS Music and which you are now extending for A2.

Before starting work on this topic you need a thorough understanding of the material on *Music for small ensemble* in the AS Guide (pages 53–66). Remember that for A2 the topic draws on works from across the **entire** Area of Study, not just those in one of the two lists, A or B.

English counterpoint

> *NAM 13*   CD2 Tracks 1–2
> Rose Consort of Viols

Holborne's dances date from a time when music for an instrumental consort was essentially little different from contemporary multi-part vocal compositions. A comparison of the texture of bars 34–43 of *NAM 34* (published in 1598, just a year before *NAM 13*) with the texture of bars 34–38 of the paduana supports this contention. Both passages exemplify a type of counterpoint in which four of the voices engage in imitation based on a rising scalic motif. In both passages the fifth voice (the alto part in Weelkes, the bass viol in Holborne) is allotted a subordinate, non-imitative role.

Such similarities are evident on a larger scale. For instance, just as Weelkes varies his texture by introducing homophonic passages (eg 'All shepherds in a ring' in bars 32–35), so the homophonic second strain of Holborne's galliard (bars 9–16) contrasts with the intense imitative polyphony of the first strain (bars 1–8).

Holborne's music was published as suitable for a variety of instruments, as indicated at the head of *NAM 13*. This was common practice for English consort music of the time, and such adaptability was made possible by the use of a limited range for each part.

A comparison of the ranges covered by each instrument in the pavane with the ranges of each voice in the madrigal shows more parallels between Elizabethan consort and vocal music. The compass of the top two parts in *NAM 13* is, like the two soprano parts in *NAM 34*, a ninth. The compass of the bass in both works is a twelfth.

If you compare the melodic intervals and general melodic contours in the pavane and madrigal you will notice that Holborne's consort music is as vocal in style as Weelkes' ballett. The melodies of both are mainly conjunct, but both contain leaps of an octave (easier to sing than a 7th – an interval found in neither composition). When there is a leap of more than a 3rd the melodies of both pavane and madrigal tend to return within the interval. The only glaring exception to this rule (and so the only unvocal line) occurs in the fourth viol part in bar 31 of the pavane. The same generalisations are true of the galliard. Although the ranges are higher (as befits a jollier dance) none of them exceeds an 11th.

Holborne's instrumentation is thus not idiomatic – the parts are not specifically designed to exploit the characteristics of strings. But what it lacks in idiomatic instrumental writing it makes up for in the intensity of its polyphony.

Roman clarity

> *NAM 15*   CD2 Track 4
> Fitzwilliam Ensemble

There could hardly be a greater contrast between *NAM 13* and the string writing of Corelli. The violin had been perfected by Italian craftsmen such as Nicolo Amati, and the violin family soon ousted viols in 17th-century continental Europe. The two families are quite different. Viols have six strings and a fretted fingerboard, violins have four strings and no frets. The tone of viols is intimate and plaintive, the violin family (including the viola and cello) is capable of a much wider pitch and dynamic range. Notice how both violins, and the violone (which in late 17th-century Italian music usually means a bass violin or cello) in *NAM 15* use a range of two octaves or more.

Just as significant is the fact that the violins share almost the same range, which is some two octaves above the range of the violone. This polarised texture (high melody instruments separated by an octave or more from the bass, with a continuo filling the gap between) is typical of much middle and late baroque music, and is quite unlike the dense, evenly-spaced textures of *NAM 13*. By the time *NAM 15* was published in 1689 the bass instrument, while still fulfilling its functional harmonic role, had begun to share some of the melodic interest with the treble instruments. In this piece the cellist is allowed to participate in the fugal entries at the start of both sections, but the rest of the part consists of repetitions of the three-note quaver figure heard in the first bar together with entirely functional passages such as that in bars 35–38.

It would be possible to sing Holborne's dances or play them on a variety of instruments. But try singing Corelli's sonata movement and you will soon discover how unvocal it is. Try playing it on the piano and you will discover how unpianistic it is. We are here at the start of idiomatic writing for specified string instruments.

Although Haydn's string writing in *NAM 16* is only a little more technically demanding than Corelli's, and the range of his string parts is only a little greater, there are some significant differences. Apart from a handful of dynamic marks Corelli, like most baroque composers, leaves interpretation to the performers, while Haydn's liberal and detailed markings for both dynamics and articulation (slurs, staccato, etc.) give clear and specific directions. Varied articulation and dynamics are, of course, essential elements of the musical jokes that Haydn foists on his unsuspecting listeners.

The greatest differences are in scoring and texture. *NAM 16* includes a viola part, which completes a balanced quartet of bowed string instruments that can offer four-part harmony and makes a continuo unnecessary to fill out the middle of the texture. Where Corelli's violins are accompanied by a partially melodic cello part and improvised continuo chords, Haydn's melody is supported by string chords forming a homophonic texture. While Corelli writes contrapuntal parts for two equal violins, Haydn mainly confines his melodies to the first violin (the other instruments are allowed only brief spells of melody). Where Corelli's texture is varied only by the introduction of rests before contrapuntal entries, Haydn's textures are varied by contrasting detached and sustained chords, by a reduction in the number of parts, and by total silence. These are some of the elements that make Corelli's sonata movement and Haydn's quartet movement so typical of their respective periods.

The origins of larger-scale chamber music with wind instruments are to be found in 18th-century compositions with titles such as divertimento or serenade. These multi-movement works could be played indoors or outdoors with instrumental forces of varying size. That tradition lived on in works (such as this septet) which are so

Viennese classicism

NAM 16	CD2 Track 5
The Lindsays	

The viola often had a very limited role in much baroque music – it doesn't feature in trio sonatas such as *NAM 15*, and when it did appear it often doubled the bass (see the music example on page 65).

Larger-scale chamber music

NAM 17	CD2 Track 6
Berlin Philharmonic Octet	

sonorous that a very large 'chamber' indeed is required for their adequate performance. And it is not just the addition of three wind instruments which makes this ambience essential for Beethoven's septet since the work also includes a double bass (sounding an octave lower than printed), extending the total string compass to nearly six octaves (as against four in *NAM 16*). In addition Beethoven freely uses double, triple and even quadruple stopping (ie chords on a single string instrument) to produce vibrant textures.

Here are just a few examples of Beethoven's string writing – you should be able to discover many more for yourself:

- in bars 1–4 *tutti* chords are contrasted with an unaccompanied acciaccatura figure on the first violin, and then a violin melody accompanied by a soft, sustained chord

- in bars 8–11 an antiphonal effect is achieved by thin three-part string chords in close position alternating with *tutti* chords supported by cello and bass octaves

- at the start of the *Allegro* the texture reduces to that of a string trio (but this melody-dominated texture is quite unlike that of Corelli's contrapuntal trio)

- when this passage is repeated (bars 28–39) the strings adopt a subordinate role with syncopations that are typical of classical accompanimental figures

- the complete emancipation of the viola is evident in bars 70–73 where its melody is supported by the broken chords of the violin playing an octave and more below

- in bars 111–115 strings (and woodwind) play in octaves, but the double bass merely shadows the other parts in two of these bars

- dynamics, articulation and other nuances are comprehensive and explicit throughout and include the famous Beethovenian *subito piano* (eg the syncopated chord at the end of bar 83).

Romantic fusion

NAM 18   CD2 Track 7
Guarneri Quartet with
Peter Serkin (piano)

The fact that Brahms first scored his Op. 34 for string quintet (1862), then for two pianos (1864) before releasing it in its final form as a piano quintet (1865) tells us much about his musical thinking. More than any other romantic composer Brahms was primarily interested in music as form rather than as colour. This does not imply that instrumentation and scoring were unimportant to him, it simply means that his initial concepts were motifs, melody, harmony and structure. In fact it is probably because of the work's difficult genesis that much of the string writing is so original. In bars 100–109, for instance, the percussive battle of the two-piano version is rendered as a battle between string and piano octaves. But when Brahms augments the six-note semiquaver motif of bars 101–102 to a six-note crotchet motif (bars 105–108), the sustaining power of the first violin and viola in octaves allows this transformation to be heard more clearly than in the two-piano version.

As with Beethoven's septet, it would take many pages to describe the whole gamut of Brahms' string textures, so what follows is intended to do no more than draw attention to string writing that is quite unlike any that we have yet encountered.

- The movement begins with a pale texture created by a pizzicato pedal on the lowest string of the cello, above which bowed violin and viola play a quietly syncopated melody in bare octaves.

- Violin 1 and viola announce a second theme (bars 13–18), still **pp** and in octaves. The viola is left to complete the melody while the other strings provide a pizzicato accompaniment of four-part chords (made possible by the use of double stopping).

- In the fugato (bars 67–99) textural clarity is ensured by staccato articulation in both strings and piano, but from bar 84 legato phrasing and crotchets in the piano part conflict with the continuing staccato semiquavers in the upper strings. It is this textural conflict which helps bring about the climax at bar 100.

- Bars 146–157 reveal the wide range demanded of the strings and indicate that this is chamber music for highly-skilled players.

- The whole Scherzo is dominated by insistent semitonal figures. In bars 176–193 Brahms maximises the sinister power of these semitones (B♮–C and D♭–C) by scoring them for low unison violins, playing on their darkly-coloured lowest string. These, with increasing support from viola and cello, are powerful enough to withstand the assaults of the massive, syncopated Neapolitan chords of the piano.

- The opening of the trio also features a pedal on the bottom note of the cello (this time bowed). Note the sustained lyricism of the melody in bars 210–225, followed by a contrast between high legato violins in octaves over staccato cello and piano.

Private study

1. (i) What is meant by the word idiomatic?
   (ii) Why could the string writing in *NAM 15* be described as more idiomatic than that in *NAM 13*?

2. On page 69 the bass part in bars 35–38 of *NAM 15* was described as 'entirely functional'. What does this mean?

3. Why do you think the violin rose to such prominence following the development of this instrument in 17th-century Italy?

4. List some of the different string textures used by Haydn in *NAM 16* and state the bar numbers in which each can be found.

5. Comment on the role played by the double bass in *NAM 17*.

Sample questions

In the exam there will be two questions on this topic, from which you must choose to answer **one**.

(a) Why is the string writing in *NAM 18* so much more dramatic than that in *NAM 15*?

(b) How do Haydn's string textures differ from those of Holborne?

(c) To what extent is it true to say that Beethoven combines string and wind instruments in *NAM 17*, while Brahms contrasts strings and piano in *NAM 18*?

Warning. Photocopying any part of this book without permission is illegal.

> **For examination in summer 2004 and 2005**

> **Special Focus Work for 2004 and 2005**
> NAM 17 CD2 Track 6
> Berlin Philharmonic Octet

Music for small ensemble

This part of the chapter deals with the special focus work and topic set for examination in summer 2004 and 2005. If you are taking the exam in summer 2002 or 2003 turn to page 64.

Beethoven, Septet in E♭ (first movement)

Before starting on this section you should work through (or revise) the information about the context and structure of this music given on pages 60–62 of the AS Guide. Make sure that you understand all of the terminology used on those pages.

When Beethoven offered his new septet to a publisher in 1800 he described all of the instrumental parts as obbligato parts. By this he meant that they were all essential for a satisfactory performance of the work. He needed to make this clear because six-movement compositions of this sort originated in earlier divertimenti for wind and strings that could often be performed without one or more of the instruments, or with substitute instruments (Beethoven himself permitted the performance of the wind parts on string instruments).

You can see what he meant if you compare the double bass and cello parts. In most of the work the double bass merely strengthens the cello. There are, however, passages in which the cello is allowed an independent melodic role. For example, in bars 148–150 the cello engages in dialogue with the woodwind and viola while the double bass provides a non-melodic, but nevertheless essential bass for the whole ensemble. But these passages are few and far between, and when the double bass is independent of the cello (or horn or bassoon) it is never allowed to participate melodically.

Do you agree that the violin and clarinet parts have most of the melodic interest? The bassoon, horn and viola fulfil dual roles as accompanists (most of the time) and as participants in the thematic argument (although they are often doubled with another instrument). In listening to these parts you will also discover that while Beethoven's textures are varied, there is very little counterpoint. Passages such as bars 249–264, where a version of the first subject is contrapuntally combined with a theme from the codetta, are rare. For the rest the phrase 'melody and accompaniment' aptly describes Beethoven's main textures. So, in saying that all instruments are obbligato, he meant only that they are essential, not that all instruments have an equal share in the musical argument.

The effective (but decidedly late 18th-century) scoring also helps us to understand why Beethoven's mature view of the septet was so different to the views of those contemporary critics who greatly admired the work: 'In those days I did not know how to compose. Now I think I do know'.

The septet was written in the last year of the 18th century and the first year of the 19th century, but it really belongs to the world of Mozart and Haydn rather than the new age of romanticism that Beethoven helped usher in. This is true of both the structural and stylistic elements outlined below.

> **Warning.** Photocopying any part of this book without permission is illegal.

The movement begins with a slow introduction linked to the Allegro by a common motif (the figure marked *p* in the first violin part of bars 8–9 which becomes the first motif of the Allegro), a pattern established in several of Haydn's symphonies of the 1790s.

The sonata form of the Allegro corresponds with the proportions established as a norm in the late 18th century (proportions that Beethoven overthrew in many later works). The recapitulation at 78 bars balances the length of the exposition (80 bars), and these flank a modest development section of 43 bars. The only indication of what was to come is the inflation of the coda to 55 bars. It consists of a transposed repeat of the codetta (bars 233–245 = bars 98–110) followed by what amounts to a brief second development (bars 246–277) and a passage consisting entirely of perfect cadences decorated with a new trill motif (bars 277–288). The point at which this 'second development' begins (bar 246) is marked by a shift towards the subdominant (found in many closing sections throughout the 18th century) and a dramatic augmented-6th chord (bar 248). The idea of development is generally confined to the simple sequential treatment of easily recognisable melodic fragments from the exposition (see, for example, Beethoven's extension of the melody of bars 98–102 in bars 116–124).

Only closely related keys are used. In bars 116–124, for instance, sequential development leads from the relative minor (C minor) to the subdominant (A♭ major); the only other key in the development is the supertonic (F minor in bars 132–136). The use of the tonic minor in bars 10–11 is purely decorative and similar passages can be found in Haydn's earliest and lightest galant-style compositions.

The harmony is largely diatonic, almost always functional, and heavily reliant on I and V in all inversions. Like much late 18th century music the rate of change of chords is usually slow in the first half of a phrase then faster towards the cadence (which often contains the classical fingerprint of a cadential six-four chord). For instance, in the first phrase of the Allegro (bars 18–29) chord I lasts for four bars. The rate of change then speeds up to one chord per bar (IV–II–V–V^{7}d in bars 23–26), then one chord per minim beat (Ib–IIb–Ic–V–I in bars 27–29). All of these chords are diatonic, and there is a preponderance of key-defining chords – I, II and V. Chromatic chords do appear, but nearly all of them are decorative secondary dominants (such as V^{7}c of IV in bar 5), and they all resolve regularly to the diatonic chord to which they are related. The German augmented-6th in bar 7 is a striking exception, but it too resolves to the expected dominant in the next bar.

While most chords are diatonic, melodic chromaticism abounds. The opening of the Allegro (bars 18–21) consists of the tonic triad with upbeat quavers featuring lower auxiliary notes, two of them chromatic. These and the three chromatic passing notes in bar 26 are typical, not of Beethovenian struggle, but of galant pleasure.

Equally typical of the late-18th century are the periodic phrasing and antecedent-consequent pairings that prevail throughout most of the movement. In the main development section, for instance, the melody of bars 116–136 consists entirely of sequential pairs of two-bar phrases. At the start of this passage two of these phrases

When studying these passages remember that the clarinet in B♭ sounds a tone lower than printed, and a horn in E♭ sounds a major 6th lower than printed.

form a four-bar antecedent (clarinet, bars 116–120) that ends with a perfect cadence in C minor. This is answered by a consequent from the horn (bars 120–124) that ends with a balancing perfect cadence in A♭ major. Frequent melodic exchanges are typical of the dialogue technique that Haydn learned from Mozart and that both bequeathed to Beethoven (see, for instance, the violin and woodwind parts in bars 61–65).

Private study

1. To what extent are the cello and double-bass parts independent?
2. Which two instruments have most of the melodic interest?
3. What is meant by (i) functional harmony, and (ii) a cadential six-four? Find an example of each in *NAM 17*.
4. Write a paragraph comparing bars 52^4–56^3 with bars 56^4–60^1. Include the following terms in your answer: periodic phrasing, antecedent, consequent, and rate of harmonic change.
5. What is notable about the coda of this work?

Sample questions

In the exam there will be three questions on this work, from which you must choose to answer **two**.

TIP: See the AS Guide, pages 60–62.

(a) Outline the form and tonality of this movement.

(b) Discuss Beethoven's use of instrumentation in *NAM 17*.

(c) To what extent is *NAM 17* typical of 18th-century classicism?

Topic for examination in 2004 and 2005

Continuity and change in harmony and tonality

You do not need to study this topic unless *Music for small ensemble* is the Area of Study that you undertook for AS Music and which you are now extending for A2.

Before starting work on this topic you need a thorough understanding of the material on *Music for small ensemble* in the AS Guide (pages 53–66). Remember that for A2 the topic draws on works from across the **entire** Area of Study, not just those in one of the two lists, A or B.

Pavane and Galliard

NAM 13   CD2 Tracks 1–2
Rose Consort of Viols

Throughout most of the past four centuries the form of instrumental music has been determined by tonality as much as by thematic repetition and contrast. The beginnings of the structural use of tonality can be traced back at least as far as the typical three-strain structure of dances such as this pavane and galliard. This is evident at the start of the pavane, where a five-bar phrase is defined by the inverted perfect cadence in bars 4–5. The same sort of cadence in A major is heard in bars 10–11, and the first strain ends with a definitive perfect cadence in D (bars 14–16). The second strain begins in G major and ends in A major. The return to D major in the third strain is emphatic: a tonic pedal lasting for six bars is followed by an ascent in the bass from tonic to dominant and a perfect cadence in bars 41–42. This progression is balanced at the end by a four-bar dominant pedal and another definitive perfect cadence in the last four bars. Thus the D-major tonality of strains 1 and 3 enclose a tonally more ambiguous central section.

Warning. Photocopying any part of this book without permission is illegal.

It is only when we look more closely at other harmonic progressions that we realise how strong is the legacy of renaissance harmony and modality. Holborne, like his forbears, uses only root-position and first-inversion triads. These are varied by frequent suspensions which provide the only on-beat dissonances in the two dances.

The other dissonant effect – the false relation – though musically expressive, is also symptomatic of the clash of modality with the emergent major- minor tonal system. Thus the apparent modulation to the dominant in bars 10–11 is immediately followed by a modal C♮ (the flat seventh degree of the mixolydian mode on D) that causes a false relation with the C♯ on the previous beat. In fact such clashes have as much to do with Holborne's linear thinking as with chords considered as vertical entities. Notice how, in the third viol part of bars 10–11, a C♯ is used in the ascending patterns of both bars, but the first viol takes C♮ because the melody then immediately falls. Similar considerations govern the formation of the false relation (G♮–G♯) in bar 13. Where there are chromatic inflections they are most often contradicted shortly afterwards in another part (whether or not they form false relations). See how many instances you can find (and how many exceptions to the rule there are).

The galliard contains more examples of melodic lines in which chromatic inflections change chords from modal minor triads to tonal major triads (or *vice versa*). It also contains two harmonic progressions that are typical of this period of tonal change. In the 16th and early 17th centuries it was an almost unbroken rule that the last chord of a definitive cadence should be a bare octave, a bare 5th or a major triad. This avoidance of minor triads at a cadence often gave rise to the tierce de Picardie at cadences. In bars 13–14 a modal progression of six root-position triads includes four chords containing C♮, but the phrase ends (bar 16) as expected with a major chord containing a Picardy 3rd (C♯). But in bar 17 Holborne immediately reverts to the modal-sounding F-major triad of bars 13–15. The consequence is a false relation between the tierce de Picardie at the end of one phrase and its unaltered modal form at the beginning of the next (in this case C♯ in bar 16 and C♮ in bar 17). It is one of the most characteristic sounds of the period.

The other characteristic progression found in the galliard is the phrygian cadence (IVb–V in a minor key). This occurs in bars 15^3–16, where a G-minor chord in first inversion (decorated with an accented passing note) resolves to chord V of D minor.

Note that apparent second inversions (like IVc at the start of bar 5) arise from the use of suspensions on other triads.

Many of the points we made about Holborne's harmonic and tonal style also apply to Gabrieli's *Sonata pian' e forte* (unsurprisingly, since it was published just two years before Holborne's dances). Gabrieli's chord vocabulary is similarly limited to root position and first-inversion triads, and apparent second inversions are actually the product of suspensions (eg bar 2, beat 3). Most of the on-beat dissonances are suspensions, the chief exception being decorative accented passing notes (see the example overleaf). Like Holborne, Gabrieli's phrases end on a bare 5th or with a tierce de Picardie. Bar 14 illustrates both of these features: *Coro 1* ends on a bare 5th as *Coro 2* enters and supplies the tierce de Picardie (B♮); the phrygian cadence is a stylistic fingerprint (bars 16–17).

Sonata pian' e forte

NAM 14 CD2 Track 3
His Majesty's Sagbutts and Cornetts
Directed by Timothy Roberts

Warning. Photocopying any part of this book without permission is illegal.

There are, however, several important differences between the harmonic and tonal styles of the dances and the sonata. In the sonata (though not in many of his other compositions) Gabrieli avoids false relations while Holborne revels in them. In particular the type of false relation formed between a tierce de Picardie at the end of one phrase and its contradiction at the beginning of the next is evaded by overlapped phrases, with one of the choirs beginning or ending on a bare 5th (eg bar 14).

Another difference is a cadential formula characteristic of the time which occurs frequently in the *Sonata pian' e forte* but not at all in *NAM 13*. Normally at this time a fourth from the bass was regarded as a dissonance that required both preparation and resolution. The exception was a cadential formula in which a 4th from the bass was treated as though it were a concord. This 'consonant 4th' was approached and quitted by step as shown *left*. There are many examples in the sonata, including syncopated versions such as the second note of the cornett part in bar 75.

① 7–6 suspensions
② accented passing note (on A)
③ consonant 4th
④ tierce de Picardie

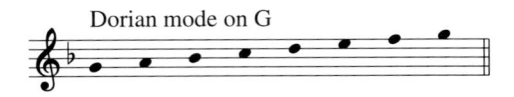

Dorian mode on G

Perhaps the most significant difference between the dances and the sonata is Gabrieli's modality compared with Holborne's more tonal style. The sonata is in the dorian mode on G (see *left*). It is often chromatically altered in order to form cadences on the first degree (eg the plagal cadence in bars 79–80), the second degree (eg the phrygian cadence in bars 16–17), the fourth degree (eg the perfect cadence in bars 30–31) and the fifth degree (eg the perfect cadence in bar 54). Cadences on the third degree (eg first choir, bars 42–43) and the seventh degree (eg bars 20–21) do not require chromatic alteration of the mode.

Trio Sonata in D

NAM 15   CD2 Track 4
Fitzwilliam Ensemble

A brief glance at the editorial figuring shows that Corelli was as reliant on root-position and first-inversion triads (amply seasoned with suspensions) as were earlier composers. But in this sonata modal ambiguity has been dispelled by diatonic harmony. There is no mistaking Corelli's tonal structure. The first section of his binary form is elucidated by a firm move to the dominant key of A major in bar 9, and this key is maintained until the perfect cadence in bars 18–19. The second section begins in the dominant but soon moves back to the tonic (bars 23–24). It then moves through closely related minor keys (B minor in bars 26–28, and E minor in bars 29–32). Finally a modulating circle of 5ths (E minor, A major, D major and G major in bars 32–35) prepares for the inevitable return of the tonic key of D major in bars 36–37. This is the key that is maintained throughout the rest of the movement.

Finale of 'The Joke' Quartet

NAM 16   CD2 Track 5
The Lindsays

Bars	Chords	
1–2	E♭–B♭^{7}–E♭	I–V^7–I
3–4	B♭–F^7–B♭/D	V–V^7 of V–Vb
5–6	A♭–B♭^{7}/A♭–B♭/D	IV–V^{7}d–Ib
7–8	Fm–B♭^{7}–E♭	II–V^7–I

By 1781, when Haydn wrote the six quartets of Op. 33, functional harmony reigned supreme, dominant-7th and six-four chords were used without preparation (though the dissonances they contained usually resolved by step) and key-defining tonic and dominant chords were predominant. Take a look at the first eight bars and you will find the progression shown *left*. Of the 12 chords, six are tonic triads, four are dominants and just two are of subdominant function (IV and II).

In bar 1 the 7th of V^7 (A♭ in the second violin part) is unprepared but resolves by step to G in the next bar. The F^7 chord in the second half of bar 3 is a secondary dominant (in this case, the 'dominant of the dominant'). The aural effect is of fleeting chromatic colour rather than modulation. The F^7 chord doesn't destabilise the E♭-major tonality of these bars. Instead it strengthens it by highlighting the importance of B♭ as the dominant of E♭ major ($F^7 \rightarrow B\flat \ldots \rightarrow E\flat$). A similar secondary dominant can be found on the second beat of bar 13 (V^7c of II, resolving to II). Finally, notice the typical classical cadence (Ic–V) in bar 16, in which the 4th from the bass (E♭) is unprepared but resolves by step to a concordant D. Chords of these types help define the simple tonal structure of the whole movement (see *right*, and also read the section beginning on page 64).

Bars	Form	Key
‖: 0–8	A	E♭ major
8–36	BA	E♭ major :‖
36–70	C	A♭, Fm, E♭
71–79	A	E♭ major
79–99	B	E♭ major
99–107	A	E♭ major
107–140	C^1	E♭ major
140–148	A	E♭ major
148–152	Adagio	E♭ major
152–172	A^1	E♭ major

Enough has been said about Beethoven's harmony and tonality in the section starting on page 72. All we need now is an outline plan of the way his tonal structure relates to, and helps determine, the sonata-form structure of the Allegro. If this looks complicated, start with the simpler plan on page 61 of the AS Guide. Remember that it is important to try to *hear* the relationship between key centres, and how these key centres relate to the structure, as you listen.

Septet, movement I

NAM 17   CD2 Track 6
Berlin Philharmonic Octet

Form	Bars	Section	Keys
Exposition	18–39	First subject	E♭ major
	40–52	Transition	E♭ major modulating to B♭ major
	53–98	Second subject	B♭ major
	98–111	Codetta	B♭ major
Development	111–153	B♭ major (bars 111–113) modulating (114–115) to C minor (116–120). Then modulating (121–123) to A♭ major (124–128) and next modulating (129–131) to F minor (bar 136). Finally Beethoven modulates (in bar 136) back to E♭ major (bars 138–140). The development ends with extended dominant preparation (bars 140–153).	
Recapitulation	154–181	First subject	E♭ major and A♭ major
	182–187	Transition	V of E♭ major
	188–233	Second subject	E♭ major
Coda	233–288		E♭ major, A♭ major and E♭ major

Although the structure is much more complex than Haydn's finale there is never any doubt about the succession of keys, thanks to Beethoven's strongly functional harmony. Two important features should be noted. Firstly the above analysis shows the two clearly defined keys of the exposition and the tonal instability of the development. Both features are typical of hundreds of classical sonata-form structures. Secondly, and more unusually, there are strong moves towards the subdominant in the recapitulation of the first subject and in the coda. These movements to the flat side balance the even stronger move to the sharp side in the exposition.

Like Haydn and Beethoven before him, Brahms' harmony is functional and helps define the complex inner workings of the A section of his ternary structure (Scherzo in C minor, Trio in C major, Scherzo in C minor). As might be expected his harmony is often more chromatic than that of Haydn and Beethoven, there is less reliance on tonic–dominant progressions, and strong emphasis on augmented-6th chords and Neapolitan 6ths (both are identified in the schematic tonal analysis which follows).

Piano Quintet, movement 3

NAM 18   CD2 Track 7
Guarneri Quartet with
Peter Serkin (piano)

> **Warning.** Photocopying any part of this book without permission is illegal.

Form		Bars	Tonality
Scherzo	A	1–12	C minor coloured by an implied augmented 6th in bar 5
	B	13–21	C minor coloured by a modal version of chord V (bar 19^2)
	C	22–37	C major coloured by Vb of ♮VI (E major first inversion, resolving to A minor) and V of V (D major, resolving to G major) in bars 26–29 and 34–37
	A^1	38–45	C major or minor: a German augmented 6th twice resolving to V
	A^2	46–57	C minor modulating to V of G minor
	B^1	57–67	G minor modulating through B♭ minor and D♭ major to V of E♭ minor
	Fugato	67–100	E♭ minor with transitory modulations (bars 88–98)
	B^2	100–109	E♭ minor
	C	109–124	E♭ major
	A^3	125–158	E♭ major/minor and C minor, both keys coloured by augmented-6th chords
	B^3	158–193	C minor with modulating sequences, prominent Neapolitan 6ths (piano bars 177–185) and frequent Picardy thirds
Trio	D	193–255	C major with sequential modulations through G major and B major (bars 202–209) and a diatonic circle of 5ths (bars 213–219)
	E	225–241	V of C major (note the dominant pedal in the piano then cello parts)
	D^1	241–261	C major coloured by the subdominant key (bars 242–246), and chromatic chords borrowed from the tonic minor (bars 252–257)

Sonata for Horn, Trumpet and Trombone, movement 1

NAM 19 — CD2 Track 8
Nash Ensemble

Poulenc's harmonic style differs from earlier styles we have studied in his free and witty use of dissonance as a means of parody. In the example below, for instance, the first bar could have come straight from a dreamy piano piece by Schumann, but in the next bar the melody wilfully crashes into the accompaniment (as shown by the encircled notes):

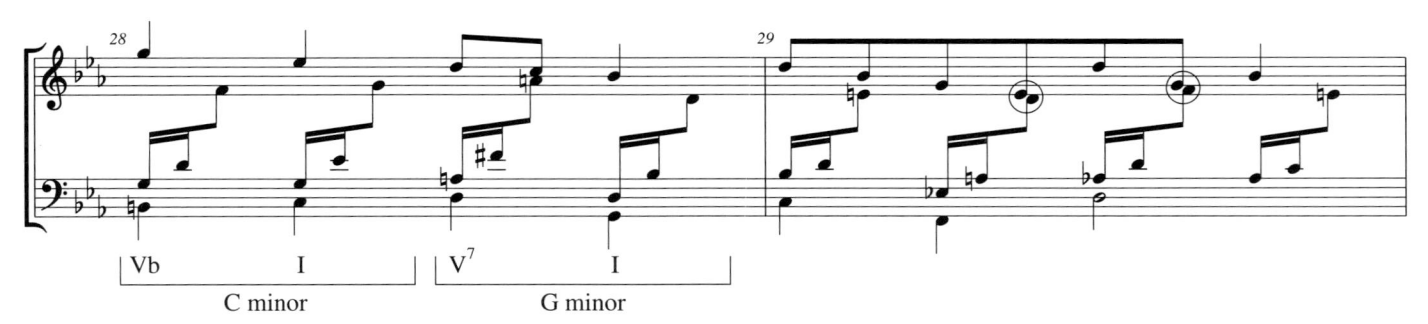

Also notice the 7ths between the two lower parts and the 9ths between tune and bass (both on the first two beats of bar 29), and the 9th between the top two parts on the last beat. Yet for most of the movement simple diatonic chords clearly define the tonality, and this in turn helps define the ternary structure.

The A section (bars 1–25) is mostly in G major. The first eight bars divide into two balanced four-bar phrases. The first is an antecedent ending with a cliché Ic–V^7–I cadence (or it would have been had the horn not sabotaged the six-four chord with a dissonant C – see the music example on page 65 of the AS Guide). The second is a consequent, modulating to a perfect cadence in the conventional dominant key of D major. The remainder of the section is made up of a series of false starts each prematurely terminated by a perfect cadence (bars 11, 14, 15, 17 and 21). There is also much chuntering about the relative merits of minor or major versions of chords II^7

and IV (minor in bars 10–11, major in bar 12, minor in bar 15 and minor again in bar 17). This confusion is echoed in bars 21^4–25, in which the opening motif peters out in first major then minor versions of the tonic chord.

The B section contrasts with the flanking sections by being in flat keys (E♭ major with a tendency towards B♭ major; then B♭ major with a tendency towards F major). At the end of this section (bars 54–57) an attempt is made to stop this drift towards sharper keys (ie keys with fewer flats) by a bold assertion (*fff*) of the dominant 7th of D♭ major. Shocked by the impudence of this tonal coup, the trumpet apologetically slides down an incomplete D♭-major scale, but the descent is continued in the horn's incomplete G major scale. This apology for a modulation turns the tonality back to G major ready for a modified recapitulation of the A section (bars 57^4–85).

The coda (bars 86–89) begins with two atonal bars in which a 'very discreet' chromatic scale accidentally crashes into the repeated B♭s in the horn and trumpet parts, but an end is put to this nonsense by the return of the tonic chord in the last two bars.

Private study

1. What two types of dissonance are used in *NAM 13*?

2. (i) How does the dorian mode differ from the minor scale?
   (ii) Which work in this Area of Study uses the dorian mode?

3. In the first trombone part of *NAM 14* an E♭ occurs in bar 9, followed by an E♮ in bar 10. Why is this **not** a false relation?

4. (i) What is meant by a consonant 4th in renaissance music?
   (ii) Give two examples of a consonant 4th on page 196 of *NAM*.

5. (i) Explain what is meant by functional harmony.
   (ii) Give an example of a functional chord progression from one of the works you haved studied.

6. What makes the development section of Beethoven's septet less tonally stable than the exposition? How does Beethoven balance this period of tonal instability?

7. What do you notice abut the rate of harmonic change in bars 154–164 of Beethoven's septet?

8. What does the term 'atonal' mean?

Sample questions

In the exam there will be two questions on this topic, from which you must choose to answer **one**.

(a) Compare and contrast *NAM 13* and *NAM 14* in terms of both harmony and tonality.

(b) Explain the importance of tonality to the structure of music in the classical period, using examples from either *NAM 16* or *NAM 17*.

(c) How can you tell from the harmony and tonality of *NAM 18* that this quintet is a later work than *NAM 17*?

> **For examination in summer 2002 and 2003**

Keyboard music

The first part of this chapter deals with the special focus work and topic set for examination in summer 2002 and 2003. If you are taking the exam in summer 2004 or 2005 turn to page 88.

Shostakovich, Prelude and Fugue in A, Op. 87, No. 7

> **Special Focus Work for 2002 and 2003**
> NAM 25   CD2 Track 17–18
> Tatiana Nikolayeva (piano)

Before starting on this section you should work through (or revise) the information about the context and structure of this music given on pages 75–77 of the AS Guide. Make sure that you understand all of the terminology used on those pages.

Neo-classicism

The various styles of 20th-century neo-classicism are sometimes lumped together as products of the 'Back to Bach' movement. But a comparison of Debussy's nostalgic evocation of a French baroque sarabande (*NAM 24*), Shostakovich's tribute to Bach (*NAM 25*) and Stravinsky's reworkings of 18th-century music (*NAM 7*) reveals that this is a misleading tag for a movement that was as multifaceted as the earlier music that stimulated the creative imaginations of these 20th-century composers. Neo-classical composers are sometimes accused of pastiche – 'Bach with wrong notes'. Yet there is not one 'wrong note' in the fugue of *NAM 25*. In fact its luminous serenity can in large measure be attributed to the fact that it is constructed throughout from major and minor triads without a single discord.

Note that if your edition of *NAM* has C♭ in bar 58 it is not a solitary discord – it is a misprint for C♮.

Prelude

Of course there are many discords in the prelude, but they mostly reinforce rather than detract from the simple harmonic progressions implied by the pedal notes. The example *left* shows how the dissonances in bar 1 are effectively auxiliary notes that decorate the root and third of the tonic chord of A major (B and G♯ on either side of A; D and B on either side of C♯). Similarly chord VI (implied by the pedal F♯ in bars 4–5) is decorated with the auxiliaries D, B and G♯. Such harmonically charged melodies were common in the baroque era, as shown in the example by Bach on the next page.

A major: I ⎯⎯⎯⎯⎯⎯→

When the bass takes up the melodic line, accompanied by right-hand chords (bars 3 and 6) the harmony becomes explicit: chord I in bar 3, and chord III in bar 6 (both decorated with an auxiliary F♯ on the third beat of the bar). The pedal in bars 8–9 implies chord V, but the same pedal also supports two unrelated triads – C major and B♭ major in bar 10. Diatonic chords in A major return in bars 11–12, but when the next pedal appears (C♯ in bars 13–15) the C♯ major triad implied at the start is soon negated by a descending chromatic scale, itself decorated with chromatic auxiliaries.

Up to this point A major tonality prevails: note that the four pedal notes are all diatonic in this key, and three of them (A, E and C♯) outline chord I. But from bar 13 foreign chords (such as F major in bar 18 and A♭ major in bar 19) and chromatic melodies almost negate tonality. Almost, but not quite, because:

> **Warning.** Photocopying any part of this book without permission is illegal.

+ the implied triad of C♯ major in the first two beats of bar 13 is related to chord I of A major by the common note C♯

+ the chord of F major is a triad on the flattened sixth of the scale of A major (a chromatic chord not uncommon in Bach's music)

- the chord of A♭ major contains the leading note of A (A♭=G♯)
- the chord of D♭ major (bars 21–22) contains the third of the tonic chord of A major (D♭=C♯).

It is the enharmonic equivalence of D♭ and C♯ which facilitates Shostakovich's jump straight from this last chord back to chord I of A major, implied by the left-hand melody in the first three beats of bar 23. From here to the end an inverted dominant pedal is heard above three plagal cadences formed by chords IIb and I, the last of which is over a tonic pedal.

Thus Shostakovich creates a simple ternary structure that is largely defined by his tonal scheme:

A	bars 1–12	diatonic A-major tonality
B	bars 13–22	tonally ambiguous chromatic harmony
A'	bars 23–28	diatonic A-major tonality

Like many of the preludes in Bach's *Well-tempered Klavier* (the model for Shostakovich's own 24 Preludes and Fugues) the whole structure is unified by two motifs:

It would be very useful to compare this Shostakovitch prelude with some of Bach's preludes – particularly the D-major prelude in the second book of *The Well-tempered Klavier*, which has an opening motif that begins with the same rhythm.

The first is the semiquaver figure *x*, heard in 14 of the prelude's 27 bars. In bars 1, 3, 4, 6, 11, 16, 18 and 23 it is heard in its original form. Elsewhere it is subjected to the sort of manipulation heard in bar 5 (*x'*) where the first four semiquavers are an inversion of *x* beginning on the beat, with two more semiquavers added before the motif reaches its final quaver. But no matter how Shostakovich manipulates motif *x* it is always recognisable because it always consists of a group of conjunct semiquavers leading to a quaver.

The second motif is the leaping quaver figure (*y*). This is subjected to more radical change. For instance the leaps are smoothed out to a descending triad (*y' above*), to a scalic figure (bar 12, left hand) and to an auxiliary-note figure (bar 14). But motif *y* retains its identity because it always begins on the beat and always consists of three quavers (except for the passage in bars 16–17, where one motif is tied to the next in a descending sequence).

The next example shows how closely Shostakovich modelled the motivic style of his melodic material on Bachian practice. It begins with a semiquaver figure (*x*) which, in varied form (*x'*) is similar to *x* in the example *above*. It also has a three-quaver on-beat figure (*y*) outlining the tonic triad (like *y above*) and is subjected to a manipulation (*y' below*) in which the leaps are as angular as those heard in Shostakovich's prelude. It is as if Shostakovich is transferring the wide leaps in Bach's cello writing to a keyboard idiom.

Bach: *Gigue* from Cello Suite, BWV 1009

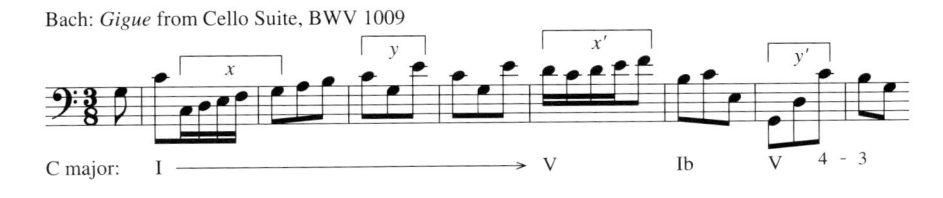

C major: I ⟶ V   Ib   V   4 - 3

48 bars from this gigue may be heard in track A90 of the *Rhinegold Dictionary of Music in Sound*.

Fugue Before starting work on this section reread the entry on Fugue in the glossary of the AS Guide and make sure you understand the difference between a Subject, Countersubject and Answer.

Shostakovich has made half a dozen pre-compositional decisions which determine the style of this remarkable fugue:

- the triadic subject (bars 1–4) is entirely constructed from the notes of a single chord (chord I in the exposition)

- the answer is real, so it exactly replicates the subject a 4th lower (left hand, bars 5–8), and thus outlines the dominant chord

- the only tonal (melodically modified) entries of the subject are those that do not start on the root of a triad, eg the final entry of the subject at bar 96 (which starts on the fifth of chord I)

- most entries of the subject are accompanied by a regular (unchanging) countersubject which is also entirely triadic

- the only modifications of the regular countersubject are those necessitated by the limitations imposed by the range of notes that can be covered by the performer's hand (eg bars 21–24, uppermost voice) and octave displacements necessitated by the crossing of parts (eg bar 47, where the countersubject passes from the right hand to the left hand at the same time as the subject passes from the left hand to the right hand)

- the episodes are derived from motifs in the subject and countersubject, so the whole fugue is constructed from a series of triads heard in root position and in first and second inversion.

These ground rules mean that the rate of change of chords is slow (every four bars) whenever the subject or answer is stated. This is an important factor in determining the serene mood of the fugue. Shostakovich reserves faster harmonic rhythm for the intervening episodes (where chords change on average every two beats). This is an important factor contributing to variety throughout the fugue. The ground rules also mean that the only method of generating tension is side-stepping to unrelated keys and the juxtaposition of triads that Bach would have considered to be unrelated. Both of these devices are used with great skill in the central section of the fugue (bars 41–61) in which the dynamic level rises from *piano* to *fortissimo*. Yet even here there are connections between chords in the shape of common notes. In bars 42–43 chords of A major and F major share the common note A. Similar tertiary relations are apparent in the chromatic chords that colour the otherwise diatonic harmony in the final section (bars 62–99):

> The term tertiary refers to keys or chords that are a third apart.

- in bars 82–84 triads of A major and C major are linked by the common note E

- in bars 84–87 triads of A major, C♯ major, F♯ major and F♯ minor are linked by the common note C♯

- in bars 87–88 triads of D major and F♯ major are linked by the common note F♯.

These general observations should be born in mind when reading the following analysis of the whole fugue.

First section	Exposition	The subject, on the tonic chord.	Bars 1–4
Entirely diatonic – A-major tonality.	A three-voice fugal exposition	The answer (lower part of bars 5–8) with a regular countersubject on the dominant.	5–8
		Codetta based on chords IV and I.	9–10
		A further entry of the subject (lowest part of bars 11–14) with the regular countersubject (middle voice), and a second countersubject (uppermost voice) on the tonic.	11–14
	First episode	Built on a chain of alternating and falling first inversion triads changing every two beats (Vb, IVb, IIIb, IIb and Ib).	15–20
	First set of middle entries	The subject (middle voice, bars 21–24), a variant of the regular countersubject (uppermost part) and the second regular countersubject (bass) on chord VI of A major.	21–24
		The answer (in the middle voice for the first three beats of bar 25, then in the uppermost part until the end of bar 28) and regular countersubject (bass) on chord III of A major.	25–28
	Second episode	From here to bar 50 the texture reduces to two parts.	29–32
	Second set of middle entries	The subject (lower part of bars 33–36) and regular countersubject on I of A major.	33–36
		The answer (upper part of bars 37–40) and regular countersubject (varied in the first bar) on V of A major.	37–40
Second section	Third episode	The first move away from A major (to F major) occurs at bar 43.	41–46
The tonal centres are much more fluid, moving from A to F major and then B♭ major before a series of unrelated chords leads back towards to A major.	Third set of middle entries	The subject (lower part in the first two beats of bar 47, then the upper part) and regular countersubject (upper part in the first two beats of bar 47, then the lower part),	47–50
		The music moves to B♭ at bar 51. The subject, regular countersubject and second countersubject in the bass, alto and treble respectively.	51–54
	Fourth episode	As in the other episodes, chords change twice per bar.	55–57
	A set of false entries. These are incomplete statements of the subject, each entering a bar apart.	The return to the tonic is engineered by means of a modal-sounding progression of unrelated chords (Cm, B♭, E♭, C♯ and F♯m. The last of these is chord VI of A major and leads to the return of the home key in bar 62.	58–61
Closing section	Restatement in the tonic	Begins with the complete subject and regular counter-subject. A dominant pedal runs throughout bars 62–69.	62–65
Remains in the tonic despite the intrusion of the chromatic chords discussed earlier.	Fifth episode	The dominant pedal continues.	66–69
	Stretto entries at the octave	Both *dux* (the leading part) and *comes* (the follower) are incomplete, as is the subject in the bass of bars 76–78.	70–73
	Final entry	The complete subject appears in bars 79–82. From here to the end the first bar of the subject is heard in almost every bar, supported by long bass notes that refer back to the same pitches that were pedal notes in the prelude (A, F♯, E and C♯) – all asserting the A major tonality	79–99

Private Study

1. What do you understand is meant by neo-classical style?

2. What are pedal notes? What is their role in the prelude?

3. What is the form of the prelude and how is this form defined?

4. What is meant by a tertiary relationship?

5. Explain the difference between a subject and a real answer. How does a countersubject differ from the subject?

6. What is (i) an episode, (ii) a false entry and (iii) a stretto?

7. Why might the fugue in *NAM 25* be described as one of the most tonal fugues of the 20th century?

Sample questions

In the exam there will be three questions on this work, from which you must choose to answer **two**.

(a) To what extent is Shostakovich's use of motivic development in the prelude modelled on techniques used by Bach?

(b) Outline the form of the fugue in *NAM 25*.

(c) Compare and contrast the prelude and the fugue, mentioning any features that the two movements have in common.

Continuity and change in keyboard textures

Topic for examination in 2002 and 2003

You do not need to study this topic unless *Keyboard music* is the Area of Study that you undertook for AS Music and which you are now extending for A2.

Before starting work on this topic you need a thorough understanding of the material on *Keyboard music* in the AS Guide (pages 67–77). Remember that for A2 the topic draws on works from across the **entire** Area of Study, not just those in one of the two lists, A or B.

Sweelinck's Pavana Lachrimae

NAM 20   CD2 Track 9
Peter Seymour (harpsichord)

Many of the earliest keyboard pieces were transcriptions of vocal compositions. These worked perfectly well with only minor alterations when played on the organ, but when performed on keyboard instruments with plucked strings the lack of sustaining power meant that slow music was less effective. Yet harpsichords, spinets and virginals were the keyboard instruments most likely to be found in 16th- and 17th-century homes. In order to overcome this problem particularly long notes in the original vocal music were embellished with a variety of ornaments, especially at cadences. These could be improvised or composed. You can see the process at work if you look at the music example on page 68 of the AS Guide and compare the cadences in bars 10 and 14 of the *Pavana Lachrimae* with the corresponding bars in Downland's *Flow My Teares* (*NAM 33*). Notice how Sweelinck uses a written-out trill and turn in bar 14.

Compare the melody in bars 42–43 with its variation in bars 58–59 to see how Sweelinck often retains the notes of the original melody in their correct metrical positions, but fills them out by adding passing notes (*p*) and an auxiliary note (*a*):

Original melody

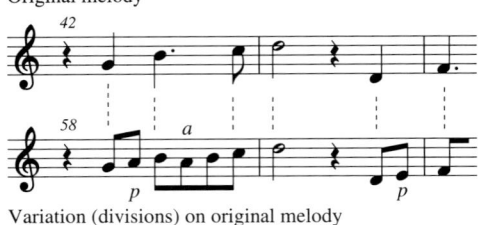

Variation (divisions) on original melody

Pitch ranges
17th-century harpsichord   NAM 20

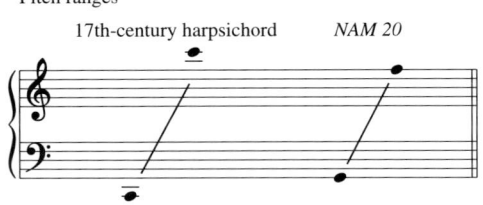

It is a short step from this sort of ornamentation to variation in which almost every note of the original is encrusted with elaborate figuration. This technique, known in England as divisions, was one of the earliest types of variation. The music example on page 69 of the AS Guide shows how Sweelinck uses this technique at the start of his first variation (bars 17–32), which corresponds with the repeat of the first verse in Dowland's original song. As well as fragmenting long notes into scalic patterns of semiquavers Sweelinck creates new motifs which pass from one part to another. In bars 17–19, for instance, a three-note figure (two semiquavers and a quaver) is heard in the uppermost part, the bass and the uppermost part again. This quasi-contrapuntal texture contrasts with the more homophonic texture of bars 26–27 where continuous decorative semiquavers are supported by a simple subordinate accompaniment. At the other extreme Sweelinck takes the largely homophonic texture of bars 33–35 and develops from it an entirely new quaver figure which he treats in three-part imitation in bars 49–51.

The pitch range of the whole pavane is well within the four-octave compass of contemporary Flemish harpsichords (see *left*).

By 1700 composers had developed keyboard textures that were not only independent of vocal models, but which incorporated totally integrated melodies which grew organically from a limited number of motifs heard at the start. See how the little three-note figure at the start of bar 1 reappears in inversion and with an additional note in bar 5, how it gains two demi-semiquavers in bar 17, and how it is then repeated to form a rising sequence. Similarly the walking bass acquires a three-note motif (two semiquavers and a quaver) in bar 5, and, having achieved melodic status, this too is treated sequentially in the next two bars.

Unlike Sweelinck, whose four-part texture varies from homophony to imitative counterpoint, Bach's two-part counterpoint evolves throughout the sarabande, interrupted only by pairs of homophonic bars to signal the starts of the three structural sections of rounded binary form (bars 1–2, 13–14 and 29–30). Although the sarabande works splendidly on the harpsichord and exploits most of the compass of contemporary instruments, it has to be admitted that this is not entirely idiomatic keyboard writing. Apart from a few low melody notes it could, for instance, be equally effective played on a violin with continuo accompaniment.

It is much harder to think of a combination of instruments that could perform this dance as effectively as a harpsichord or piano. Here, instead of maintaining fugal textures consistently in three contrapuntal strands, Bach introduces contrasting chords as early as the last entry of the subject in the exposition (bars 16–21). He exploits this texture to the full in the first episode (bars 22–35) and allows the semiquavers of what has now become a *perpetuum mobile* (a piece featuring rapid continuous motion) to run straight through the first bar of the next (incomplete) entry of the subject (bars 36–41). In bars 41–48 and 89–96 the texture thickens to four- then five-part chords which alternate with unaccompanied arpeggios and two-part counterpoint. Even when a learned double fugue seems imminent (bars 49–60) Bach breaks off to allow a similar variety of idiomatic keyboard textures.

Much that has been said about Bach's textures is also true of this prelude. Compare bars 6–7 or 11–12 with bars 20–25 of Bach's gigue, and notice the similar texture of dotted-crotchet chords in the right hand accompanying left-hand triplet figures.

There are, however, two important textural differences. Firstly Bach exploits most of the compass of contemporary harpsichords while Shostakovich only makes use of just over four of the seven octaves available on modern pianos. But within this fairly narrow range there is plenty of contrast. Notice particularly the polarised textures at the start (where the melody floats as much as three octaves above the pedal notes), and the ethereal texture at the end (where the music is confined to the uppermost register of the compass Shostakovich works in). The second important difference is the inclusion of much longer notes in *NAM 25*. The longest note in Bach's sarabande is a minim while the longest note in Shostakovich's prelude lasts for 12 dotted crotchet beats. This difference is, of course, explained by the greater sustaining power of the modern piano compared with the baroque harpsichord.

Bach's Sarabande

NAM 21   CD2 Track 10
András Schiff (piano)

Bach's Gigue

NAM 21   CD2 Track 11
András Schiff (piano)

Shostakovich's Prelude

NAM 25   CD2 Track 17
Tatiana Nikolayeva (piano)

Warning. Photocopying any part of this book without permission is illegal.

Shostakovich's Fugue

NAM 25   CD2 Track 18
Tatiana Nikolayeva (piano)

Like the fugal exposition in Bach's gigue, this is a three-voice fugue, but, where Bach abandons contrapuntal textures and introduces four- and five-part chords, Shostakovich never uses more than three parts and his textures are consistently contrapuntal. For textural variety he relies on the contrast between dense three-voice counterpoint and the two-part counterpoint of bars 1–10 and 29–50, two-part counterpoint above pedal notes (bars 62–69 and 96–99) and two-part counterpoint above other long non-thematic notes (bars 82–89). Variety is also ensured by the exploitation of different registers, especially to generate the climax of the fugue – bar 50 being in mid-register with the following bars gradually rising until the *ff* in bar 61 where all three parts are in the highest register.

Mozart's Piano Sonata

NAM 22   CD2 Track 12
Alfred Brendel (piano)

Like Bach's sarabande, this sonata movement is mainly composed of a variety of two-part textures. But, whereas Bach is consistently contrapuntal (the bass having a melodic life of its own), Mozart's texture is dominated by the treble melody, while the left hand provides a homophonic broken-chord accompaniment. Even when the left hand is given melodic snippets (eg bars 35–36) it soon reverts to providing a functional bass (bar 37), block chords (bars 45–49), or the cliché figuration of the Alberti bass (bars 57–58 and 71–80). Mozart uses almost the full range of the contemporary piano (his preferred instrument, as the dynamic markings indicate). Within this range Mozart uses contrasting registers, sometimes designed to emphasise important structural articulation. See, for instance, how he plunges from the highest register to the lowest immediately before the second subject (bars 22 and 118).

Schumann's character pieces

NAM 23   CD2 Tracks 13–15
Alfred Brendel (piano)

When Mozart wrote his sonata in B♭, K333, in 1783 the piano was still a relatively new instrument. 55 years later, when Schumann composed *Kinderscenen*, pianos could be found in middle-class homes throughout western Europe, and composers were exploiting its characteristics in their music. This is immediately evident in 'Von fremden Ländern und Menschen'. Here the articulation of the uppermost part as a song-like melody depends on the performer's ability to play it louder than the lower parts (despite the fact that the highest notes of the accompaniment must be played with the right-hand thumb). Although it is possible to give a *cantabile* rendition of the melody without the sustaining pedal, Schumann's romantic style demands the sustained resonance that can only be achieved through its careful use. The artful two-part counterpoint between the outer parts in bars 9–14, with continued harmonic filling, is typical of romantic textures that are entirely dependent on the sustaining power that pianos had by this time achieved.

Note that the F♯ in bar 11, beat 2 (left hand) should have a down-stem to show that it is part of the bass countermelody and is to be sustained as a crotchet.

'Hasche-Mann' and 'Fürchtenmachen' show how far keyboard textures had developed from the melody-dominated homophony of Mozart. The first of these pieces achieves its suggestion of a child running blindfold by its difficult leaping accompaniment (rather like a jazz stride bass). The second piece contrasts the chromatic counterpoint of the refrains (bars 1–8, 13–20, 29–36 and 41–48) with a bass melody combined with staccato chords in the first and last episodes (bars 9–12 and 37–40). The central episode (bars 21–28) is differentiated from the other sections by syncopated *sforzandi* which, by 1838, had become a cliché of piano textures.

Warning. Photocopying any part of this book without permission is illegal.

There could hardly be a greater contrast of keyboard textures than that between the sarabandes of Bach and Debussy. The first is in two parts and is almost consistently contrapuntal. The second is based on thick, resonantly-spaced chords, requiring the use of the sustaining pedal, and is almost entirely homophonic. The first spans a range of just over four octaves. The second has a compass of more than five octaves (though this by no means covers the complete range of the pianos that were available in 1894). Within these parameters Debussy uses most of the textural changes available to him. There is the immediate contrast of the parallel six-part chords of the opening bars and the bare octaves in bars 5–6. These are followed by contrary motion chords that open up to the first climax (bar 8). In bars 9–10 a treble melody is supported by block chords and almost the same melody is harmonised by a parallel stream of 'dominant 7ths' in the next two bars. Contrary motion chords return in bars 13–14, but the effect is different because they are in a much lower register.

In bars 23–26 the quartal harmony supports two subtly differentiated melodies (rising and falling minor 3rds in the treble and an inner part defined by semiquaver movement) while the bass part achieves some independence as a link between the two-bar phrases. These are but a few examples of the wonderful array of Debussy's piano textures, perhaps the most magical of which is the series of chords based on fourths that rises from the lowest register to the highest in the last six bars.

Debussy's Sarabande

NAM 24   CD2 Track 16
Zoltán Kocsis (piano)

Quartal harmony is harmony in which the chords are based on superimposed fourths.

Private study

1. Which of the six works in this area of study were originally intended to be played on a plucked string instrument such as the harpsichord, and which were intended for the piano?

2. To what does the term texture refer and what does the word idiomatic mean (as used in paragraph two on page 85)?

3. What is rounded binary form? In which work is it used?

4. List some of the different textures used by Mozart in *NAM 22* and state the bar numbers in which each can be found.

5. How can you tell, other than from the date, that the pieces in *NAM 23* are romantic works written specifically for the piano?

6. What is meant by quartal harmony?

TIP: look up Textures in the Glossary of the AS Guide.

Sample questions

In the exam there will be two questions on this topic, from which you must choose to answer **one**.

(a) Compare and contrast the contrapuntal textures in the fugue of *NAM 25* with those in the gigue of *NAM 21*.

(b) How do Schumann's piano textures differ from those of Mozart?

(c) To what extent do the textures of piano music differ from those found in music for plucked string keyboard instruments such as the harpsichord? Refer to bar numbers of specific works in the *New Anthology* to support your arguments.

Warning. Photocopying any part of this book without permission is illegal.

> For examination in summer 2004 and 2005

Keyboard music

This part of the chapter deals with the special focus work and topic set for examination in summer 2004 and 2005. If you are taking the exam in summer 2002 or 2003 turn to page 80.

Bach: Partita BWV 828 (Sarabande and Gigue)

> **Special Focus Work for 2004 and 2005**
> NAM 21   CD2 Track 10–11
> András Schiff (piano)

Before starting on this section you should work through (or revise) the information about the context and structure of this music given on pages 69–71 of the AS Guide. Make sure that you understand all of the terminology used on those pages.

Sarabande

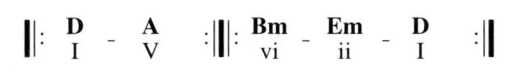

You have already studied the overall rounded binary form of this dance and you will have noticed how, with the exception of the repetition of passages from the first section in bars 29–38, the form is largely determined by Bach's key scheme (see *left*). Now we must look more closely at the structure of the melody.

As in most baroque movements Bach's melodic line seems to grow and develop organically with no contrasting themes. Just as the shape of a sapling largely determines the shape of the mature tree, so melodic ideas heard in the first few bars of the sarabande seem to determine the contours of the rest of the melody. This is because Bach consistently manipulates a few melodic fragments (motifs) and characteristic rhythms throughout the dance. Let us trace the evolution of the very first motif, the descending slide heard on the first beat of the first bar (motif *x* in the example, *left*).

What two changes are made to *x* when Bach reuses this motif at the start of bar 5? How does bar 6 relate to bar 5? What new change is made to the motif on the first beat of bar 7?

All of these variants move by step, but, provided the rhythm remains unchanged, it is possible to change the pitches of a motif (eg to fit different chords) without altering its relationship to a version heard earlier. If you compare our motif *x* in the *last* beat of bar 7 with the version in the first beat of bar 5 you will see that Bach has maintained the same rhythm but augmented the interval between the last two notes from a descending 2nd to a descending 6th. Pitch changes become more radical at the start of bars 9 and 10, but the connection with *x* in bar 5 is still clear.

We have discussed all but one of the appearances of motif *x* in the first part of the sarabande. Find and describe the missing one.

One way in which baroque composers 'grew' their melodies was to repeat an established motif in a sequence. In bar 17 Bach inverts the variant of motif *x* heard at the start of bar 7 then repeats it in a rising sequence. See if you can find another such sequence in the second part of the sarabande.

The melodic lines of baroque slow movements for harpsichord tend to be highly ornamented, partly because of the instrument's limited ability to sustain long notes. Ornaments in baroque music may be indicated by symbols or written out in full. In this sarabande (as in many of his other works) Bach preferred to write out most of the ornamentation. This is true of motif *x*. In England this ornament was known as a slide and the French (who had a variety of symbols for it) called it a *coulé sur une tierce* (a slur over a third). The only symbol for an ornament Bach uses in this movement is a wiggly line (bars 1, 13 and 29). Most folk call this an upper mordent, often played as shown in example 1, but Bach called it a *trillo* and wrote out an example of it for one of his sons in the manner shown in example 2. You will see that it begins on the beat with the upper note and that it is extended into a sort of trill. However the precise interpretation of this symbol depends upon its context and the good taste of the performer. For instance, if the sign appears above a note that is slurred to the previous note (as it is in bar 1) a common interpretation in a piece in moderate tempo and in French style (like this sarabande) could be that shown in example 3. In fact, because of his very slow tempo, András Schiff on CD2 chooses to interpret the *trillo* in the manner shown in example 4, and in the repeat he turns the ornament into an extended trill.

1 Upper mordent

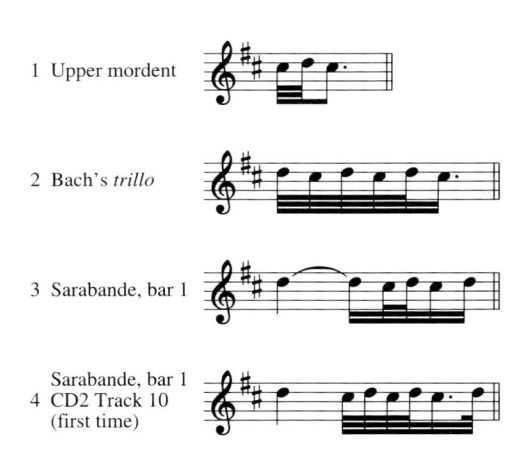

2 Bach's *trillo*

3 Sarabande, bar 1

4 Sarabande, bar 1 CD2 Track 10 (first time)

Listen to the same ornament in bars 13 and 29. Is Schiff consistent in his interpretation of this ornament?

We know from accounts written in the 18th century that it was usual for baroque performers to add extra ornamentation, according to the known and understood conventions of the time, especially when a section was repeated. Listen to the repeats on CD2, paying particular attention to Schiff's added ornaments. The first of these is an ascending slide inserted between the sixth and seventh semiquavers of bar 3, which mirrors Bach's descending slide in bar 1. There are many more of them for you to identify, and they are all in keeping with the French style of Bach's sarabande.

J. S. Bach's second son, C. P. E. Bach, wrote about ornamentation in his *Essay on the proper method of playing keyboard instruments* (published 1753): 'It is not likely that anybody could question the necessity of ornaments. They are found everywhere in music, and are not only useful, but indispensable. They connect the notes; they give them life. They emphasise them … when there are few or no signs, the piece must be ornamented according to its proper style.'

The texture – mainly two-part counterpoint – looks thin, yet when heard it sounds much richer than it appears on paper. This is because the melody is harmonically charged. At its simplest this means that Bach outlines chords in triadic melodic lines such as that in bar 9, where a triad of A major emerges from the figuration (with passing notes between C♯ and A). We can tell that this is chord I of A major because Bach outlines V^7 in this key in the melody of the previous bar and because the leading note (G♯) appears as a lower auxiliary three times in bar 9. Can you work out which chord in A major is outlined by the melody in bar 10?

Accidentals can signify modulation, but sometimes they just add chromatic colour. The difference is important because modulation is a structural device, but chromaticism merely adds colour. For example, bars 1–2 are based on the progression I–VIIb–Ib, with a 7–6 suspension (D–C♯) on the second chord and the addition of C♮ to chord Ib. C♮ seems to turn the tonic chord into V^7 of G major, and, indeed, that is the chord implied on the first beat of bar 3. But notice that C♮ is cancelled by C♯ in the next beat. No modulation has taken place, Bach has simply added chromatic colour by his use of an incomplete secondary dominant in bar 2.

Almost every diatonic triad can be preceded by such a secondary dominant without a modulation taking place. Look, for instance, at bar 6, beat 3, in which every note of V^7 of E major is sounded. But when this dominant 7th resolves to an E-major chord in the first

Note that secondary dominants are a useful way to introduce colour into many styles of composition, from Bach chorales to 20th-century popular songs.

beat of the next bar Bach immediately cancels the effect of the D♯ with D♮ in the bass, turning the E-major chord into E^7, the dominant of A major, thus introducing the second main key of the movement.

Two other types of chromaticism occur in the sarabande. The first is a note borrowed from the tonic minor (F♮ in bar 12). Whole chords can be borrowed in this way without affecting the major tonality of the music. The other is a major triad in first inversion based on the *flattened* second degree of the scale. In E minor the flattened second degree is F♮. The major triad on F♮ consists of the notes F, A and C, and in first inversion the third of the chord (A) will be the bass note. This is the Neapolitan-6th chord, heard on the third quaver of bar 23. All of the other notes in this bar belong to the prevailing key of E minor, but this brief flash of chromaticism contributes much to the expressiveness of the melody at this point.

Gigue

Bach introduces the same secondary dominant that he used in the second bar of the sarabande (V^7 of IV) into bar 2 of the gigue. This is unlikely to be coincidence since Bach does exactly the same in the first two bars of another dance in this Partita, the Allemande – an example of a unifying device that is rare in baroque suites and partitas. To counteract this hint of the subdominant Bach outlines the 'real' dominant 7th of D major in bar 5.

The movement begins with a complete three-voice fugal exposition (bars 1–21), with a real answer (an answer that precisely replicates every interval of the subject) in the left-hand part of bars 7–12, a codetta (bars 13–15), and the subject again (left-hand, bars 16–21).

The countersubject is constructed from motifs heard in the subject:

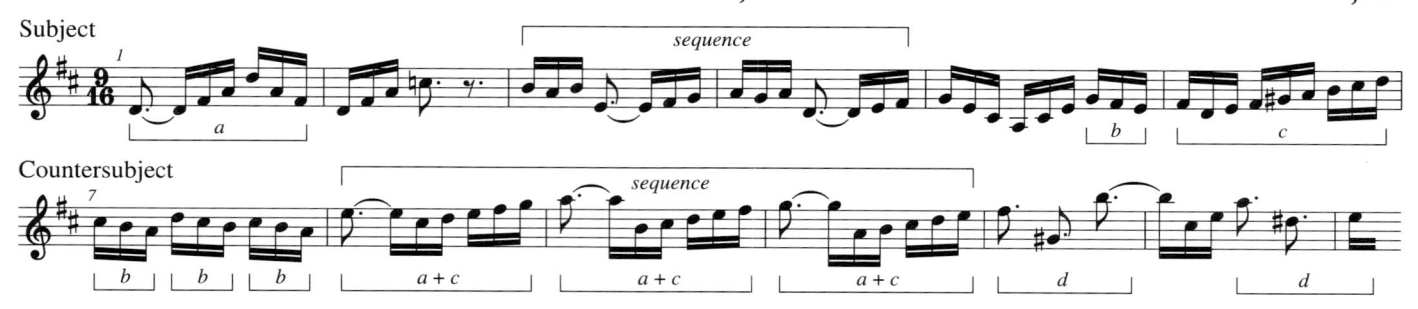

> Like many phrases in the sarabande, the fugue subject is so harmonically charged that a complete progression is implicit in its unaccompanied melody. Try to identify the chord progression that it outlines.

It begins with repetitions of the tiny three-note motive (*b*) from the end of bar 5. It continues (bars 8–10) with a sequential treatment of a motif that has the rhythm as bar 1 (*a*) and the ascending scale pattern of bar 6 (*c*). It ends with a new motif (*d*) that consists of three on-beat dotted crotchets.

Bach creates an extraordinary sense of unity by fashioning most of the remainder of the dance from these four motifs. For example in:

✦ the (adapted) countersubject in bars 17–21 (stems down on the treble stave), which follows the same pattern described above

✦ the first episode, in which motif *d* in the right hand is heard above *b* (bar 22) and then above *c* (bar 23) in the bass; at bar 27 motifs *b* and *d* (right hand) are combined with *a* in the bass

✦ the closing section of the first part of the gigue (bars 41–48), where manipulations of motif *a* in the bass are followed by motif *d* (bar 45) and then motif *a+c* (bar 46, left hand).

In the AS Guide we discussed the introduction of a second fugal subject in bars 49–54 and noticed how Bach combined it with the first subject in bars 55–60. Try to identify how often Bach utilises an inversion of motif *b* in this new subject. In fact the whole of bars 21–24 appears freely inverted in bars 70–73, and the movement ends with a restatement of the closing bars of the first part, now in the tonic and with the final arpeggio inverted.

Private Study

1. What are the characteristics of (a) a sarabande, and (b) a gigue?
2. Describe what is meant by rounded binary form, outlining the main keys (tonic, etc.) you would expect in each of its sections.
3. To what extent is the sarabande based on the ornamentation of simple harmonies?
4. What is meant by a fugal exposition?
5. Earlier on this page we indicated that bars 70–73 of the gigue are a free inversion of bars 21–24. What does this mean?

Sample questions

In the exam there will be three questions on this work, from which you must choose to answer **two**.

(a) (i) Comment on the harmony and tonality of bars 1–12 of the sarabande.
 (ii) Briefly explain how the music in these 12 bars is used in the second part of the sarabande.

(b) Describe how Bach creates a sense of unity in the gigue.

(c) Justify the statement that the gigue is a synthesis of binary form and fugal style.

Continuity and change in the handling of short forms

> **Topic for examination in 2004 and 2005**

You do not need to study this topic unless *Keyboard music* is the Area of Study that you undertook for AS Music and which you are now extending for A2.

Note that 'short forms' includes sonata form for the purposes of this examination topic.

Before starting work on this topic you need a thorough understanding of the material on *Keyboard music* in the AS Guide (pages 67–77). Remember that for A2 the topic draws on works from across the **entire** Area of Study, not just those in one of the two lists, A or B.

This set of variations on Dowland's ayre (*NAM 33*) can be represented as AA' BB' CC', in which A, B and C are free transcriptions of the three strains of the song, each of which is followed by a figural variation (A', B' and C'). Almost every note of Dowland's three strains are retained in the variations, often buried in elaborate figuration. You can see how Sweelinck approaches the art of variation by the mechanical exercise of spotting common notes in corresponding bars as we did in the AS Study Guide (page 69) but a quicker method is to hear the original and the variation simultaneously, perhaps by playing the recording of *NAM 20* on CD while performing Dowland's original strains on a keyboard. The result

Pavana Lachrimae

NAM 20		CD2 Track 9
Peter Seymour (harpsichord)		

Bars		
1–16	A	Dowland bars 1–8
17–32	A'	Variation on A
33–48	B	Dowland bars 9–16
49–64	B'	Variation on B
65–81	C	Dowland bars 17–24
82–98	C'	Variation on C

will be heterophony (and occasional cacophony!) that will show where the composer has embellished simple melodic lines with florid ornamentation. Having done this you should focus on particular passages and identify the types of melodic decoration used by Sweelinck. For instance, bar 17 (shown left) is based on the chord of A minor from bar 1. Sweelinck's decoration includes chord notes (known as essential notes, and marked *e*), passing notes (*p*) that move between essential notes, and an accented passing note (*a*) which resolves on to an essential note. The example from bar 23 shows auxiliary notes (*x*) which decorate the minims from bar 7.

Sarabande and gigue

NAM 21 CD2 Tracks 10–11
András Schiff (piano)

The clear tonal scheme of Bach's binary form movement is shown on page 88. This assured handling of tonality as a structural device distinguishes Bach's dance from Sweelinck's variations, written more than a century earlier and which remain in a modal A minor almost throughout. The two composers also handle figuration differently. Sweelinck's ornate melodic lines derive from Dowland's simpler melodies, but Bach's figuration arises out of his manipulation of a number of motifs that run through the whole dance. This process of continuous manipulation of motifs (which Germans call *Fortspinnung* – 'spinning out') is even more evident in the gigue, as we saw earlier. Notice, for instance, the way motif *b* (see page 90) in its original and inverted forms dominates the second fugal subject (bars 49–54). As in many a baroque gigue, Bach combines rounded binary form (like that in the sarabande) with fugal textures.

Sonata

NAM 22 CD2 Track 12
Alfred Brendel (piano)

Bars	
1–63	An **exposition** of the main themes, grouped into two opposing tonal centres (tonic and dominant: B♭ and F)
63–93	A **development** of these themes passing through several keys (notably F minor, C minor and G minor in bars 63–86)
93–165	A **recapitulation** of the principal themes in the tonic

There is a direct connection between Bach's rounded binary form and Mozart's sonata form. Both start with a section that modulates to the dominant, and both return to the tonic by way of a tonal journey through several related keys. Both also include restatements of some (Bach) or all (Mozart) of the first section with modifications and transpositions to ensure that the recapitulation remains in the tonic key. But there are two obvious differences. Firstly, Mozart's sonata movement is much longer than either of Bach's dances. Secondly Bach's monothematic elaboration of a few pervasive motifs is replaced by a number of clearly differentiated and self-contained themes in Mozart's sonata. Movements in sonata form have three main sections (shown left), yet a comparison of Bach's sarabande with Mozart's sonata movement reveals the historical truth that sonata form developed from baroque binary form.

Kinderscenen

NAM 23 CD2 Tracks 13–15
Alfred Brendel (piano)

'Von fremden Ländern und Menschen' is a miniature example of rounded binary form – ‖:A:‖:BA:‖ – and is thus obviously related to Bach's sarabande and gigue, but there are significant differences:

+ The periodic phrasing (2+2+4 in the first section) is typical of classical music (eg the two-bar phrasing at the start of *NAM 22*).

+ Unlike Bach's dances, the first A section does not modulate and the second (bars 15–22) is an exact repetition of the first.

+ The B section (bars 9–14) is melodically distinct from section A and makes only fleeting reference to a different key (E minor) whereas Bach's dances pass through several related keys.

'Hasche-Mann' is another rounded binary form movement, but it contains tell-tale signs of romanticism, such as the sudden intrusion of an unrelated key (C major in bars 13–15) and the abrupt shift (there is no modulation) from the C major chord to the dominant 7th chord of the home key (B minor) in bar 15.

The ABACABA rondo form of 'Fürchtenmachen' is classically symmetrical. The periodic phrasing is also similar to many classical phrase structures (regular two, four and eight-bar phrasing is a characteristic feature of Schumann's style). But the rondo theme is less integrated with the episodes (B in bars 9–12, repeated in bars 37–40, and C in bars 21–28) than the much longer and more complex sonata-rondo structures of classical music.

Pour le piano: Sarabande

NAM 24   CD2 Track 16
Zoltán Kocsis (piano)

This is the longest and structurally the most complex of the binary-form keyboard pieces in the *New Anthology*. It differs from Bach's monothematic binary forms in two respects – it has several independent themes (instead of Bach's continuously evolving melody) and its modal melodies and ambiguous harmonies do not permit clear-cut cadences in well-defined keys. So, although the music pays homage to French baroque music, the clear tonal structures of that period are blurred by a profusion of themes and by modes that lack the presence of a key-defining leading note.

The melody of the first section (bars 1–22) begins with the fourth degree of the aeolian mode on C♯ and ends on the *finalis* (the modal equivalent of the tonic). Between these two points phrases cadence on the fifth degree (bars 2, 4, 16 and 18), seventh degree (bar 8) and second degree (bar 14). There are hundreds of plainsong melodies of this sort, but no baroque binary-form movements that are so tonally ambiguous. At the start of the second section (bars 23–72) modality evaporates in a welter of chromatic discords, and when the first theme returns (bar 42) the first bar is harmonised with a D-major chord that is foreign to the aeolian modality of the melody. Finally the movement ends with a modal cadence (B to C♯).

Form	Bars	
	1–8	A1
	9–14	A2
	15–22	A1 '
	23–41	B1
	42–49	A1 "
	50–55	B2
	56–62	A2 '
	63–72	Coda

The return of the opening theme in the second section hints at rounded-binary structures such as those in *NAM 21*, but the introduction of a completely new theme (bars 50–55) is quite foreign to baroque practice. In fact, if we concentrate solely on the thematic structure, the rondo-like form shown *above right* emerges. Given the length of the central section (bars 23–41), the lack of repeat marks, and the fact that both themes of the first section are recapitulated, it is possible to hear the piece as a ternary structure (ABA, where the final A section starts at bar 42).

Don't worry if the form at first seems a little confusing. Examiners know that there is no single correct answer that will adequately explain the form of a complex work such as this. They will be more interested in your ability to present the arguments for different points of view, and your ability to back them up with evidence from the music itself.

Although larded with discords and modulations to unrelated keys the tonal structures of these neoclassical pieces are much less ambiguous than Debussy's sarabande. The prelude is an improvisatory movement based, like Bach's dances, on a limited number of motifs that are heard in a variety of guises throughout most of the piece. In this case there are just two, and both are heard in the first bar (the semiquaver figure and a three-note leaping quaver figure).

Prelude and Fugue

NAM 25   CD2 Tracks 17–18
Tatiana Nikolayeva (piano)

The ternary structure of the prelude is determined by its key scheme. In the first section A major is firmly established by pedals that form the simple progression I (bars 1–3), VI (bars 4–5) and V (bars 8–9). The central section is based on a series of unrelated chords (eg C major in bar 10, C♯ major in bar 13, A♭ major in bar 19 and

D♭ major in bar 21. D♭ is the same pitch as C♯, the third of chord I of the home key, A major. It is through this common note that Shostakovich banishes tonal uncertainty with a short closing section (bars 23–28) that remains in A major to the end of the prelude.

Bach followed his sarabande with a gigue in fugal style – in other words, it uses elements of fugue. However Shostakovich follows his prelude with a complete three-voice fugue. A full analysis is given on page 83, but the three important elements are:

- A fugal exposition (bars 1–14) that consists of a subject (bars 1–4), an answer (left hand, bars 5–8), a regular countersubject (right hand, bars 5–8), a codetta (bars 9–10) and finally the subject combined with regular and new countersubjects (bars 11–14, bass, middle and upper parts respectively).

- A set of episodes in which motifs from the exposition are manipulated in a variety of keys, eg A major in bars 15–20, and D and F major in bars 41–46. These alternate with middle entries in a variety of keys, eg F♯ minor in bars 21–24 (lower part on the treble stave), and B♭ major in bars 51–54 (bass).

- A closing section (bars 70–99) which, despite some colourful chromatic triads, remains throughout in the tonic key of A major and includes stretto entries (bars 70–75) and a return of the pedals that dominated the prelude.

Private study

1. What determines the structure of *NAM 20*?
2. Why can Bach's sarabande be described as monothematic?
3. What is rounded binary form? How does it differ from standard binary form? In which works that you have studied is it used?
4. Why is sonata form described as a development of rounded binary form rather than an extension of ternary form?
5. Show how Shostakovich uses tonality to structure his prelude.

Sample questions

In the exam there will be two questions on this topic, from which you must choose to answer **one**.

(a) Compare and contrast the form of **either** 'Von fremden Ländern und Menschen' **or** 'Hasche-Mann' with the form of Bach's dances in *NAM 21*.

(b) Using *NAM 22* as an example, explain why sonata form offered composers a means of constructing movements of considerable length and drama.

(c) To what extent does Debussy's Sarabande reflect the forms of baroque dance music, such as Bach's Sarabande in *NAM 21*?

(d) To what extent does Shostakovich make use of traditional structures in the fugue of *NAM 25*?

(e) Discuss the relationship between tonality and form, referring to appropriate examples from the works you have studied.

Sacred vocal music

For examination in summer 2002 and 2003

The first part of this chapter deals with the special focus work and topic set for examination in summer 2002 and 2003. If you are taking the exam in summer 2004 or 2005 turn to page 102.

Stravinsky, Symphony of Psalms, III

Special Focus Work for 2002 and 2003

NAM 31   CD3 Track 9
Choir of Westminster Cathedral
City of London Sinfonia
Conducted by James O'Donnell

Before starting on this section you should work through (or revise) the information about the context and structure of this music given on pages 86–88 of the AS Guide. Make sure that you understand all of the terminology used on those pages.

The last movement of the *Symphony of Psalms* is constructed from a number of sharply defined musical ideas, like the brilliantly coloured pieces of glass and stone that go to make up a mosaic. And, like a mosaic of Christ in majesty in a Byzantine church, the *Symphony of Psalms* is dedicated by its creator 'to the glory of GOD' (the capitals here and in the word DOMINUM in the Latin version of Psalm 150 are Stravinsky's own). We begin by identifying the most important elements (some no more than melodic fragments) that are juxtaposed and combined to form this hymn of praise.

A homophonic setting in bars 2–3 of *Alleluia* ('God be praised'). This is of the utmost simplicity, accompanied only by the notes G and C (cellos and basses). Stravinsky said it was inspired by music he heard in Russian Orthodox churches as a child.

Motif A

A hypnotically repeating melodic ostinato D–E♭–B♭ (tenor and bass from bar 4) ending on a repeated C (see example *below right*). It has the narrow range and repetitive patterns typical of many Russian folk songs, such as the following (which has the same four pitches):

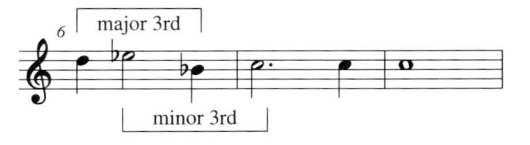

Motif B

Stravinsky's ostinato is accompanied by an orchestral bass defining a conflicting chord of C major (bars 4–8). It reappears in bar 12, and from bar 14 onwards it is accompanied by a three-note ostinato oscillating between the tonic and dominant of C (bars 14–20).

Motif C (soprano, bars 9–11) alternates between the two notes of a minor 3rd. This is accompanied by lower parts that form alternating chords of C minor and C major.

Motif C

Motif D is an even simpler melody, consisting of just two notes a semitone apart (horns, bars 14–19). It refers back to a chant-like melody heard at the start of the whole symphony:

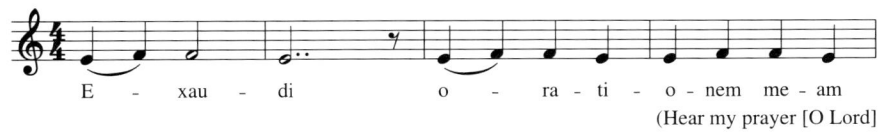

Motif D

E - xau - di   o - ra - ti - o - nem me - am
(Hear my prayer [O Lord])

These are the elements that are juxtaposed and combined to form the slow introduction. In themselves they are simple, but the way they relate to each other is anything but simple. The next example shows that the pitches of the vocal parts in bars 14–19 derive from the aeolian mode on C (as do the pitches of the horn melody and orchestral ostinato in these bars).

Warning. Photocopying any part of this book without permission is illegal.

[Musical example: bars 14–19 showing Horns, S/A, Aeolian mode on C, T/B, and Db. etc., with labels ①, ②, ③ marking the three ostinati.]

Notice how the three ostinati shown *above* are so constructed and combined that the first notes of all three never coincide. Aeolian modality gives way to the tonic (C) plus a tierce de Picardie (E♮) on the word *DOMINUM* (though the modal B♭ is retained in the cellos in bars 21–22 as a link to the next section).

In the fast section starting at bar 24 two more simple elements are introduced:

Motif E   This is a six-note quaver rhythm, first beard in bassoons and horns at bar 24. In bar 27 this is metrically displaced, by starting the pattern on the first beat of the bar instead of the second, and the sixth note is greatly extended in the first bassoon part.

Motif F   Triplet rhythms which take the form of triadic figures (bars 40–43 and 46–47) and semitonal/chromatic figures (bars 44–45).

These are the six basic elements of the whole movement. But just as the primary colours of fragments of glass can be superimposed to form secondary colours in a mosaic, so Stravinsky combines and transmutes these elements to form more complex musical ideas. With them he builds a complete and totally original structure from what, at first hearing, seem disparate elements.

The fast section begins in bar 24 with element E expressed as a series of triads stepping up from C major (the tonal centre of the whole movement) in bars 32–36 (horns), through D major (horns, bar 37) to E major (horns, bars 40–43). These chordal motifs are linked by elements B and C, expressed in the simplest terms as a minor 3rd followed by a major 3rd (G–B♭ and A♭–C in trumpet and harp, bars 33–34) and in more complex form as interlinked 3rds (C–A♭ and B♭–D in bar 38).

Notice how interlinked major and minor 3rds are encapsulated within the original version of B, shown in the music example on the previous page.

Element F (bars 40–47) leads to the first climax – another tonal conflict, this time consisting of a D-major triad superimposed on a bass G♯ (bars 48–49). Sopranos, then altos, enter with element D, now with its minor second enlarged to a major second. Element E appears in altos, tenors and divided strings in bars 65 and 68–69.

Typically Stravinskian hockets (in which syllables of single words are divided by rests) appear in bars 66–71, linked with element E by a bass ostinato (harp, piano and strings). Variants of E (orchestra, bars 72–86) then lead to a second climax, consisting of a combination of element C (sopranos, bars 87–98, now all major 3rds) with element E (orchestra in the same bars – by now the ear accepts all repeated-note quavers as related to the original six-note pattern).

A recapitulation begins at bar 100, starting with a reference to the wind chords and *Alleluia* from bars 1–3, followed by a return to the fast section, consisting of:

- element E (wind, bars 104–108)
- element C (trombone and piano, bars 109–112)
- a choral version of element E, this time stepping up from C major (bar 121) through E major (bars 126–128), to B♭ major (bars 132–133). This process (it is not a modulation) is interleaved with elements B+C and F, and continues to rise in the orchestra through E♭ major (bars 134–137) to reach the greatest climax of the movement in the E major triad (conflicting with A♯ in the bass) of bars 144–146.

In bars 150–162 the tempo again returns to that of the opening, but the beat is now a minim in triple time rather than a crotchet in quadruple time. G major is briefly established in bars 150–156, and a swaying triadic melody is introduced. It is possible that this is the only example of word painting, the *choro* (dance) of the text being expressed through the grave triple metre of music that sounds like a sarabande. Whether or not this is so, the passage acts as a link between the E-major tonality of bars 144–146 and the E♭ major tonality of the coda (bars 163–212). Over an ostinato for double bassoon and bass trombone that anchors the music in G major, a solemn canon unfolds in treble and bass parts (bars 150–156). Imitation continues in bars 157–160 as the sopranos climb up two six-note segments of octatonic scales (consisting of alternating semitones and tones) and tonality is almost obliterated by the dissonances in the last climax of the movement (bars 161–162).

Stravinsky described the coda (bars 163–212) as a

> hymn of praise [that] must be thought of as issuing from the skies [in which] agitation is followed by 'the calm of praise'.

Using a four-note ostinato (E♭–B♭–F–B♭) repeated 30 times, the sopranos explore the diatonic and chromatic contents of a minor 3rd (element C). Then the *Alleluia* returns (bars 205–206) and we now realise that this too is related to element C (its melody rises through the interval of a minor 3rd). Finally the ostinato figure B returns and all tonal tension is released in the C-major chord that for Stravinsky symbolises the alpha and omega of all things – *DOMINUM* – the Lord.

Private study

1. How can you tell that *NAM 31* was intended for performance in the concert hall rather than in a liturgical context?

2. Stravinsky, in common with other Russian composers such as Borodin, Tchaikovsky and Rachmaninov, sometimes uses modal melodies of a narrow range based on repeating patterns. What is the likely influence for this style of melody?

3. Explain each of the following terms and give an example of its use in *NAM 31*: hocket, octatonic scale, canon.

Warning. Photocopying any part of this book without permission is illegal.

Sample questions

In the exam there will be three questions on this work, from which you must choose to answer **two**.

(a) Discuss how Stravinsky uses ostinato both as a structural device and as a way to establish mood in *NAM 31*.

(b) Explain how tonal conflict, and its resolution, plays an important part in this movement.

(c) (i) What is unusual about Stravinsky's choice of instruments in the orchestra for *A Symphony of Psalms*?
   (ii) Choose and discuss three passages in *NAM 31* that you consider are interesting examples of orchestration.

Continuity and change in the handling of voices and/or instruments

Topic for examination in 2002 and 2003

You do not need to study this topic unless *Sacred vocal music* is the Area of Study that you undertook for AS Music and which you are now extending for A2.

Taverner

NAM 26   CD3 Track 1
Christ Church Cathedral Choir
Oxford
Conducted by Stephen Darlington

Taverner's handling of voices is typical of 16th-century styles in:

+ the preponderance of arch-shaped melodies (treble, bars 1–4)
+ melodies in which intervals greater than a 4th are rare, and in which leaps are usually followed by movement in the opposite direction (treble, bars 7–10)
+ the avoidance of melodic tritones, major 6ths, 7ths and intervals greater than an octave
+ contrasting groupings of voices, with antiphonal exchanges between these groups (bars 1–10)
+ contrasting homophony (bars 38–42) and imitative polyphony (bars 56–65).

Gabrieli

NAM 27   CD3 Track 2
Gabrieli Consort and Players
Directed by Paul McCreesh

It is easier to see change rather than continuity when comparing the *seconda prattica* style of *NAM 27* with the renaissance vocal polyphony of the *prima prattica* seen in *NAM 26*. It is true that most of Gabrieli's vocal melodies are predominantly conjunct and that a leap is most often followed by a return within the leap, but tritones such as those in bars 72–73 (D–G♯) are a much more modern feature, as are the echo effects in bars 55–60. Instead of Taverner's chaste melodic lines Gabrieli's melodies are often encrusted with ornamentation (eg bars 68–69). Instead of the flexible imitative textures of renaissance polyphony (eg *NAM 26*, bars 56–65) Gabrieli's use of imitation is often stiffly metrical and short-lived (eg alto I and tenor in bars 10–11). But the greatest innovation is Gabrieli's use of continuo accompaniment for monodic passages such as bars 1–5, and the *concertato* contrasts between vocal solos and duets, the two vocal choirs, and the instrumental choir.

Bach

NAM 28   CD3 Tracks 3–6
Yorkshire Bach Choir, Fitzwilliam
Ensemble, Clare Mathias (alto)
Conducted by Peter Seymour

Bach is famous for the synthesis of different styles he achieved in his sacred vocal music, so it is not surprising to find both continuity and change when comparing these four movements taken from Cantata 48 with Gabrieli's motet. Like *NAM 27*, the first movement of *NAM 28* contains a continuo part, and an instrumental ensemble that is both contrasted and combined with the vocal ensemble. But

Bach's textures are unlike the polychoral textures of Gabrieli. Four-part strings form the core of the ritornello form movement, around which Bach weaves imitative entries for four-part choir plus a chorale melody treated in canon by the wind. There is no similar use of a pre-existing melody as a cantus firmus in *NAM 27*.

The recitative that forms Bach's second movement derives from early baroque monody, but rather than being part of a continuous sacred concerto (like *NAM 27*) it forms a separate movement. Instead of a simple continuo accompaniment, a complete string ensemble acts as an expressive background to an angular, chromatic melody quite unlike Gabrieli's vocal solos and duets. And while there are homophonic passages in *NAM 27*, there is nothing comparable to the chorale harmonisation in Bach's third movement.

While still reliant on a continuo ensemble, the aria is quite unlike solo passages in *NAM 27*. This becomes immediately apparent if the second vocal solo of *NAM 27* (bars 13–24) is compared with the vocal part of Bach's aria. Gabrieli's melody is made up of four short unrelated phrases, the first two treated sequentially, the third repeated and the last containing two perfect cadences. In contrast Bach's phrases are not only longer, they are more coherent because they are all built from motifs derived from the oboe solo in the first ritornello (bars 1–16).

A full account of Haydn's handling of voices and instruments will be found among the notes on the *Quoniam*, starting on page 102. Haydn perpetuates some of the traditions of earlier sacred vocal music. In general terms, the use of a four-part choir and four-part strings, with contrasting vocal textures (solo voice, homophonic choral writing and counterpoint) can be found in many sacred choral works throughout the 18th century. More specifically, the desire to include the bright sounds of trumpets in D (which then dictate the key of the movement) and the traditional fugal ending to the *Gloria* can be found in many baroque masses – including Bach's *Mass in B minor* (1733). However Haydn's essentially symphonic style owes little to baroque precedent and neither did it have any influence on Stravinsky's neo-baroque style.

Although Bruckner wrote his *a cappella* motets under the influence of the Cecilian movement (see page 108) and his liturgical intentions were similar to those of Taverner, his homophonic handling of voices in this motet owes little to sacred music of the renaissance. The wide-ranging melodic lines are interrupted by frequent and dramatic silences with equally dramatic leaps from one phrase to the next. Particularly striking are the contrasts between the diatonic melodies of bars 30–39, the chromatic counterpoint of bars 40–42, the total silence in bars 43–44[1] and the return to simple diatonic melodies in the last phrase.

Stravinsky said that he wanted to write a work in which a four-part chorus and a large orchestra would be equal partners in a three-movement symphony. From the start he had in mind the clear tone of treble voices and a wind-dominated orchestra. To satisfy both of these requirements he dispensed with violins and violas (too much vibrato that could spoil the clarity of treble voices) and all types of clarinet (too smooth-toned compared with the more biting timbre

Haydn

NAM 29   CD3 Track 7
Barbara Bonney (soprano)
London Symphony Chorus
City of London Sinfonia
Conducted by Richard Hickox

See also the 'Hallelujah' chorus in Handel's *Messiah* (1742). It too is in D major and has a central fugal section, but its baroque style and ritornello form are very different to the symphonic style of Haydn. Unlike Bach's *Mass in B minor*, *Messiah* was a work that Haydn knew and greatly admired.

Bruckner

NAM 30   CD3 Track 8
Christ Church Cathedral Choir
Oxford
Conducted by Stephen Darlington

Stravinsky

NAM 31   CD3 Track 9
Choir of Westminster Cathedral
City of London Sinfonia
Conducted by James O'Donnell

of the double-reed instruments that dominate the middle and bass registers of his orchestral textures). With typical eccentricity there are no cymbals (despite a reference to them in the text) and the bass drum plays only two notes in this movement. To provide percussive incisiveness to the orchestral ostinati he included parts for two pianos. Several examples of his handling of these forces have been discussed in the analysis starting on page 95 and the music example on page 96 shows how he realises the equal partnership of voices and instruments in a fairly complex texture.

Stravinsky stated that he did not wish to follow the symphonic writing of composers such as Haydn (*NAM 29*) in which the chorus is allotted a simplified version of a self-sufficient orchestral texture (bars 3–22), or in which voices and instruments double each other in contrapuntal textures (bars 22–61). However continuity with earlier traditions is evident from a comparison of the concertato style of *NAM 27* with the neo-baroque style of Stravinsky:

- both works contain a homophonic *Alleluia* that punctuates more complex textures, like a refrain
- both have purely orchestral sinfonias dominated by wind and supported by string bass instruments
- both include massive tutti chordal passages (Gabrieli, bars 102–103 and Stravinsky, bars 161–162)
- both include passages in which a vocal duet is accompanied by a complex instrumental texture (Gabrieli, bars 39–61 and Stravinsky, bars 80–86)
- both contain canonic passages involving both instruments and voices (Gabrieli, bars 114–118 and Stravinsky, bars 150–156).

Of course the differences are as striking as the similarities:

- in the symphony there is no equivalent of Gabrieli's continuo group or of his use of monody (see bars 1–5 of *NAM 27*)
- the ostinati that so dominate many of Stravinsky's textures are not found in Gabrieli's motet
- in the symphony the solo–tutti contrasts of the motet are absent
- in the motet there is little instrumental doubling of the type seen in bars 157–161 of *NAM 31*, and neither is there any equivalent of Stravinsky's heterophonic textures – such as that seen in bars 150–154 of *NAM 31*, where the oboe shadows the soprano, and the bassoon shadows the bass.

Stravinsky's innovative handling of the natural phenomenon of harmonics requires explanation. While we tend to hear one main pitch when a single note is sounded, above this 'fundamental' a hierarchy of quieter 'harmonics' is also present (unless the sound is a pure electronic tone). The relative strengths of these overtones helps to give a note its distinctive timbre, making a trumpet note sound different to the same pitch played on the flute, for instance. In the following example the first E♭ is a fundamental and the other notes are its harmonics (the presence of higher harmonics tends to make a note sound brighter and more reedy):

The notes printed in black are out of tune with the corresponding pitches in the type of equally-tempered scale that is used in most western music today.

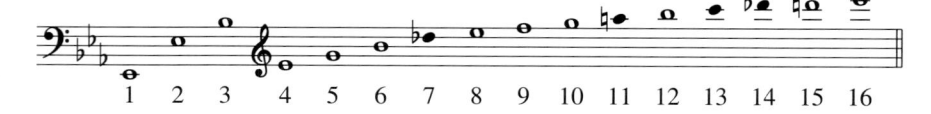

In bars 187–198 there are as many as ten independent contrapuntal strands with many dissonances. Yet when you listen, instead of harsh clashes, do you notice that what you hear is a bass ostinato and homophonic voices wreathed in an aura of high-pitched sound? In the three chords at the word DOMINUM Stravinsky uses all of the harmonics shown in the example on page 100, other than the 9th and 11th. Nowhere does he use pitches not shown in the harmonic series except for B♮ (and this only as a lower auxiliary note lasting one beat). Some of the higher harmonics are doubled at a lower octave, but by and large Stravinsky maintains the spacing of the harmonic series (octaves at the bottom decreasing gradually until they reduce to semitones at the top). This is but an extreme example of Stravinsky's original and imaginative handling of voices and instruments that is evident throughout the *Symphony of Psalms*.

As a young man Tavener was bowled over by a performance of Stravinsky's *Canticum Sacrum*, so it should not be surprising to find elements of continuity between *NAM 31* and *32*. This is obvious in the first two bars of the soprano part, where a chant-like melody of just four pitches extending over a perfect 4th replicates the pitches in the tenor part of bars 4–8 of Stravinsky's symphony (transposed and in the minor). When this melody is repeated in bars 11–12 it is doubled at the octave by tenors in much the same way as Stravinsky's tenor is doubled at the octave by the bass and, as in the symphony, this simple melody is repeated many times. There are, however, no parallels in the vocal parts of *NAM 31* for Tavener's other melodic techniques, which include:

Tavener

NAM 32	CD3 Track 10
Westminster Abbey Choir	
Directed by Martin Neary	

✦ simultaneous melodic inversion of the theme (bar 2)
✦ chromatic extension of the theme (bars 3–4) and simultaneous melodic inversion of this extended melody (bars 5–6)
✦ homophonic accompaniment of the theme in the pure aeolian mode (bars 7–8) – unlike Stravinsky's tonal conflict
✦ rhythmic augmentation of the theme (bar 10).

Private study

1. What type of voice is a mean (*NAM 26*)?

2. Explain how the following terms relate to *NAM 27*: (i) *sinfonia*, (ii) *cori spezzati*, (iii) *stile concertato* and (iv) *basso continuo*.

3. What is meant by the terms (i) *a cappella*, (ii) liturgical church music, (iii) *prima prattica* and (iv) *seconda prattica*?

4. What is unusual about the instrumentation of *NAM 31*?

Sample questions

In the exam there will be two questions on this topic, from which you must choose to answer **one**.

(a) Compare and contrast the vocal writing of Taverner (*NAM 26*) with that of Tavener (*NAM 32*).

(b) Show how Haydn's symphonic writing in *NAM 29* differs from the instrumental accompaniments of Bach in *NAM 28*.

(c) Outline the difference between the *prima prattica* and the *seconda prattica*, as exemplified by *NAM 26* and *NAM 27*.

TIP: reread the section headed 'The new style' on page 81 of the AS Guide.

Sacred vocal music

For examination in summer 2004 and 2005

This part of this chapter deals with the special focus work and topic set for examination in summer 2004 and 2005. If you are taking the exam in summer 2002 or 2003 turn to page 95.

Haydn, Quoniam tu solus sanctus

Special Focus Work for 2004 and 2005
NAM 29 — CD3 Track 7
Barbara Bonney (soprano)
London Symphony Chorus
City of London Sinfonia
Conducted by Richard Hickox

Before starting on this section you should work through (or revise) the information about the context and structure of this music given on pages 84–85 of the AS Guide. Make sure that you understand all of the terminology used on those pages.

The text

The text of *NAM 29* forms the last section of an ancient Christian hymn of praise beginning with the words *Gloria in excelsis Deo* ('Glory to God in the highest'). The Gloria is the second main text of the ordinary (ie the unchanging part) of the mass. It is said or sung (to plainsong or in a choral setting) in all celebrations of the mass, except when a joyful hymn of praise would be inappropriate, such as during the penitential seasons before Christmas and Easter. For the same reason, it is omitted from the Requiem (a mass for the souls of the dead). The text is thus liturgical – that is to say it is officially approved for use in church services. (Not all sacred music is liturgical; the text of *NAM 32*, for instance, is a setting of non-liturgical poetry by William Blake.)

The term *Gloria* is also used for a much shorter text, beginning *Gloria Patri et Filio* ('Glory be to the Father and to the Son') added to the end of psalms in services such as vespers (Roman Catholic) and evensong (Anglican).

In order to understand the text of *NAM 29* (and hence Haydn's setting of it) you need to be aware that for most Christians there is one God, who is manifest in three persons: the Father (whom no living human has seen), the Son (who took human form), and the Holy Spirit (who dwells in everyone). The words of the *Gloria* fall into three sections. The first praises the Father, the second is addressed to Jesus the Son, and the third (our text) acknowledges the unity of the trinity: *Jesu Christe* (Jesus Christ), *Sancto Spiritu* (the Holy Spirit), and *Dei Patris* (God the Father).

The musical setting

Try to hear the whole of the *Nelson* mass, or at least the entire Gloria, so that you get an idea of the context of the extract in *NAM 29*. Remember that in a liturgical setting other parts of the church service take place between the main musical movements of the mass; these do not all follow straight on from each other as they do when you listen to a CD or hear a concert performance of the mass.

In common with most baroque and classical settings Haydn allots a separate movement to each of the three sections of the *Gloria*, which in its entirety forms a ternary structure (ABA^1), *NAM 29* being the final A^1 section. The music of bars 1–15 of *NAM 29* appears at the beginning and end of the first A section (thus symbolising oneness), but the central movement (B) is a contrasting adagio in B♭ major. All three movements could be performed by orchestra alone without detracting too much from Haydn's conception. This is what is meant by the common term 'symphonic mass'. Even in the 18th century there were those who criticised such elaborate settings of liturgical texts as being too long, too ornate and too worldly. But all six of Haydn's great masses written between 1796 and 1802 (including the *Nelson* mass of 1798) were specifically composed to celebrate the name day (an event like a royal 'official birthday') of Princess Maria, the wife of Haydn's employer, Prince Nicholas II of Esterházy. These days you are far more likely to hear the *Nelson* mass in the context of an Anglican communion service than in a Roman Catholic mass – and more likely still to hear it in a concert than a church service of whatever denomination.

Warning. Photocopying any part of this book without permission is illegal.

Haydn's setting of the Quoniam falls into three distinct sections, just as his setting of the whole Gloria falls into three movements. These tripartite divisions are not accidental – in this and many other mass settings they reflect the doctrine of the Trinity, and each section also contains its own musical symbolism.

Section 1

Haydn begins the first section (bars 1–22^1) with alternating solo and tutti phrases, the latter echoing the former. The single soloist reflects the text 'For you alone are the Holy One', a statement that tutti chorus and orchestra then affirm in a homophonic version of the soloist's phrase. These solo/tutti alternations reflect the ancient versicle-and-reponse formula in which a cantor makes a statement (in a versicle such as 'The Lord be with you') to which all respond with a phrase such as 'And also with you'. This section is itself divided into three sub-sections:

- the solo/tutti alternations (bars 1–9^1)
- a choral repeat of the first sub-section (bars 9–15^1)
- a hushed choral setting of the final sentence over a tonic pedal moving at the last moment to the dominant (bars 16–22^1).

Section 2

The second section (bars 22–61) is an extended four-voice fugato. The example *right* shows the first entry of the fugal subject and countersubject. Both are sequential melodies. The orchestral part is called a regular countersubject because it accompanies the subject almost every time it appears. Nearly all of the contrapuntal strands of the fugato derive from one or other of these two melodies. Such thematic integration is one of the most common features of fugal writing, and it helps explain why so many baroque and classical composers chose to end settings of the Gloria with a fugue. Just as the text speaks of the many (Father, Son and Holy Spirit) being one God, so the many voices of a fugue are united in their proclamation of the same idea. Let us explore some of the ways in which Haydn exploits the material shown in the example *right*.

A fugato is a fugal passage within a longer structure. The terms 'fugal' and 'fugue' are explained in the glossary of the AS Guide.

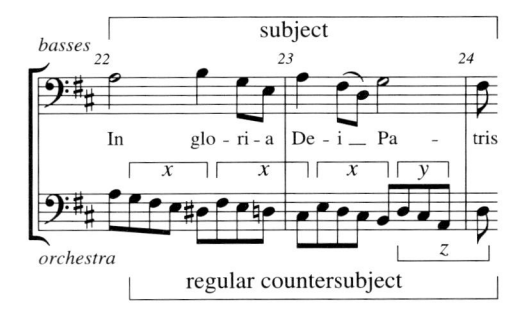

How does the tenor entry in bar 24 relate to the bass entry two bars earlier? Do you see that it is a transposed version of the subject? In a fugue this is known as the answer, and you hopefully spotted that it isn't an exact transposition (which would be called a real answer) – compare the opening intervals. This modification is made to avoid an unwanted modulation, and the result is known as a tonal answer. Meanwhile the basses, having completed the subject, continue with a transposed but otherwise exact repetition of the countersubject.

The altos enter (bar 26) with the subject while the tenors take over the countersubject. Meanwhile the basses sing a free part consisting of sequential treatment of an inversion of motif *y* plus a version of motif *z* in which just the first interval is inverted.

The soprano statement of the answer (bars 28–30^1) is accompanied by the countersubject and the same free part as that sung by the basses in bars 24–25. Technically this marks the end of the fugal exposition (the opening statement of the subject/answer by all fugal voices), but the term has little meaning here since the entire fugato is so dominated by entries of the subject.

In bars 30–31 the melodic strands of bars 26–27 are contrapuntally inverted, the uppermost part (subject) becoming the lowest, the

Warning. Photocopying any part of this book without permission is illegal.

middle part (countersubject) becoming the highest, and the lowest (the free part) becoming the middle part. Three-part counterpoint that can be inverted in this way is known as triple counterpoint (the Trinity again?). The ends of the countersubject and free part are bent to form a phrygian cadence (IVb–V) in B minor.

In bars 32–34 the first pair of stretto entries appears in the tenor and soprano parts. Haydn does not take advantage of the fact that, with imitation at the octave and two parts entering one bar apart, it is possible for them to state his complete subject and make perfectly good counterpoint. This is not an oversight. If Haydn were to do this consistently the counterpoint would become four-square and predictable. Instead he exploits the potential of the three motifs shown earlier by introducing inversions of *y* and *x* (alto) and by allowing the tenor to end its three-bar phrase with an inversion of *y* and a varied form of *z*. For the same reason he varies the end of the subject in the bass part of bars 35–36, setting against it a soprano part derived from his setting of the word *gloria* in the subject, immediately followed by motif *x*.

Similar modifications of the subject ensure variety and increase excitement. In the soprano entry at bar 40, for instance, the falling sequence of the original subject becomes a rising sequence, and in bars 54–55 the subject has only just started in the soprano part when it is suddenly displaced by a whole octave.

Short fugal episodes (bars $42-44^2$ and $50-51^2$) give momentary relief from the otherwise omnipresent thematic ideas which derive from bars 22–23. By doing so they make the stretto entries that follow even more effective. The fugato ends with a coda (bars 57–61) in which contrapuntal tension unwinds as the sopranos descend a whole octave in 3rds with the altos but out of step with the tenors (so forming a series of 7–6 suspensions). Meanwhile the basses sing a descending sequence derived from the inverted form of motif *y*.

Throughout the fugato notice how textural variety is achieved by Haydn's use of almost every permutation of two, three and four-part counterpoint.

Section 3 The third section (bars 62–82) is a coda to the whole movement, in which the triadic setting of the word *gloria* (see the previous music example) is transformed into continuous tonic–dominant figuration in the strings. Above this male soloists sing a simple round derived from the bass part of bar 36 joined to the last two notes of the fugue subject. Above them the solo soprano sings a descant that also comes from the setting of the word *gloria* (the four quavers at the start of bar 65 being a retrograde of the four quavers played by the violins at the same time). The rising sequence of bars 68–70 is similarly built on an alto part that also ultimately comes from Haydn's setting of the word *gloria* in the fugal subject (via the version of it in the first two beats of the soprano part in bar 55). The symbolism could not be clearer: for Haydn (by now aged 66, but still with some of his finest works before him) everything derives from the glory of God. As in many a symphonic coda, so in this closing section the tonic is strongly affirmed by tonic pedals (which in this case occupy 13 of its 22 bars), underpinning the affirmation of faith in the final word *Amen* ('so let it be').

Private study

1. (i) There are normally five main sections in musical settings of the mass. Which of these five is the *Gloria*?
   (ii) Which part of the *Gloria* of the *Nelson* mass is the music of *NAM 29*?

2. (i) Why is this work often described as a symphonic mass?
   (ii) Why is it rarely performed in a liturgical context?

3. Identify the key in bar 4, explaining the effect of the note D♯ in the tenor part of this bar.

4. In bar 9 the choir begins a varied repeat of bars 1–8. How does Haydn achieve a smooth transition from the first eight bars?

5. (i) What is the difference between a subject and an answer in a fugue?
   (ii) Explain the following terms: fugato, tonal answer, regular countersubject, triple counterpoint, stretto.

6. What were the circumstances that prompted Haydn to write sacred music on such a grand scale in the *Nelson* mass?

Sample questions

In the exam there will be three questions on this work, from which you must choose to answer **two**.

(a) Give a detailed account of bars 22–61, identifying the features which identify this as a passage of fugal writing.

(b) Comment on the variety of vocal textures in *NAM 29*.

(c) To what extent do you feel that Haydn regards musical form and drama more highly than religious devotion in *NAM 29*?

Continuity and change in the setting of Latin words

Topic for examination in 2004 and 2005

You do not need to study this topic unless *Sacred vocal music* is the Area of Study that you undertook for AS Music and which you are now extending for A2.

Before starting work on this topic you need a thorough understanding of the material on *Sacred vocal music* in the AS Guide (pages 78–90). Remember that for A2 the topic draws on works from across the **entire** Area of Study, not just those in one of the two lists, A or B.

Taverner's setting of this votive antiphon addressed to St William, a 12th-century Archbishop of York, is more commonly associated with a text addressed to Jesus Christ, hence its alternative title of *O Christe Jesu, pastor bone*. This tells us something about the way early 16th-century composers often approached the setting of Latin words. For them music was expressive in much the same way as gothic architecture is expressive – both raise the soul to the contemplation of things eternal, but neither attempts to comment on the concrete images of the scriptures or other liturgical texts. This is particularly true of Taverner's simple and austere style that is represented by this antiphon. It is written in the transposed ionian mode, which, to all intents and purposes, is the same as F major.

O Wilhelme, pastor bone (O Christe Jesu, pastor bone)

NAM 26   CD3 Track 1
Christ Church Cathedral Choir
Oxford
Conducted by Stephen Darlington

Warning. Photocopying any part of this book without permission is illegal.

The first chromatic alteration is the flattened 7th heard in bar 15 on the first syllable of *agone* (anguish or strife). It is so expressive that we may be tempted to interpret this as word painting. That this interpretation is erroneous is proved by Taverner's use of the same flattened 7th in such totally different contexts as bar 36, when referring to Thomas Wolsey (the composer's employer), and bar 60, in connection with *aeternae vitae* (eternal life).

The setting is syllabic, only becoming melismatic in the final bars, and then only after the text about the reward of eternal life has first been heard in the syllabic setting of bars 56–58. Such repetition of the text was, incidentally, highly unusual at this time although it later became common (see *NAM 27*) and it forms a fundamental part of the style in works such as *NAM 29*.

The chief means of articulating individual clauses of the text is by vocal scoring. Thus the first clause (*O Wilhelme, pastor bone*) is treated antiphonally, the two-voice counterpoint of upper voices being answered by the three-voice counterpoint of lower voices (the uppermost voice of each group having the same melody). Taverner reverts to two-part counterpoint for the second clause (*Cleri pater et patrone*), but this time the trebles are answered by the full five-part choir. In bar 16 the three lowest parts introduce the next section of text, to be answered by the two upper parts in bar 20. Once again the rest of the choir joins in, but this time the entries are staggered, starting with basses in bar 22.

Vocal textures vary from pure homophony (bars 16–18), through homorhythmic duets (bars 20–24) to the imitation of bars 57–65. Among these is an ancient English musical device known as gymel – two parts of similar range, which here freely cross one another (trebles, bars 43–47). They are supported by the mean to form a homophonic three-voice texture in a relatively high register for the words *Et ecclesiam piorum*, which this time is answered by the full choir. Notice how Taverner holds in reserve three devices to create a climax for the final line of the text, *Aeterna vitae praemium* (the reward of life eternal) – melismatic writing, imitation and (in bar 64) the full three-octave range of the choir.

In ecclesiis

NAM 27 CD3 Track 2
Gabrieli Consort and Players
Directed by Paul McCreesh

The contrast between Taverner's austere a capella antiphon and Gabrieli's exuberant concerted motet is as striking as the difference between renaissance and baroque music. The latter is particularly reflected in Gabrieli's use of solo voices, instruments, a rondo structure and devices such as sequence and ostinato, but there are also notable differences in his approach to word-setting.

NAM 27 is divided into five sections by choral refrains to the word *Alleluia*. In the first two of these sections the texture is thin (solo voice accompanied by the newly-invented continuo ensemble), and the word-setting is mainly syllabic – a combination which ensures that the text is delivered in a dramatic and clearly audible fashion. The fourth section (bars 68–94) is also accompanied by continuo alone and, despite being scored for vocal duet and containing more melismatic writing, the text is again clearly audible. Elsewhere Gabrieli's luxuriant multi-voice counterpoint and florid melismas impress, but they tend to obscure the text in both solo and tutti passages (bars 39–61 and 114–118 respectively).

The variety of textures available to Taverner was limited by the resources of the small chapel choir at Cardinal College (now Christ Church), Oxford – although, as we have seen, he achieves variety by dividing the five-part choir into various smaller groupings. In contrast, the lavish resources available at St Mark's, Venice enabled Gabrieli to use 14 contrapuntal strands, grouped in three contrasting choirs – comprising a four-voice solo choir, a four-voice choral choir, and a six-voice instrumental choir. With the addition of the omnipresent continuo accompaniment these polychoral resources allowed a much wider range of textures including:

- monody for the deceptively simple start (bars 1–5)

- solo vocal duets with echo effects and imitative counterpoint supported either by six-voice instrumental counterpoint (bars 39–61) or a simple continuo accompaniment (bars 68–94)

- choral homophony in antiphonal exchanges with either a solo voice (bars 6–10), or with a duet supported by homophonic instrumental parts (bars 62–66)

- choral polyphony with a single solo part (bars 10–12), or with two soloists and six-part instrumental polyphony (bars 66–68)

- instrumental homophony (bar 31) and imitative counterpoint (bars 32–39)

- massive tutti homophony for the dramatic setting of *Deus* (God) to the two unrelated chords of F major and D major (bar 102)

- antiphonal exchanges between various different groupings of all 14 parts (bars 103–114).

For the climactic setting of *in aeternum* ('for evermore') in bars 114^4–118, Gabrieli uses the baroque device of a dominant pedal to underpin his mastery of renaissance-style counterpoint, displayed in a 'canon 8 in 3' (three simultaneous canons spread among eight parts). This comprises (i) a canon for the four solo voices, (ii) a two-voice choral canon (alto II and tenor) and (iii) a canon for the two cornetts. This entire panoply of 'surround sound' (achieved in Gabrieli's time by positioning the various groups of musicians around spacially separated galleries in St Mark's) comes to rest on a tierce de Picardie in bar 118. Its A-major chord is immediately followed by a dramatic and unrelated F-major triad as the final *Alleluia* kicks in.

There is no obvious word painting in Taverner's antiphon, but in Gabrieli's motet these joyful and dramatic interjections of *Alleluia* (Praise the Lord) are highlighted by choral homophony and a change to triple time every time they occur. Elsewhere in the motet there is no overt word painting, but the textural variety described above amply reflects the sentiments of the jubilant Latin text.

Finally note that there is considerable variety in the sacred music of the late renaissance and the early baroque. Many renaissance motets include much more imitation and melismatic word-setting than *NAM 26*, and polychoral church music was not unknown at this time. And not all early baroque motets require the resources of *NAM 27* – many were written for just solo voice and continuo.

'Quoniam tu solus sanctus' from the Nelson Mass

> NAM 29   CD3 Track 7
> Barbara Bonney (soprano)
> London Symphony Chorus
> City of London Sinfonia
> Conducted by Richard Hickox

Enough has been said in the section starting on page 102 to show that Haydn's symphonic setting of Latin words is, in most respects, radically different from both Taverner's *a cappella* antiphon and Gabrieli's polychoral motet. Yet there are some common elements:

- both Taverner and Haydn set their texts in a basically syllabic style until they reach the crucially important words at the end (*aeternae vitae praemium* in Taverner's antiphon and *Amen* in Haydn's 'Quoniam')

- Haydn's alternation of solo and choral homophony (bars 1–10) is similar to the exchanges between solo voice(s) and chorus in the *Alleluia* sections of Gabrieli's motet

- Haydn's fugal writing in his middle section (bars 22–57) finds its counterpart in Gabrieli's imitative writing (bars 32–62) and canonic counterpoint (bars 114–118).

However these superficial similarities are more than out-balanced by the major differences in musical style between the renaissance polyphony of Taverner, the early baroque *stile concertato* of Gabrieli and the classical symphonic writing of Haydn.

Locus iste

> NAM 30   CD3 Track 8
> Christ Church Cathedral Choir
> Oxford
> Conducted by Stephen Darlington

The Cecilian movement was dedicated to the reform of Roman catholic church music in the 19th century through the revival of a capella choral singing and the restoration of ancient forms of plainsong. The movement flourished in France, Germany and Austria and was named after St Cecilia, the patron saint of music.

After what they saw as the excesses of baroque and classical church music, priests and composers who belonged to the 19th-century Cecilian movement advocated a return to the more austere styles of renaissance polyphony and the reinstatement of plainsong in church services. Bruckner was familiar with Haydn's symphonic masses and he himself wrote masses that are as much at home in the concert hall as in church. However several of his motets were written in accordance with the precepts of the Cecilian movement: they are simple, unaccompanied and intended for liturgical use. *Locus iste* is perhaps the most perfect of them. It is a gradual (a motet sung between readings in a mass) written for the dedication of a church. Its restrained style, particularly its hushed, meditative ending, is designed to prepare the congregation for the Gospel reading that follows. Among the works we have studied it is closest in both function and style to Taverner's antiphon, as the following comparisons show:

- both are written for a cappella voices

- both are designed to be sung at specific points in (Bruckner) or after (Taverner) the roman catholic liturgy

- both are short and restrained in style

- both are mainly syllabic, allowing the words to be heard clearly

- both contain a melismatic passage towards the end (bars 40–42 in *Locus iste*, where Bruckner responds to God's name with expressive chromaticism followed by awe-struck silence).

But Bruckner's motet is not pastiche, for it combines renaissance features of much more recent musical styles:

- wide-ranging, aspiring and often disjunct melodies (Taverner's treble part has a compass of a 9th and never leaps more than a 5th whereas Bruckner's soprano part has a compass of a 13th and includes leaps of a 6th and a 7th in the first ten bars)

> **Warning.** Photocopying any part of this book without permission is illegal.

- expressive dissonances that highlight important words (such as the soprano appoggiatura on G in bar 4 and the alto entry on E, against the soprano F♯ in bar 22)

- mainly four-bar phrasing (bars 21–29 and 38–48 are the only exceptions), with modulating sequences that give structure to sections of repeated text (eg bars 12–20)

- intense chromaticism that temporarily masks a sense of tonality (bars 21–25)

- detailed performance directions (an indication of tempo and copious dynamic markings).

Stravinsky's *Symphony of Psalms* was not intended for liturgical performance as its title suggests, but the double dedication ('to the glory of God and to the Boston Symphony Orchestra on its 50th anniversary') reveals Stravinsky's intentions clearly. It requires a massive symphonic orchestra (significantly without the romantic timbres of violins and violas), but his setting of Latin is much nearer to Taverner's restrained style than to that of Gabrieli, Haydn or Bruckner. This is apparent right from the start of this movement and at every point thereafter.

Symphony of Psalms

NAM 31 — CD3 Track 9
Choir of Westminster Cathedral
City of London Sinfonia
Conducted by James O'Donnell

- Both Gabrieli and Stravinsky use a repeated setting of the word *Alleluia* as a refrain. But whereas Gabrieli changes to dancing triple metre, and adds more voices and instruments to each successive appearance of the refrain, Stravinsky's hushed and simple chordal setting remains unchanged.

- Stravinsky's slowly revolving melodies owe more to the repeating cells of Russian folk music and Orthodox chant (see page 95) than to earlier art music (compare the soprano part in the first 22 bars with Haydn's utterly different soprano part in the first 15 bars of *NAM 29*).

- Like Bruckner, Stravinsky highlights the name of God (DOMINUM in, for example, bars 7–8 and 210–212). But whereas Bruckner (in bars 40–42 of *NAM 30*) opts for melismatic and highly chromatic writing, Stravinsky prefers the simplicity of a syllabic setting, with the choir singing hushed bare octaves on C (to which an E is added very high in the orchestra).

- Like Taverner, Stravinsky eschews almost all temptations to use images in the text as an excuse for word painting. The most extreme example comes in bars 163–168 where his setting of the words 'Praise him in the well-tuned cymbals' is marked to be performed quietly and much more slowly. The exultant text elicits a conjunct soprano melody ranging over a minor 3rd supported by a mesmeric orchestral ostinato.

- When the voices take up the syncopated orchestral rhythms, melodic invention is reduced to a monotone (bars 65–71) to maximise the percussive impact of the word-setting.

- After the metre changes to triple time (bar 146) in response to the text (*choro* = dance) the minim beat becomes extremely slow (48 beats per minute from bar 150) so the dotted rhythms are solemn, not dancing like Gabrieli's setting of *Alleluia*.

- Even when Stravinsky uses imitative counterpoint (bars 150–160) the effect is restrained compared with the exuberance of Gabrieli's canonic fireworks in bars 114–118 of *NAM 27*.

Let Stravinsky himself have the last word: 'The Church knew what the Psalmist knew: Music praises God'.

Private study

1. What is meant by the terms monody, antiphony and gymel?
2. (i) What is the difference between liturgical church music and non-liturgical church music?
   (ii) Give one example of each of these types of church music from the works you have studied.
3. Explain the difference between syllabic and melismatic word-setting and give an example of each.
4. What were the circumstances of the original performance of the *Nelson* mass that prompted Haydn to write the work on such a grand scale?
5. The text of *NAM 29* focuses on God as a Trinity of Father, Son and Holy Spirit. How does Haydn reflect this concept in his music?
6. (i) What did the Cecilian movement advocate?
   (ii) In what ways does *Locus iste* differ from renaissance motets such as *NAM 27*?
7. The text of *NAM 31* is as joyful as that of *NAM 27*, but the music is very different in style and mood. What do you feel are the key elements that Stravinsky wants to convey in his setting of Psalm 150?

Sample questions

In the exam there will be two questions on this topic, from which you must choose to answer **one**.

(a) Compare and contrast the setting of Latin texts in *NAM 27* and *NAM 31*.

(b) The Cecilian movement objected to increasing worldliness in sacred music. Explain why it would have found *NAM 30* more appropriate for worship than *NAM 29*.

(c) To what extent do you agree that the music of *NAM 26* reflects the fact that its text is a private prayer for the members of an Oxford college while *NAM 27* uses its text as an excuse to celebrate the splendour and music of Venice?

Secular vocal music

> **For examination in summer 2002 and 2003**

The first part of this chapter deals with the special focus work and topic set for examination in summer 2002 and 2003. If you are taking the exam in summer 2004 or 2005 turn to page 120.

'Thy hand, Belinda' (recitative) and 'When I am laid in earth' (aria) from Purcell's opera Dido and Aeneas

> **Special Focus Work for 2002 and 2003**
> NAM 36   CD3 Track 14
> Carolyn Watkinson (soprano)
> with the English Baroque Soloists
> Directed by John Eliot Gardiner

Before starting on this section you should work through (or revise) the information about the context and structure of this music given on pages 97–98 of the AS Guide. Make sure that you understand all of the terminology used on those pages.

Recitative was invented by Italian composers in about 1600, and it played an important part in Monteverdi's *Orfeo* (1607), one of the earliest great operas still to be regularly staged:

Recitative

Monteverdi, Recitative from Act 3 of *Orfeo* (1607)

[musical notation: "La-scia-te ogni spe-ran - za voi ch'en-tra - - - te."]

Translation: Abandon all hope you who enter here.

Whereas arias (songs) gave an opportunity for characters to reflect on the situation that confronted them, the objective of recitative was the correct declamation and expressive treatment of dramatic moments in the libretto (the text). This distinction was maintained well into the 19th century and the following basic principles were observed in recitative throughout much of this period:

A recording of this recitative, and another longer example from *Orfeo*, is given in the *Rhinegold Dictionary of Music in Sound*.

✦ The text (usually for a soloist) should be set in such a manner that the natural inflections and rhythms of speech are observed without regard to an obvious metrical pulse. The text is not normally repeated and, although it became normal to notate recitative in common time, the singer was free to interpret the composer's rhythms with the utmost flexibility. This is true of Carolyn Watkinson's interpretation on CD3. Listen, for instance, to her dotted rendition of the even quavers in bar 1 and her lengthening of the last syllable of 'Belinda'.

✦ The affection (emotional significance) of the text should be clearly expressed without compromising correct declamation. At this point in Purcell's opera, Dido is in a state of extreme despair. The composer expresses this affection by:

  ✦ a tonally ambiguous melisma that highlights the key word 'darkness'
  ✦ anguished chromaticism and unpredictable changes of key
  ✦ short, detached phrases with silences that suggest sighs
  ✦ grinding dissonances between the solo part and the bass
  ✦ jagged rhythms that transcend the suave and elegant French style of much of the rest of Purcell's opera
  ✦ a melodic line which slowly descends a 7th to reach another key word, 'death'.

> **Warning.** Photocopying any part of this book without permission is illegal.

- The accompaniment should support the singer but not obscure the words. To this end one or two instruments played the written bass part (in the recording on CD3 a bass viol suffices) while one or two harmony instruments improvised a chordal filling between the two written parts (in this particular recording of the recitative, one archlute suffices).

Composers sometimes added a few figures to the bass part to show what intervals should be played above the bass part. Modern editors sometimes add very full figuring (as in *NAM 36*), but performers are at liberty to disregard it. The example below shows what is actually played on CD3. This figuring represents the archlutenist's improvisation and takes no account of expressive dissonances formed between the singer and the bass (such as the minor 9th at the start of bar 4). The passing modulations and frequent cadences are typical of many kinds of recitative.

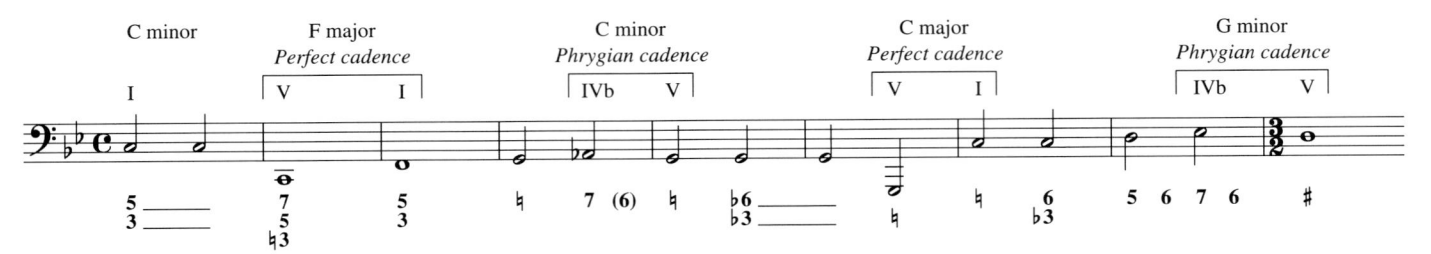

Air upon a ground

Basso-ostinato compositions were common in continental Europe throughout the 16th and 17th centuries, but the term ground bass (synonymous with basso ostinato) is usually applicable only to English instrumental or vocal compositions from the late 16th century onwards. Purcell would have been familiar with ground-bass compositions by earlier English composers such as William Byrd (1543–1623), but he acknowledged his debt to contemporary French and Italian composers in print.

Ground-bass arias do not necessarily have to remain in the same key throughout, like Dido's lament. The aria 'Ah, Belinda' from *Dido and Aeneas* uses 21 repetitions of a four-bar ground: 11 in the tonic, two in the dominant and eight in the tonic. If possible try to hear all of *Dido and Aeneas*: it is a short opera (under one hour) and is readily available in score and CD format. Videos of the opera have occasionally appeared, but may not be easy to track down.

Purcell's opera *Dido and Aeneas* reveals this rich mix of different European traditions in the composer's work. Much of the instrumental music is French in style, modelled on the dramatic music of Lully (1632–87), while the choruses are more in the style of Purcell's own English church music. The Italian influence is seen in the recitatives and the ground-bass arias. Purcell's indebtedness to Italian operatic composers such as Cavalli (1602–76) will become obvious if you perform the following example and compare it with Purcell's air in *NAM 36*.

The whole of Cavalli's aria can be found in *The Norton Anthology of Music*, edited by Claude Palisca.

Did you notice that Cavalli's four-bar ostinato is exactly the same as the first four bars of the ground bass of 'When I am laid in earth'? However Purcell's use of a five-bar pattern offers greater potential for interesting asymetric structures, with vocal phrases that often overlap and disguise the repetitions of the bass.

Purcell is not guilty of plagiarism – baroque composers often made use of formulaic bass melodies, many with names that reveal their origins as the basses of dance-types such as the passamezzo. A basso ostinato that falls in semitones from the tonic to the dominant in a minor key was a late addition to this repertoire of stock basses and, when used for vocal compositions, it was always associated with words such as 'weeping' (Cavalli) and 'fate' (Purcell).

A composer's originality was expressed through the varied melodies and harmonies added to such basses, the whole composition thus becoming a continuous set of variations. Although one cannot hope to pin down genius in words, it is possible to identify some of the elements that contribute to the expressiveness of this, the most famous air upon a ground that has ever been written.

- ✦ Purcell's extension of the stock lamenting bass implies a perfect cadence in G minor even when there is no harmony (bars 4^3–6). With the addition of the string parts this becomes a reality in the perfect cadence marking the end of the ground in bars 10–11, 15–16, 20–21 etc. By remaining in one key and by emphasising it through so many perfect cadences, Purcell underlines the implacable fate that drives Dido to kill herself.

- ✦ The melody of bars 6–14 (repeated in bars 16–24) expresses the doom-laden words through chromaticism (bars 7–8) and the drooping tritone in bar 12. The melody of bars 25–36 (repeated in bars 36–46) is fragmented (so deep is her despair that Dido is almost unable to continue her lament) yet contains the climax of the whole song when she reaches her highest note (bar 33), then falls hopelessly through a flat 7th (F♮ in bar 34) back to the tonic (bar 36).

- ✦ The pathos of the dramatic situation is underpinned by a rich harmonic vocabulary. The basic harmony of Dido's first phrase is essentially the progression I–V–IV–V but, as shown below, this is enriched with 7ths on the dominant chords, poignant suspensions in both the vocal part and accompaniment, and passing notes and an accented passing-note in Dido's melody. In addition, the chromatic movement generates harmonies such as the chord marked * (VII^7 of C – acting like a secondary dominant to the following chord of C) and, in the third bar of the phrase, first major and then minor forms of chord IV (both of which are decorated with melodic dissonances).

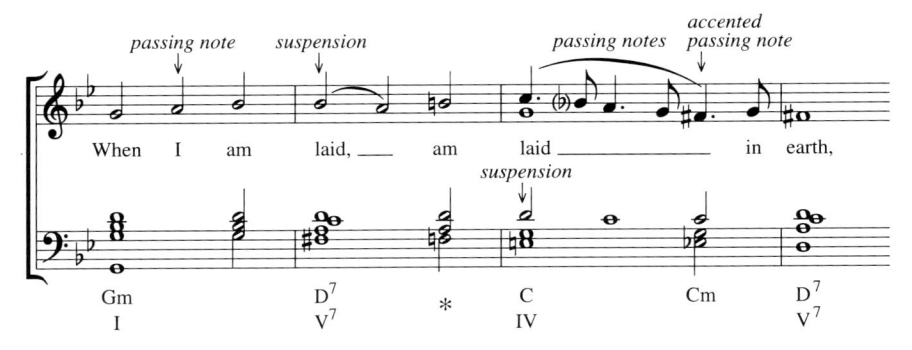

The result is a texture of deeply expressive dissonances (major and minor 9ths, 7ths, augmented 4ths, diminished 4ths and 2nds) between voice and accompaniment. In the final *ritornelle* similar discords are formed on the first beat of every bar but the last.

Private study

1. What is a libretto?

2. State in your own words what is meant by affection.

3. In the recitative the continuo instruments used on CD3 are an archlute and a bass viol. What two other instruments do you think might be appropriate to use for this continuo part?

4. What is a melisma? Give one example of a melisma in the recitative and one example in the aria.

5. What is a phrygian cadence? Where does one occur in the aria?

6. What style of music influenced the extracts in *NAM 36*? What other styles of music influenced Purcell?

7. How does Purcell achieve a sense of unity and continuity between the recitative and aria in *NAM 36*?

Sample questions

In the exam there will be three questions on this work, from which you must choose to answer **two**.

(a) What are the main characteristics of recitative?

(b) Why is 'When I am laid in earth' regarded as one of the greatest examples of a ground-bass aria?

(c) How does Purcell's music express Dido's state of despair?

Continuity and change in the setting of English words

Topic for examination in 2002 and 2003

You do not need to study this topic unless *Secular vocal music* is the Area of Study that you undertook for AS Music and which you are now extending for A2.

Before starting work on this topic you need a thorough understanding of the material on *Secular vocal music* in the AS Guide (pages 91–105). Remember that for A2 the topic draws on works from across the **entire** Area of Study, not just those in one of the two lists, A or B.

Ballett

NAM 34   CD3 Track 12
Purcell Consort of Voices
Directed by Grayston Burgess

The ballett (or ballet) was a simple, binary-form madrigal which developed from an Italian instrumental dance known as the *balletto*. The earliest extant collection of vocal balletts is Gastoldi's *Balletti a cinque voci … per cantare, sonare e ballare* (Balletts for five voices … for singing, playing and dancing) which dates from 1591. Just four years later Morley, one of the first and most prolific of English madrigalists, imitated Gastoldi in his *Balletts to Five Voyces*. For both composers the most important musical elements of the vocal ballett were the characteristic dance-like rhythms of the original instrumental *balletto*. You can hear these in simple form in the canzonet printed opposite. Notice particularly the fast triple metre, the lively ♩ ♪ rhythms, the syncopation in bar 7 (a second-beat accent) and the hemiola in bars 25–26.

A recording of Morley's canzonet, *Though Philomela lost her love*, can be found in *The Rhinegold Dictionary of Sound*. Note that exam questions will not require you to know music outside *NAM*, but knowledge of other relevant pieces may help you to provide a fuller answer.

Weelkes knew Morley's madrigals intimately, and a comparison of this canzonet with *Sing we at pleasure* (published in 1598) reveals

Warning. Photocopying any part of this book without permission is illegal.

Morley, Canzonet *Though Philomela lost her love* (1593)

something of the continuity and change that occurred during the incredible flowering of English music which took place in the last few years of the reign of Queen Elizabeth I. Dancing dotted rhythms occur in more than half of the 85 bars of *Sing we at pleasure*, syncopated second-beat accents can be heard in bar 21 (and elsewhere), and there is a hemiola in the alto part of bars 20–21.

But there are significant changes as well. By slurring together the quaver and crotchet of some of the dotted rhythms (eg 'praises' in bar 30), Weelkes creates a peculiarly English syncopation to highlight this important word. A second-beat syncopation occurs just before the three most important cadences, but in bar 21 it is heard against two other contrasting rhythms. The example *right* shows the second-beat accent in the soprano and bass parts. The hemiola in the alto (notated in $\frac{2}{4}$ time to show its true rhythm) not only conflicts with the metre of the other parts, it also contains within itself an off-beat syncopation (shown by an accent mark). In bar 21 only the tenor maintains unsyncopated triple-time rhythms.

Weelkes followed the advice Morley gave in his famous *Plaine and Easie Introduction to Practicall Musicke* (1597) by ensuring that the natural accentuation of English speech is maintained in the musical rhythms of his setting. He also followed the older composer's advice by expressing the significance of important words through the shape and rhythms of his melodic lines. See how, in the first three

Warning. Photocopying any part of this book without permission is illegal.

bars, the strong–weak rhythm of the all-important word 'pleasure' is reflected in an ascent to the highest pitch followed by a fall of an octave to the unaccented second syllable. Notice that in bar 23 'Love' falls on an accented minim (again on the highest note) in a simple chordal texture which allows the words to be clearly heard.

The rising 4th of 'Sweet Love' is replicated in the imitative setting of 'Whilst we his praises sound', so making 'we' the principal accent in these phrases. It is in this passage (bars 25–29) that we hear the most complex rhythms of the whole ballett. Because the parts enter at a beat's interval, accents are thrown on all beats of the bar: the third beat in the bass, the first beat in soprano 1 (cantus) and the second beat in soprano 2 (quintus). For five chaotic bars the triple-time metre seems to disappear as Weelkes evokes the clamorous shouts of praise for the God of Love. Finally notice how, in bars 35–41, the two chief means of celebration, dancing and singing, are represented by the syncopated setting of 'dancing' and the scalic ascent through a 7th to reach, once more, the highest and longest note on the word 'sing'.

Ayre

NAM 33   CD3 Track 11
James Bowman (countertenor) with David Miller (lute) and bass viol.

Dowland's ayre was published in 1600, only two years after *Sing we at pleasure*, but there could hardly be two more contrasting songs. About the only thing they have in common is their origin in dance forms. But where *Sing we at pleasure* derives its rhythmic drive from the balletto, a fast dance in triple time, Dowland's *Flow my teares* derives its solemn tread from the pavane, a slow dance in duple time (sometimes notated, as here, in $\frac{4}{4}$).

Dowland used the music of the *Lachrimae Pavan* yet again in his 1604 publication, *Lachrimae ... Seven Passionate Pavans ... for Lute, Viols or Violins*. This work, and the influence of *Lachrimae* on a wide variety of other composers, is discussed in *Dowland: Lachrimae (1604)* by Peter Holman. Cambridge Music Handbooks. Cambridge University Press. ISBN: 0-521-58829-4. See also *NAM 13* and *NAM 20*.

The song is an adaptation by Dowland of a lute solo called the *Lachrimae Pavan* (the Tearful Pavane) that he had written in the early 1590s and which rapidly achieved fame throughout Europe. This helps explain the lack of metrical regularity in the text, which was presumably written to fit the existing melody, and the way in which the five verses are set. The *Lachrimae Pavan* is written in a type of variation form, common in Elizabethan England, in which three phrases are each followed by a variation (AA' BB' CC'). In *Flow my teares* the first two verses are set strophically (bars 1–8), and so are the next pair (bars 9–16). Dowland also intended that the last verse (bars 17–24) should be repeated to maintain the overall form of the *Lachrimae Pavan*, but this final repeat is not observed on CD3. James Bowman does, however, introduce typical cadential ornamentation at the end of the fourth and fifth verses (see *left*).

Dowland's verses, unlike Weelkes' doggerel, are worth studying for their own sake. *Flow my teares* was written in Denmark, where, having failed to obtain a post at the English court, Dowland was court lutenist. This gives special resonance to the phrase 'Exilde for ever'. It also helps to know that Dowland's personal motto was *Semper Dowland, semper dolens* (Always Dowland, always doleful), which he also used as the title of one of his lute pieces. Although he could compose cheerful ditties (like the famous *Fine knacks for ladies*), he was chiefly famed for giving expression to the black streak of melancholy that ran through Elizabethan culture. Certainly the images – springing tears, the black bird of night, the shadows of souls that forever lament their fate in hell – vividly evoke a nightmare-world of hopeless grief.

Dowland's melodic lines fit the verses like (black) gloves. Falling tears are represented by the initial descent of a perfect 4th in the first three beats. The upward leap of a minor 6th adds a musical accent to the repetition of 'fall', and the fall itself is intensified by the contraction of the perfect 4th to a diminished 4th (C–G#). Having established the connection between falling tears and falling perfect and diminished 4ths at the start, these intervals serve as musical images of grief throughout much of the rest of the ayre (for example in the settings of 'Exilde' in bar 3 and 'infamy sings' in bar 6). Simultaneously they unify the three eight-bar phrases.

Even when the melody briefly visits a major key (perhaps reflecting the highest spire of contentment) at the start of the second phrase, falling fourths make their presence felt. When, at the start of the third phrase, the motif is inverted (bar 17) it intensifies the poet's address to the souls in hell, but, having reached C, the melody once again falls back through a diminished 4th to G#.

The climax of the whole ayre is reached with the bitter hyperbole 'Happie they that in hell Feele not the world's despite'. Up to this point the highest note has been the C an octave above middle C. Now the singer enters on a high E then sinks exhausted through a series of falling 4ths (E–B, D–A, C–G#) back to the note on which the ayre began. Among many other melodic representations of the text the suggestion of grief-induced hyperventilation evoked by the rests between the mounting 3rds in bars 12–13 is particularly notable. There is even persistent syncopation (bars 1 and 9, beat 4; bars 6 and 11, second quaver, etc), but, unlike the jolly syncopation in *NAM 34*, these rhythmic disturbances directly reflect the emotional disturbance of the tortured poetry.

Recitative and Air

NAM 36   CD3 Track 14
Carolyn Watkinson (soprano)
with the English Baroque Soloists
Directed by John Eliot Gardiner

Many aspects of this special focus work were discussed earlier. Continuity is evident between *NAM 34* and *NAM 36* in genre (ayre and air) and in the serious mood of both pieces. There is also a connection in the two composers' common use of rests to suggest sighing. But these links are superficial when compared with the profound differences between Dowland's metrical setting and the freely declaimed rhythms of Purcell's recitative or the ominously insistent repetitions of his ground bass. Dowland's word-setting is syllabic, with certain words subtly emphasised by syncopation, while Purcell incorporates expressive melismas and features on-beat dotted rhythms. Dowland's expressive use of the diminished 4th occurs in the context of a diatonic melody, while Purcell expresses Dido's resigned grief through chromaticism (in the recitative) and tritonal intervals (in the air). Finally, the texture of Dowland's song is freely contrapuntal, whereas Purcell's string accompaniment is mainly homophonic.

Canzonetta

NAM 37   CD3 Track 15
Elly Ameling (soprano)
Jörg Demus (piano)

My mother bids me bind my hair was one of a series of settings of English verses that Haydn wrote to commission on a visit to England. His elegant yet superficial galant melody accurately reflects the vacuous text of the first verse of a poem that was originally called a 'pastorale' (a work about simple countryside pleasures). While their servants laboured for 12 hours or more every day, it was fashionable for 18th-century aristocrats to amuse themselves by contemplating or even enacting the supposedly idyllic lives of

Warning. Photocopying any part of this book without permission is illegal.

rural peasants. It is a characteristic scene from such a never-never land that is portrayed in this canzonetta (little song).

The periodically phrased antecedent and consequent of bars 8^6–16 is notable for its triadic and scalic figures (eg bars 9 and 11 respectively), its appoggiaturas (eg the first note in bars 10, 11 and 12), and its decorative slide and acciaccatura (bar 15^1 and 15^4).

Haydn's craftsmanship is evident in the way the falling diatonic figures of the third phrase (bars 17–19) become a falling chromatic phrase at the start of the fourth phrase (bars 22–24) to reflect the tears of the bashful maiden. There is a link here with Dowland's ayre, both in the falling fourths of 'tie up my shoes with ribbands rare', and in the rests that punctuate the chromatic melody and the melody of the last 17 bars. But where Dowland is in dead earnest, Haydn, the witty composer of the *Surprise* symphony, seems to be gently mocking the sham pathos of the poem – as well he might given the inanity of 'I scarce ... *(gasp)* ... can go ... *(gasp)* ... or creep ... *(tenuto)*, ... while Lubin is ... *(gasp)* ... away'. The strophic setting does nothing to help the singer when, in the second verse, she is supposed to be saddened by the loss of Lubin. The same porcelain melody has to do service for the diametrically opposed sentiments of 'My mother bids me bind my hair with bands of rosy hue' and ''Tis sad to think the days are gone, when those we love were near'. Finally, although the maiden is supposed to be mortified by Lubin's absence, Haydn sets the concluding words to a melody that outlines the conventional chords (I, IIb, Ic, V^7 and I in A major) with which any galant trifle might be expected to end.

Blues

NAM 41   CD3 Track 19
Leona Mitchell (soprano)
Cleveland Orchestra and
Cleveland Orchestra Chorus
Conducted by Lorin Maazel

This lullaby, the first number of *Porgy and Bess*, is set as a 16-bar blues. If we strip away Gershwin's luxuriant vocabulary of blue notes, added notes and chromaticism, and identify just one main chord per bar, the basic chord sequence in B minor is:

bars	8	9	10	11	12	13	14	15	16	17	18	19	20	21	22	23
chord	Bm	Bm	Bm	Bm	Em	Em	F♯	F♯	Bm	Bm	Bm	Bm	D	E	Bm	Bm
	I	I	I	I	IV	IV	V	V	I	I	I	I	III	IV	I	I

This is much easier to hear than to analyse from the score. Listen to CD3 and see if you can spot the characteristic start of the blues sequence that begins in bar 8 – four bars of chord I, followed by two bars of chord IV. Now compare this with the 12-bar blues in *NAM 48* (see the AS Guide, page 121) and the minor-key blues in *NAM 49*, both of which were recorded less than eight years before Gershwin wrote *Porgy and Bess*.

Although all four phrases are four bars long (and so superficially similar to Haydn's periodic phrasing), there is a subtle tension between text and music, as the following diagram shows:

Musical form	Text	Rhyme scheme
A	Summer time an' the livin' is easy,	A
B	Fish are jumpin', an' the cotton is high.	B
A	Oh yo' daddy's rich, an' yo' ma is good-lookin'	C
C	So hush, little baby, don' yo' cry.	B

Like Haydn's canzonetta in *NAM 37*, this lullaby is strophic, but, whereas Haydn simply writes repeat signs, Gershwin re-writes his melody for the second verse, making subtle alterations, not only to accommodate the differing number of syllables, but also to provide delightful rhythmic variants. For instance, compare the cross rhythm of bar 25 with the straight rhythm of bar 7, and the extra syncopation in bar 30 compared with bar 12.

The lyric is a white man's attempt to transcribe southern American drawl. This laid-back speech is reflected in the minor pentatonic melody and in the singer's interpretation of dotted rhythms as jazz quavers in bars 9, 13 and elsewhere, while gospel ecstasy is evoked by the portamento to and from the wonderful high B heard in bars 41–43. Some might perceive a connection between these quasi-improvisational alterations and James Bowman's added ornamentation in *NAM 33*, but the link is, to say the least, tenuous.

In opera, the (entire) text is known as the *libretto* (Italian for a little book). In musicals a distinction is often made between the text of songs (the lyrics) and the spoken dialogue between musical numbers (the book) since each may be written by a different author. The lyrics of *Porgy and Bess* were written by Dubose Heyward, but the book was a collaboration between Heyward and George Gershwin's brother, Ira Gershwin.

It has to be admitted that in the five pieces discussed in this section it is easier to spot change than continuity. Even with two pieces published a couple of years apart (*NAM 33* and *34*) it is immediately obvious that the handling of rhythm and melodic contour is quite different. Nevertheless you should be prepared to find connections where you can. For example, despite the lack of a key signature, Weelkes' melodies are as clearly in G major as Haydn's melodies are in A major. But do not try to defend an untenable position in your answers: at advanced level you are asked to think for yourself and argue from a position you know you can support with evidence contained in the music itself.

Private study

1. What is (i) a hemiola, and (ii) a strophic setting?

2. How do *NAM 33* and *NAM 34* reflect the dance styles on which they are based?

3. What is (i) an ayre, (ii) a canzonetta, and (iii) a ballett?

4. What is meant by the galant style? Why could *NAM 37* be described as galant?

5. Which features of 'Summertime' are typical of a traditional blues, and which are not?

TIP: reread page 104 of the AS Guide.

Sample questions

In the exam there will be two questions on this topic, from which you must choose to answer **one**.

(a) State what is meant by word-painting in music and explain the use of this technique by Dowland in *NAM 33*.

(b) 'Summertime' is a theatrical interpretation of a lullaby sung by a black mother in the hot, deep south of the United States. How does Gershwin's music reflect the lyrics of this song?

(c) *NAM 33* and *34* are both derived from renaissance dance music. Compare and contrast the word-setting in the two pieces.

(d) *NAM 36* and *NAM 41* are taken from works that were both intended for the stage. Outline similarities and differences in the ways that Purcell and Gershwin use dissonance to heighten the expressive impact of their chosen texts.

Warning. Photocopying any part of this book without permission is illegal.

> For examination in summer 2004 and 2005

Secular vocal music

This part of the chapter deals with the two special focus works and the topic set for examination in summer 2004 and 2005. If you are taking the exam in summer 2002 or 2003 turn to page 111.

Schubert, Der Doppelgänger

> Special Focus Work 1 for 2004 and 2005
>
> NAM 38　　　　　　CD3 Track 16
> Peter Schreier (tenor)
> András Schiff (piano)

Before starting on this section you should work through (or revise) the information about the context and structure of this music given on pages 100–101 of the AS Guide. Make sure that you understand all of the terminology used on those pages.

Heinrich Heine (1797–1856), one of the most important German poets of the early 19th century, was born in the same year as Schubert and shared many characteristics with his contemporary. Both felt themselves to be outcasts, Heine because of his Jewishness (he left Germany for good in 1831 to avoid antisemitism), Schubert because of the disease (probably syphilis) that killed him a couple of months after writing *Der Doppelgänger*. Both were overawed by the long shadows thrown by the greatest of their predecessors, Goethe and Beethoven. Heine's first great success was *Das Buch der Lieder* (The Book of Songs, 1827). It contained the six poems (including *Der Doppelgänger*) that Schubert set in August 1828.

Most poems written for musical setting in Germany at this time were sentimental effusions, designed for culture-conscious amateurs to present to one another in the drawing-rooms of the middle classes. *Der Doppelgänger*, though intended for domestic performance, most definitely does not fall into this category. It is, in fact, one of the most sinister little poems of the early 19th century.

> The poem (with a translation) is printed on page 539 of *NAM*.

Can you see how Schubert's setting follows the structure of Heine's poem? The first two verses (bars 5–22 and 25–42 respectively) remain in the tonic key of B minor throughout. The rhyme scheme of the first verse (ABAB) is clarified by rests in the vocal part between each couplet (bars 13–14 and 23–24), while the similar rhyme scheme (CDCD) in the second verse is articulated by very loud chromatic discords at the end of each couplet (bars 32–33 and 41–42). Only in his setting of the third verse (bars 43–56) does Schubert move away from B minor (to the distant key of D♯ minor in bars 47–50) and allow the singer to run through the first three lines so that the return to B minor is delayed until bars 51–52. This throws the greatest emphasis on the final line of the poem, in which Heine recalls the torment of unrequited love.

By any standards Schubert's harmony is remarkable – every note of the piano part is calculated to express the horror of self-loathing engendered by the realisation that it is a reflection of his own haggard image that the poet sees in the window of his beloved's house. There are two ostinato figures. The first (bars 1–4) consists of chords I, Vb, Ib and Vc: common enough, apart from the fact that Schubert breaks almost every convention of 'correct' harmony. There is no third in the first and last two chords, no fifth in the second chord, and no root in the third chord. The leading note is doubled an octave and two octaves below and instead of 'leading'

> **Warning.** Photocopying any part of this book without permission is illegal.

to the tonic it leaps up a diminished 4th. This ostinato appears six times, the last time (bars 56–59) with a significant change. Instead of a bare 5th on the dominant, the fourth chord is a major triad on the flattened supertonic (C♮). In first inversion this is the fairly common chromatic chord known as a Neapolitan 6th, but in root position, particularly with parallel octaves, it is extremely rare. Its tonal effect undermines the key of B minor in a manner similar to the way in which the double-image destabilises the poet's mind. It takes four slow bars for Schubert to regain the tonic key (by the use of V^7 of IV, IVc and I with a tierce de Picardie in bars 60-63).

The second ostinato (bars 9–12) is notable for chords containing the flattened leading note (A♮ in chord Vb and III in bars 10–11). The first two statements of this ostinato are each followed by two-bar piano interludes (bars 13–14 and 23–24) that bring together both forms of the leading note to form plangent false relations (A♯ and A♮). In the third statement (bars 29–33) Schubert changes just one note of the final chord (C♯ is lowered to C♮ as in the last statement of the first ostinato) so that V^{7}c of B minor becomes the French augmented 6th of E minor. This is a chord in which the root is the flattened submediant (C♮ in E minor) above which is placed an augmented 6th (A♯), with a major 3rd (E) and an augmented 4th (F♯) as the other two notes of the chord. In the normal way of things augmented-6th chords resolve to dominant harmony (V or Ic–V), but Schubert's French 6th simply sinks back to the tonic chord of B minor (which for the first time contains its 3rd). This strange progression is repeated in bars 41–43, but here Schubert uses the more common German 6th in which the augmented 4th (F♯) is replaced by a perfect 5th above the root (G♮).

Bars 43–47 have the effect of a modulation to D♯ minor (though it is really just a chromatic slide with the common note F♯ acting as an anchor between the triads of B minor in bar 43 and D♯ minor in bar 47). This new key is affirmed by alternating tonic and dominant chords (bars 47–50). The return to the tonic key is achieved by the sudden intrusion of the German augmented 6th of B minor (bar 51) which now resolves 'correctly' to Ic (bars 52–53) followed by the only conventional perfect cadence in the whole song (bars 55–56).

Having grasped Schubert's remarkable tonal and harmonic strategy you should now go on to look at how the vocal part relates to the chords you have identified. Do you notice that not one discord disturbs the stillness of night in the first couplet (bars 5–12)? In the second couplet a grinding appoggiatura (G against F♯) appears at bar 16 as the poet recalls how long (*längst*) ago his beloved left the house. There are no further discords between voice and piano in the first verse, but the growing anguish of the poem is mirrored by four equally telling appoggiaturas in the second verse (bars 25–42). Perhaps because of the increased level of chromaticism and tonal instability there is again just one bitterly dissonant appoggiatura in the last verse (bar 50).

Private study

1. Translate the German words *lied* and *lieder*.
2. What is meant by the term ostinato? How does Schubert's use of ostinati contribute to the mood of this song?

For a more typical example of a Neapolitan 6th, see *NAM 18*, bars 184–186, where the chord of D♭ major (first inversion) is a Neapolitan 6th in the key of C.

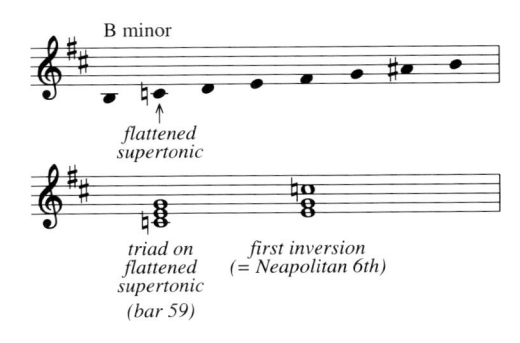

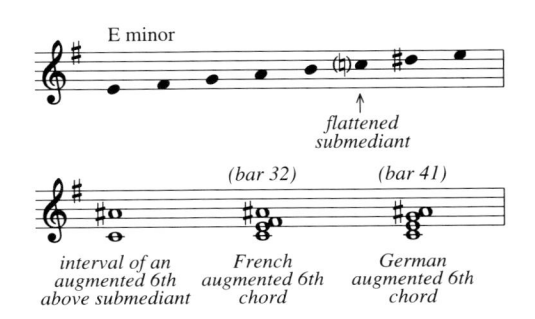

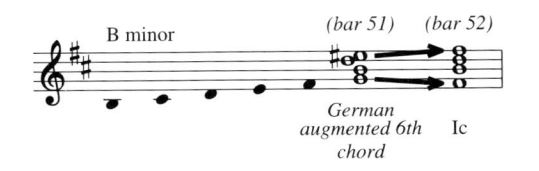

A minor

3. What is a tierce de Picardie? Which chord would you use to form a tierce de Picardie at the end of a piece in E minor?

4. Label the four chords in A minor printed *left* to show which is (a) a Neapolitan 6th, (b) a German augmented 6th, (c) a French augmented 6th, and (d) a diminished 7th.

5. Is this song strophic or through-composed? With what type of cadence does it end?

6. Reread page 100 of the AS Guide, and the material above, and then list exactly how Schubert's music reflects Heine's poem. Include the dark mood, the initial atmosphere of a still night, the obsessive nature of the poet's thoughts, his pain at remembering his lost love, the increasing anxiety, the climactic terror of the reflection and the concluding torment of self-loathing.

Schoenberg, 'Der kranke Mond' from Pierrot Lunaire

Before starting on this section you should work through (or revise) the information about the context and structure of this music given on pages 102–103 of the AS Guide. Make sure that you understand all of the terminology used on those pages.

Special Focus Work 2 for 2004 and 2005

NAM 40 CD3 Track 18
Yvonne Minton (reciter)
Michael Debost (flute)
Directed by Pierre Boulez

The comic theatrical entertainment known as the *commedia dell'arte* flourished in Italy from about 1545 to 1800.

One of the most famous melodramas occurs in the Wolf's Glen scene in Weber's opera *Der Freischütz* (1821), part of which appears in *The Rhinegold Dictionary of Sound*. Above a sinister diminished 7th a spoken incantation summons the devil, who then appears, shouting 'Why do you call for me?' to the accompaniment of a loud minor chord with trombones and tremolo strings

Schoenberg defined expressionism as 'the art of the representation of inner occurrences'. In order to represent the inner occurrences of Pierrot, the mad clown of the *commedia dell'arte*, Schoenberg resorted to melodrama. As a musical term melodrama has several meanings, the most common being a passage in a German opera in which dialogue is spoken to the accompaniment of atmospheric instrumental music. But for the 21 melodramas of *Pierrot Lunaire* Schoenberg, seeking the most direct musical expression of the mad clown's tortured imaginings, devised a type of speech-song which he called *Sprechgesang*. Many writers have attempted to explain what Schoenberg meant by his somewhat confusing description of this type of vocalisation (contained in his foreword to the score). Here is a slightly abbreviated translation of it:

> ... the speaker's melody is not meant to be sung ... the performer must transform it into speech melody, while paying due regard to the written pitches. This is done as follows: The rhythm is observed with absolute exactness, as though the performer were singing ... 'singing tone' maintains the pitch without modification, 'speaking tone' ... announces the pitch only to quit it immediately in a downward or upward direction.

There is no doubt here about rhythm (and most performers follow Schoenberg's notated rhythms accurately), but there is considerable doubt about pitch. In practice most singers give an approximate impression of the written pitches with *portamenti* (slides) between them. But on CD3 Yvonne Minton chooses to sing exact and sustained pitches with *portamenti* generally reserved for slurred notes (such as those in bar 4). If at all possible you should compare this recording with others in which the reciter follows Schoenberg's instructions more exactly (this will be useful practice for Question 2 of the Listening Test). You should also compare Minton's tremolo on each of the last five notes with other singers' interpretations of Schoenberg's mordent signs.

Warning. Photocopying any part of this book without permission is illegal.

The poem (shown on page 540 of *NAM*) falls into three non-rhyming stanzas with a refrain (*Du nächtig todeskranker Mond*) in each of them. For Schoenberg this is too structured to express madness, so he tends to disregard obvious opportunities for musical repetition (one notable exception being *an Sehnsucht* and *tief erstickt* in bars 14–15). Each line of the poem contains four metrical feet (eg *Du nächtig todeskranker Mond*), but this is again too conventional for Schoenberg's expressionist setting. Instead he avoids any sort of melodic symmetry by writing phrases of 9, 13, 8½ and 8 beats in his setting of the first stanza (and his settings of the others stanzas are equally irregular). Whichever way *Sprechgesang* is interpreted, the wide range of the vocal part (nearly two octaves), its unpredictable alternations of semitonal movement (eg bars 1–2) with angular leaps (eg bar 14), and its abrupt changes of direction (eg bar 23) all express the 'inner occurrences' of the mad clown's mind.

The thin two-part texture, in which flute and voice are equal partners, allows every word to be heard. Indeed it often sounds as though the flute is trying to speak. But this is not a rational conversation since they share no common melodic material. Each is absorbed in its own form of madness (for instance, compare the manic raging of the flute in bars 5–6 with the introspective ruminations of *Pierrot* in the same passage). Nor is there any traditional harmonic logic in the intervals formed between them. In the first six bars every interval from a semitone to a perfect octave is heard, and Schoenberg studiously avoids any suggestion of 'normal' resolution of the discords. This is what was meant when he wrote about the 'emancipation of dissonance' that accompanied his first essays in atonality (of which *Pierrot Lunaire* is generally regarded as being his greatest, and certainly his most influential work).

The text that Schoenberg used is a German adaptation of a cycle of 50 poems, called *Pierrot Lunaire*, written by the French poet Albert Giraud in 1884. Schoenberg chose 21 of these poems for his work, which was commissioned by a German actress called Albertine Zehme. She was the vocalist in the first performance, which she presented in costume, with the instrumentalists hidden behind a screen.

Further reading
Look out for **Schoenberg: Pierrot Lunaire** by Jonathan Dunsby. Cambridge Music Handbooks. *Cambridge University Press.* ISBN: 0-521-38715-9.

An extract from 'Nacht' from *Pierrot Lunaire* can be found in *The Rhinegold Dictionary of Sound*.

Private study
1. Define the terms atonality, expressionism and *Sprechgesang*.
2. Concisely describe the texture of *NAM 40*.
3. How many songs are there in *Pierrot Lunaire*? How many instrumentalists are required to perform the complete work?
4. Why do you think that *Pierrot Lunaire* is regarded as one of the most signficant works of early 20th century music?

Sample questions
In the exam there will be a total of three questions on the special focus works, from which you must choose to answer **two**.

(a) How does Schubert's music reflect both the overall atmosphere and the specific detail of Heine's poem, *Der Doppelgänger*?

(b) *NAM 38* and *NAM 40* both deal with the subject of obsession. What similarities and differences do you note in the two songs?

(c) Comment on the tonality and harmony of *NAM 38*.

TIP: Use the notes you made for question 6 on the previous page as the basis for your answer.

Warning. Photocopying any part of this book without permission is illegal.

> Topic for examination in 2004 and 2005

Continuity and change in the relationships between voice(s) and instrument(s)

You do not need to study this topic unless *Secular vocal music* is the Area of Study that you undertook for AS Music. Before starting work on this topic you need a thorough understanding of the material on *Secular vocal music* in the AS Guide (pages 91–105). Remember that for A2 the topic draws on works from across the **entire** Area of Study, not just those in one of the two lists, A or B.

Dowland

> *NAM 33*   CD3 Track 11
> James Bowman (countertenor) with David Miller (lute) and bass viol.

As explained in the AS Guide, the original edition of *Flow my teares*, published in 1600, included not only a lute part in tablature but also a vocal bass part that follows the pitches (but not the rhythms) of the lowest notes of the lute part. Elizabethan vocal compositions were sometimes described as 'apt for voices or viols' so, in accordance with contemporary performance practice, Dowland's vocal bass is replaced by a bass viol on CD 3. This is fortunate since it enables us to hear more clearly the contrapuntal interplay between the outer parts. This is particularly obvious in bars 12–15 where the two parts form a canon. Indeed the bass is often as melodic as the vocal part. In bar 20 it takes the leading role in a freely imitative exchange with the voice and then descends to a low E on the word 'hell' – a clear example of word-painting. A third element in the texture is another melodic line that runs almost all the way through the uppermost notes of the lute part (sometimes descending on to the bass stave). Play any combination of voice part, treble lute part and bass part and you will immediately see that this is a typical example of late renaissance three-part counter-point occasionally thickened by non-melodic lute notes.

Purcell

> *NAM 36*   CD3 Track 14
> Carolyn Watkinson (soprano) with the English Baroque Soloists Directed by John Eliot Gardiner

The contrast between Dowland's polyphony and Purcell's homophony in the recitative at the start of *NAM 36* could hardly be more pointed. Here the spotlight is on the singer, who must ensure that the words are clearly audible, treat the rhythm with enough flexibility to give an impression of heightened speech, and convincingly portray Dido's anguish through Purcell's chromatic and fragmented vocal line. Unlike Dowland's melodic bass part, Purcell's *basso continuo* is as simple as possible – far from drawing attention to itself it is there as a mere support for the singer. The same should be true of any improvised harmonic filling. This is baroque *stile rappresentativo* (dramatic recitative) in which a soloist totally dominates a subservient continuo accompaniment. The relationship between voices and instruments is different in the air. Here there is contrapuntal interplay between the vocal part and the ground, and, although the upper string parts are more homophonic than Dowland's lute part, they play a decisive role in providing many of the heart-rending discords that we discussed in the AS Guide. At the end it is left to the strings alone to express the ultimate tragedy of the opera as Dido, alone and rejected, kills herself.

Haydn

> *NAM 37*   CD3 Track 15
> Elly Ameling (soprano) Jörg Demus (piano)

In Haydn's canzonetta the balance between singer and accompanist shifts decisively in favour of the latter. If you play the piano part alone you will discover that up to bar 27 it makes perfectly good sense without the vocal part. This is because, apart from the odd ornament, the pianist doubles the vocal melody (bars 8–21) or shadows it in a heterophonic texture with a few two-part chords (bars 23–26). Only in bars 28–29, 32–33 and 35–39 do singer and pianist become equal partners – the former providing a very simple diatonic melody, the latter an ornate accompaniment. There were good commercial reasons for this close relationship between singer and accompanist. In the late 18th and early 19th centuries ladies were expected to display their accomplishments in the elaborate courting ceremonies of the emergent middle classes. These were the young ladies Haydn hoped would buy his canzonettas. Unfortunately such enthusiastic amateurs could not be relied upon to hold a part unaided (unlike Elizabethan singers) – hence Haydn's lengthy piano introduction (which reminds the singer how the tune goes), and the doubling and shadowing (which help the singer through the tricky bits) that are so typical of pre-romantic songs.

The opposite is true of *Der Doppelgänger*, a miniature masterpiece of romantic art. The fragmented quasi-recitative of its vocal part is entirely independent of the homophonic accompaniment. Yet this accompaniment is quite unlike the bass and improvised chords of Purcell's recitative in which the vocal part totally dominates the accompaniment. In Schubert's song the vocal and piano parts are complementary – neither makes much sense without the other (compare this with a solo performance of Haydn's piano part). The element that unites melody and accompaniment is Schubert's staggering harmony. In keeping with the text ('Still is the night') the first 12 bars are entirely consonant, both voice and piano oscillating around an obsessively repeated dominant pedal (F♯). As Heine's poem becomes more tortured, the vocal fragments begin to crash into the piano part causing grinding dissonances at the start of bars 16, 28, 35, 37 and 50. The vocal part rises to a series of climaxes (bars 31–2, 41–2 and 51–2) but the potency of these climaxes is largely determined by the chromatic discords with which they are associated. It is left to the pianist to deliver the final harmonic twist of the knife in the postlude with which the song ends.

The lyrical melody of *Après un rêve* seems to float freely above a subordinate homophonic accompaniment, yet it is the interplay between voice and piano that contributes most to the effectiveness of Fauré's style. Thus in bars 1–4 the climax of the C-minor vocal phrase has as much to do with the sumptuous and unexpected chromatic chord in bar 3 (V^9 of B♭ major) as it has to do with the arch-shaped melodic phrase. The aeolian melody of bars 2–4 and 6–8 is accompanied by more chromatic dominants, the conflict between the modal flat 7th (B♭) and tonal sharp 7th (B♮) in bar 7 being particularly delectable. Fauré underpins this fusion of vocal modality and pianistic chromaticism with a circle of 5ths in bars 1–9. This gives tonal shape to what could otherwise have been simply a luxuriant melody supported by an unrelated series of smoochy chords. It also provides a contrapuntal backbone to what initally seems an entirely homophonic texture (try playing just the melody and bass of these bars and you will see that with just one exception they move throughout in contrary motion). The contrapuntal interplay between voice and bass is even more striking towards the end of the song. In bars 34–47 these parts form two-part counterpoint that guides the song back to the tonic with absolute inevitability.

Schubert

NAM 38   CD3 Track 16
Peter Schreier (tenor)
András Schiff (piano)

It would be useful to study the relationship between voice and accompaniment in some of Schubert's other lieder. He often selects an idea from the poem to illustrate with a simple figure that serves to unify the accompaniment and that can be transformed in response to the text. Thus the sparkling broken chords which depict the trout stream in *Die Forelle* ('The Trout') suddenly become dark and agitated when the sunlit water is muddied by the impatient angler. Similarly, the incessantly turning semiquavers of the wheel in *Gretchen am Spinnrade* ('Gretchen at the spinning wheel') run increasingly out of control as her fantasies take over, suddenly stopping as she thinks of Faust's kiss.

Fauré

NAM 39   CD3 Track 17
Janet Baker (mezzo-soprano)
Geoffrey Parsons (piano)

Note that in some editions of *NAM* there is a misprint in the accompaniment of bar 4. The harmony should resolve on to chord V^7 of E♭ major on the third beat of the bar, as it does in bar 19.

Warning. Photocopying any part of this book without permission is illegal.

Schoenberg

NAM 40   CD3 Track 18
Yvonne Minton (reciter)
Michael Debost (flute)
Directed by Pierre Boulez

Exactly the opposite is true of the two-part counterpoint of 'Der kranke Mond'. The two atonal lines are incapable of suggesting a key, and instead of contrary motion they overlap and intertwine, sometimes moving in the same direction, sometimes in opposite directions in an apparently random manner. There are good reasons for this (see page 122), but the most notable characteristic of the two melodies is that they appear to coexist in two different worlds, almost entirely unrelated to one another.

Gershwin

NAM 41   CD3 Track 19
Leona Mitchell (soprano)
Cleveland Orchestra and
Cleveland Orchestra Chorus
Conducted by Lorin Maazel

The relationship between vocal melody and orchestral accompaniment in 'Summertime' contributes to the luminous atmosphere of the lullaby. The added-6th chords of bars 8–10 and 16–18 are clearly subservient to Clara's melody, but what makes it appear to float freely in the shimmering heat is the huge gap between the low, closely-spaced accompaniment and her song. In the first verse the homophonic accompaniment is enlivened by fragments of melody: strings in bars 12 and 14–15, oboe in bar 19, and flute then cellos in bars 22–24. However these merely fill the gaps between vocal phrases and so are quite unlike the contrapuntal accompaniment we found in Dowland's ayre. Nor is the solo violin part in the second verse contrapuntal (even when it can be heard). It lacks the melodiousness of a countermelody and is just a figurative decoration of the same homophonic accompaniment that was heard in the first verse (though the gap between soloist and orchestra is now filled by crooning female voices).

Private study

1. What is (i) an ayre, (ii) lute tablature, and (iii) a canzonetta?

2. What contrapuntal device occurs between the vocal part and the bass in bars 12–15 of *NAM 33*?

3. Compare *NAM 33* with the recitative in *NAM 36*. What is the main difference in texture? How does this difference alter the relationship between singer and accompaniment?

4. What is the most significant feature of the relationship between singer and accompaniment in *NAM 37*?

5. Is the piano part in *NAM 38* merely an accompaniment?

Sample questions

In the exam there will be two questions on this topic, from which you must choose to answer **one**.

(a) Compare and contrast the relationship between voice and piano accompaniment in *NAM 37*, *38* and *39*.

(b) How does Gershwin achieve variety in the accompaniment to 'Summertime' without over-balancing the voice?

(c) Schubert's lieder are often described as a partnership between singer and accompanist. Why is this?

TIP: This last question could be answered by comparing *NAM 38* with *NAM 37* and *NAM 39*, but it could be a good opportunity to make relevant references to other Schubert songs that you know.

Music for film and television

> For examination in summer 2002 and 2003

The first part of this chapter deals with the two special focus works and topic set for examination in summer 2002 and 2003. If you are taking the exam in summer 2004 or 2005 turn to page 134.

Bernstein, On the Waterfront (Symphonic Suite)

> **Special Focus Work 1 for 2002 and 2003**
> *NAM 43*   CD4 Track 2
> New York Philharmonic
> Conducted by Leonard Bernstein

Before starting on this section you should work through (or revise) the information about the context and structure of this music given on pages 110–112 of the AS Guide. Make sure that you understand all of the terminology used on those pages.

On the Waterfront won many awards as a film – but not for its music. This may seem surprising, for Bernstein is often associated with the screen, not only through films of his musicals such as *West Side Story* but also through his many television broadcasts as a conductor and music presenter in which he showed a natural rapport for working with the camera. But this was his first and only film score, and the music he wrote was of such substance and intensity that it tended to dominate the screenplay. Instead of working with short and adaptable motivic fragments, Bernstein tended to prefer long melodic lines and loud, extended riffs. Inevitably, although somewhat to the composer's surprise, these often had to be cut or faded down under dialogue in the underscore. Frustrated that his music had been fragmented in the film, Bernstein arranged it into a symphonic suite for concert performance. The complete suite lasts some 22 minutes and contains six main sections, of which *NAM 43* is the first. The opening horn melody is used as a motto theme, returning in several different guises later in the work (as it does in the film).

The term 'symphonic' was used in the 19th century to describe music (such as the 'symphonic poems' of Liszt) which aspires to the type of integration and developmental processes found in symphonies. Later it was used in the expression 'symphonic jazz' to promote the style of notated large-scale jazz, fused with elements of art music, found in works such as Gershwin's *Rhapsody in Blue*. Bernstein's use of the term reflects both usages, his symphonic suite reflecting a continuity and structure that was not possible in the film score, but also acknowledging his debt to Gershwin, who was such a great influence on Bernstein's own musical style. The term 'suite' simply indicates a collection of movements intended to be performed together.

> Bernstein used the term 'symphonic' again a few years later when he arranged some of the music from *West Side Story* into a set of 'symphonic dances' for concert performance.

Although Bernstein followed in Gershwin's footsteps as a composer at the frontier between popular and art music, Bernstein's work reflects the music of his own age – the later styles of bebop jazz, with its hard-edged dissonance and driving rhythms, and the urban blues. These styles were well suited to the social realism of *On the Waterfront*, and reflect the harsh inner-city tensions and human longings of the film in an evocative and timeless way. It was a technique Bernstein was to develop three years later in a medium that gave him much fuller dramatic control than he had as a film composer – the musical *West Side Story* (1957).

> **Warning.** Photocopying any part of this book without permission is illegal.

The opening melody of the suite is unified by a succession of minor 3rds, culminating in a climactic top note in bar 4. Although these are all rising 3rds, this arch-shaped theme has a melancholy quality, largely due to its use of the blues scale on F (see *left* – remember that the horn in F sounds a 5th lower than written). The second part of the melody introduces notes outside this scale (G, A and D sounding pitches) which hint at a resolution into F major, but the melody is accompanied and lacks any sense of definitive cadence (its open-ended quality gives great scope for different treatments later in the suite). The subsequent treatment of this theme – in two-part canon and then (from bar 13) transposed up a 4th and reordered so that its second half appears first – starts to explain Bernstein's description of the work as symphonic.

The scoring of this opening for wind (and harp) contrasts strongly with the percussive Presto beginning in bar 20, although unity is maintained by again basing the ostinato on the rising minor 3rd first heard in bar 1 – and the tonal ambiguity of the opening theme is reflected in the ambiguous 3rds (major pulled down to minor) that commence in bar 24. Details of the structure of this section are given in the AS Guide, but we should add a little more about the orchestration. Bernstein tends to use his large orchestra in blocks. The riff is assigned to percussion (including piano), joined by the entire orchestra for the gloriously dissonant tutti in bar 78–87. The main melodic material of the Presto is assigned to wind – either the jazz-like timbres of alto saxophone and muted trumpet in the quieter sections, or wind mainly in octaves in the louder sections. The strings have little independent material before bar 88 and mainly double the other parts. Bernstein is of course treating the orchestra like a huge jazz band. Only in the last four pages are the strings given a role of their own, and even then it is more in the nature of a special effect, sustaining single pitches or icy dissonances against the forceful interjections of wind and percussion.

See page 131 for a short discussion about thematic treatment in *On the Waterfront*.

Private study

1. Explain the following directions in the score: con sord. (bar 7), lontano (bar 13), Presto barbaro (bar 20), flutt. (bar 105).

2. How does the trumpet part relate to the saxophone solo in bars 52–53?

3. Explain each of the following and state one example of where each may be found in the score: canon, riff, tritone, tutti, rim shot, tremolo, monophonic texture.

4. In what sense is this suite 'symphonic'?

5. Comment on the role played by the strings in this score.

Special Focus Work 2 for 2002 and 2003

NAM 46   CD4 Track 5
Conducted by Barrington Pheloung

Pheloung, Morse on the Case

Before starting on this section you should work through (or revise) the information about the context and structure of this music given on pages 116–117 of the AS Guide. Make sure that you understand all of the terminology used on those pages.

Leonard Bernstein's concentrated, powerful score was not always well suited to the role it had to play in *On the Waterfront* – many of the louder parts of the Presto Barbaro music, for instance, had to be faded down under dialogue in the actual film. In total contrast, Pheloung's sparse textures provide an adaptable and non-intrusive background for the domestic viewing of television drama. Tiny melodic cells are separated by long, sustained notes, creating an ambient style which can register at an almost subconscious level, never seeking the self-attention demanded by Bernstein's exciting but sometimes grandiloquent intensity.

NAM 46 is based on the aeolian mode (A–B–C–D–E–F–G). Tension is created by two pitches outside this set (F♯ and A♭, both introduced in a highly dissonant context) in the second half of the music. In the final bars the music gravitates towards C major, but the tonality remains ambiguous due to the persistent F♯ still sounding in bar 109 and the disappearance of a third from the final chord.

The slow evolution of melodic cells plays an important part in the design. For instance, the initial intervals in the piano part (a rising 4th followed by a descending 3rd) trigger an inversion in the strings which is extended into a long sequence of slowly descending 4ths and rising 3rds: E–B–D–A–C–G (the last note in the lower parts only). Meanwhile an extended descending 2nd in the horns (A–G, bars 12–19) is compacted and inverted by the piano and extended to form a three-note figure (D–E–A, bars 17–19) – meanwhile the first violin answers the horn's falling 2nd with a rising 2nd (C–D, bar 18). The piano then explores the major 2nd played vertically (D and E together, bar 22) which the first violin inverts melodically (D–C, bar 24) at the same time as the second violin returns to the initial rising 4th (G–C). Bar 26 sees the return of our three-note figure (D–E–A) in the piano, now shrunk to semiquavers, its outer notes also serving as the left-hand accompaniment. Meanwhile the third horn is playing an inversion of this figure (A–G–D) in much longer note values. The outer 5th of our motif next takes on more importance, first being attached to the front of D–E–A in the piano (right hand) of bar 32, and then becoming (in inversion, as A–D) the sole motivic material in bars 36–38. This is harmonised in major 9ths – the left hand reflecting the fact that it dropped a tone to C–G in the previous four bars while the right hand stayed resolutely on its own cell of D–E–A.

The close association of tiny intervallic cells like these can be found throughout *NAM 46*, their simplicity often disguised by the use of irregular note-lengths and parts changing in pitch level at different times. For instance, even when F♯ intrudes upon the diatonic calm in bar 52, the oboe is still investigating another variant of the three-note pitch set (this time, G–A–D) after which it immediately returns to the same rising 4th (A–D) heard at the start of the work. This heralds a much modified recapitulation of the opening material, in which the falling 7th of the piano motif from bar 8 is transformed into a falling diminished 5th (bar 65), which in turn is compacted by the strings into a falling third (bar 68). This process of revisiting earlier material continues throughout the final section. Compare, for instance, the piano part in bars 98–99 with that in bars 26–28. The pattern in bar 99 is reused in bars 108–109, but now metrically displaced so that it appears a quaver later in the bar. Other variants of this tiny figure can be found in bars 102–105 (violins).

Pheloung restricts most of his instruments to a very narrow range – horns never exceed a 5th, the strings are used only in their lower register, and cello, bass and harp are silent until the final section. Similarly, dynamics never rise above *mf*, except in bar 107, when the harp introduces the final appearance of the rising 4th.

Private study

1. What special effect is used by the strings throughout *NAM 46*?
2. How does the viola part relate to the violin parts in bars 1–13?
3. Compare the piano part in bars 31–35 with the piano part in bars 26–28.
4. Compare the oboe part in bars 49–60 with the horn part in bars 25–35.

Sample questions

In the exam there will be a total of three questions on the special focus works, from which you must choose to answer **two**.

(a) Show how Bernstein uses different types of melodic interval to characterise each of his main ideas in *NAM 43*.

(b) Explain how the construction of *NAM 46* is based on the slow evolution of tiny cells formed from melodic intervals.

(c) How does Pheloung achieve variety of mood in the second half of *NAM 46* (starting from bar 61)?

Topic for examination in 2002 and 2003

Continuity and change in thematic treatments

You do not need to study this topic unless *Music for film and television* is the Area of Study that you undertook for AS Music and which you are now extending for A2.

Before starting work on this topic you need a thorough understanding of the material on *Music for film and television* in the AS Guide (pages 106–119). Remember that for A2 the topic draws on works from across the **entire** Area of Study, not just those in one of the two lists, A or B.

Passport to Pimlico

NAM 42　　　　CD4 Track 1
Royal Ballet Sinfonia
Conducted by Kenneth Alwyn

Auric's underscore for this scene depends for its effect on the rapid exchange of short, witty motifs. Only at the end of the extract are these extended into a melody which could be described as a theme and even that is composed largely from the elaboration of the one-bar motif heard in bar 55. This technique can be found throughout *NAM 42*. Bar 1 is repeated to form bar 2, the pair of bars is then repeated with shorter note values (a loose kind of diminution) to form bars 3–4. The E-major motif in bar 5 is varied in bar 6 and then repeated in rhythm (but not in pitch) by cellos and basses in bar 7; this four-bar unit is then concluded with contrary-motion scales and a perfect cadence in bar 8. The four bars are then given a decorated repeat, a 3rd higher (in G major) in bars 9–12.

Much of Auric's motivic material is based on triadic and scalic figures, often outlining the first five notes of the current key. He avoids predictability by using frequent changes of texture and orchestration, and sudden changes of key. The entire excerpt is given structure by repetitions on a larger scale. For instance, the woodwind motif in bar 33 derives from the bassoon of bar 22. More subtly, bars 39–46 repeat bars 5–12, but in the wrong order (bars 9–12 are heard first, transposed to E♭ major, and are then followed by bars 5–8 in their original key of E major).

Bernstein's preference for long melodic lines is in total contrast to Auric's lively treatment of motivic fragments. The opening horn melody is formed from rising minor 3rds, but it is the entire line of this arch-shaped solo that makes an impact rather than its component parts. The melody is subjected to canonic treatment (bars 7–12) and is then heard transposed and above pedal (bar 13). Bernstein here uses the same technique as Auric, starting with the second part of his melody (bar 13 = bar 4) and then tagging the first part on the end (bar 18 = bar 1). But the effect seems totally different in the context of Bernstein's slow moving theme.

On the Waterfront

> NAM 43 CD4 Track 2
> New York Philharmonic
> Conducted by Leonard Bernstein

There are two main thematic elements in the Presto Barbaro, both related. One is the riff, which is ever-present in one form or another until the coda. The other is the saxophone theme that begins in bar 42 – its use of three four-bar phrases hints at a 12-bar blues structure (although the harmony does not). The opening notes of this theme are (at sounding pitch) B–B♭, C–G. The first of these intervals is the same falling semitone introduced into the riff by timpani 1 in bar 24. The second is a perfect 4th, the interval introduced into the riff by timpani 2 at bar 26. These intervals, heard in the saxophone's first four-bar phrase, are repeated much closer together in the next four bars (another loose type of diminution) and are followed-up with an inversion of the falling semitone (the rising minor 2nd in bar 49). Just as a blues usually concludes with a contrasting idea in its final four-bar phrase, so does Bernstein – the syncopated figure in bars 50–53.

A development of the second and third saxophone phrases starts in bar 54. It is assigned to high wind instruments, transposed up a minor 3rd (note that the riff stays at its previous pitch) and its component intervals are again rearranged, producing a five-bar phrase in bars 54–59. The three-note figure first heard in bar 52 is then heard accompanied by its own inversion (bar 64) and developed over the falling-4th motif in the bass, leading to the central tutti statement of the riff (starting at bar 78).

The motivic importance of the intervals of a semitone and a 4th is revealed by their isolation in the orchestral stabs starting at bar 88. In bars 88 and 91 the falling semitone, B–B♭, is combined with its own inversion (A–B♭). The falling 4th is set against a rising semitone in bar 94, and both rising and falling semitones are combined with a rising 4th in bar 98. Finally, the riff ends and the coda is based on a slow restatement of the saxophone motif from bar 52, heard only as a rhythm from bar 108 onwards, and separated by a massive and dissonant 'suspense motif' in brass and timpani.

Planet of the Apes ('The Hunt')

> NAM 44 CD4 Track 3
> Conducted by Jerry Goldsmith

The repetition and development of short motifs again forms the main structural principle of *NAM 44*. Particularly notable is the use of the piano figure in bar 4 – it is extended in bars 8–9, it is the basis of the semiquaver riff which starts in bar 11 (and is reused twice later), and it is used to form the ostinato patterns which begin at bar 23.

The other main motivic element is the high sustained violin note that crescendos into an off-beat semitone (bars 11–13), a device similar to that used by Bernstein. This is heard three times at different pitches and is then modified and transferred to trombones from bar 23. In bar 40 this idea is turned on its head – the opening note is reduced to a quaver and the off-beat semitone becomes the part of the motif that is sustained, this idea forming the impetus for the repeated semitonal dissonances in the next four bars.

The original form of the motif returns in the horns at bar 45, and forms the foundation for the outburst at bar 52, where the lowest instruments repeatedly rise from E♭ to E♮ against a sustained E♭. Other versions of this motif can be traced throughout the rest of the extract, sometimes much transformed. For instance, in bar 75 the strings open out from a unison G to a minor second on G and A♭, while from bar 84 onwards this idea of an alternating unison and minor 2nd is transformed into a high ostinato pattern of semiquavers in flutes and piccolo.

ET ('Flying theme')

NAM 45   CD4 Track 4
City of Prague Philharmonic
Conducted by Paul Bateman

Unlike the essentially motivic treatment of *NAM 44*, John Williams' 'flying theme' is centred on the broad eight-bar melody that begins in bar 9. His treatment of this theme, which is discussed in detail in the AS Guide, is largely conventional – a varied repeat in bar 17 includes a countermelody (heard in alternate bars) for flutes and bells that is then developed in the transition which begins in bar 25. This is followed by a return of the main theme in the dominant at bar 34. A second transition (bar 42) leads to a grand restatement of the flying theme in the tonic (starting at bar 55), with the melody in double octaves. When the theme is repeated Williams adds some brief imitation for horns (bar 63) but the repeat is curtailed by the interruption of the coda, in which an altered version of the opening of the flying theme makes two final, dissonant appearances (bars 75 and 78).

Morse on the Case

NAM 46   CD4 Track 5
Conducted by Barrington Pheloung

The minimal thematic material in *NAM 46* is in striking contrast to the broad sweep of melody found in John William's 'flying theme', but Pheloung uses his tiny melodic cells in a highly integrated, evolutionary way – details are given above, in the section starting on page 128.

Titanic

NAM 47   CD4 Track 6
City of Prague Philharmonic
Conducted by Nic Raine

Horner employs a variety of approaches to thematic treatment in this excerpt, sometimes leading to a sense of discontinuity in the music as a whole. Rising motifs are treated in imitation in the first three bars, followed by a series of short ostinato figures through the next 26 bars. Ascending scale figures from bar 21 onwards lead to a brief climactic gesture in bars 28–29.

The soprano melody which begins at the end of bar 29 recalls the ascent from tonic to dominant in the opening motif of bar 1. This theme is now used in a more structural way, reappearing in a slightly different form at the end of bar 50. On paper this appears to be an augmented version (most of its note values are twice their former length) but since the tempo has now doubled, it actually sounds much as it did before, apart from the first two notes (which really are augmented) and the changes in scoring. This melody becomes something of a motto theme, being repeated in a varied version by first violins at bar 57 and reappearing in B major at bar 86. Between the appearances of this recurring theme Horner uses a dance-like idea, based on the same melodic outline. This is much more like a folk-dance, and appears in 5/4 time at bar 37 and in 6/4 time (with much more static harmony) at bar 68.

Private study

1. Show how the melody that begins in bar 55 of *NAM 42* largely derives from the motif heard in bar 55 itself.

2. On what two types of musical figure are many of Auric's motifs in *NAM 42* based?

3. (i) What makes the opening melody of *NAM 43* sound as though it is based on the blues?

   (ii) This opening melody is treated in canon at bar 7. What precisely is a canon?

4. Explain what you understand is meant by melodic inversion and give an example of its use in the wind melody on page 378 of the *New Anthology*.

5. (i) What is a riff?

   (ii) In *NAM 43*, show how the section starting at bar 78 relates to material in the riff which began in bars 20–41.

6. In *NAM 44*, from where does the piano ostinato which begins in bar 59 ultimately derive?

7. (i) Briefly explain how the flute motif heard in bars 25–26 of *NAM 45* is developed in bars 27–33.

   (ii) Identify a passage later in the extract in which this motif is used again.

8. In the opening section of *NAM 47* tension is built up with a variety of ostinati heard over pedal points. State how the horn ostinato in bar 12 relates to the viola part in this bar.

Sample questions

In the exam there will be two questions on this topic, from which you must choose to answer **one**.

(a) Contrast Goldsmith's treatment of motivic material in *NAM 44* with Williams' approach to thematic ideas in *NAM 45*.

(b) Describe Auric's use of thematic material in *NAM 42*, showing how he achieves a sense of balance despite the many different moods being illustrated.

(c) Explain how Bernstein achieves integration of his thematic material in *NAM 43*.

> For examination in summer 2004 and 2005

Music for film and television

This part of the chapter deals with the special focus work and the topic set for examination in summer 2004 and 2005. If you are taking the exam in summer 2002 or 2003 turn to page 127.

> **Special Focus Work for 2004 and 2005**
> NAM 47 CD4 Track 6
> City of Prague Philharmonic
> Conducted by Nic Raine

Horner, Titanic ('Take her to sea, Mr Murdoch')

Before starting on this section you should work through (or revise) the information about the context and structure of this music given on pages 117–118 of the AS Guide. Make sure that you understand all of the terminology used on those pages.

Instrumentation

The 1997 film *Titanic* was designed to be a blockbuster of epic proportions and, in the long tradition of such films, the score is written for lavish resources, requiring a large symphony orchestra and choir to which are added, more unusually, parts for synthetic vocal sounds. James Horner explained the rationale for this in a radio interview in December 1997:

> We wanted to find something that would emotionally tell the story, but musically would not … bring its own baggage with it. I was very nervous about using a big orchestra because I didn't want it to be some big Hollywood 1940s sinking spectacle. I was looking for something really very personal and human, which is why I chose the voice. And I used the synths to give it a slightly contemporary feeling and also a slightly timeless feeling at the same time … To me, the big orchestra had to be used for the most spectacular things in terms of sheer size and scope, primarily the sinking. I couldn't solve those problems with synthesizers or with a more rarified approach.

Horner's style of orchestration in *NAM 47* tends to involve much doubling of parts, with little use of solo timbres. For instance, in the opening bars the choir is doubled by both woodwind and strings. Similarly, in bars 21–24 both horns and trombones play the same pitches as the upper strings, but in a simpler, more legato version. As other wind instruments are added, they too double the strings – mainly at the unison. This preference for doubling is most noticeable in the part for synthesizer, which is rarely used as an instrument in its own right. Instead it adds colour to strings in bars 37–48 (and rhythmic accents in similar later passages) or it thickens the middle of the orchestral texture in places such as bars 28–29.

Horner tends to avoid brilliance in his orchestral sound, seldom making use of the upper register in strings or woodwind. For instance, when the main choral theme is transferred to the orchestra in bar 57 he writes for unison violins in their middle register and the accompaniment is simply a triplet figure hovering around middle C, played by horns and violas in unison. Compare this with the classic scoring in bars 55–68 of *NAM 45*, in which strings sing out the theme in double octaves, supported by upper woodwind. Horner's emphasis is not on brilliance, but on the weight of the low pedal D, assigned to cellos, double basses, tuba, bassoons and double bassoon, all in their lowest register.

Tonality and use of themes

Unlike the dissonant, sometimes atonal writing in *NAM 44*, or the modality of *NAM 46*, the music for *Titanic* is unashamedly tonal in style. The first section is characterised by short sections each designed to build-up excitement by the use of techniques such as imitation of rising figures (bars 1–3), repetition of a motif over a rising bass (bars 4–7), ostinato patterns over pedals (bars 8–20) and rising scale figures (starting at bar 21) that culminate in a climax at bar 28. Equally important in this first section is the use of keys that are a major 3rd apart: E♭ major (bar 1), G major (bar 8) and B major (bar 15). The use of such tertiary modulations to produce an exhilarating effect is something of a cliché, but it effectively underpins the epic nature of the film and the exciting depiction of Titanic's maiden voyage. After the rather episodic nature of the first 29 bars, Horner settles on the tonal centre of G major for the choral melody starting at bar 30, and underpins the whole of this short section with a tonic pedal in the horn (doubled an octave lower by tenors and a viola tremolo).

The music stays in G for the dance-like refrain beginning at bar 37. It is a theme that appears in different versions at several places in the film. Here the syncopated 5/4 metre gives it an attractive lilt, but its folk-dance style remains unmistakable – the harmonisation is based mainly on root-position triads, the texture is homophonic and there is a folk-like reference to the modal flat seventh (F major) in bars 43–44. The melody is almost enirely based on the motif heard in its first bar (bar 37). This is first repeated in transposed inversion to form bar 38, and then restated a 3rd lower to form bar 39. After the imperfect cadence in bar 40, the inverted form of the motif is used again to create the sequence in bars 41–43. The third phrase (bars 45–48) sandwiches another version of the inverted motif (bar 46) between two restatements of bar 40.

The choral melody returns (still in G major) at the end of bar 50 but is interrupted in bar 57 by an orchestral variant of the same theme, now transposed to the dominant (D major). A quaver figure that tentatively appears in bar 61 gradually takes over, leading to a return of the syncopated folk-dance, now in 6/4 and in D major. This is combined with a return of the quaver figure (bar 76) and is restated in fuller scoring at bar 80. Notice more of the great clichés of film scoring being used to underpin the crescendo in bar 79 – a suspended cymbal role (plus a glittering stroke across a bell tree) and a long upward glissando from the harps. The *ff* restatement of the folk-dance music starting in bar 80 is interrupted (by the quaver figure again) after only four bars, and another tertiary modulation takes us from D major to B major (bar 86).

The last section is based on another variant of the choral melody – like the one at bar 51 this has the appearance of being augmented, because its note lengths are twice those seen in bar 30, but as the the beat is now a minim this is really just a difference in notation. Fragments of the choral melody are developed in more varied ways in these final bars – notice the syncopated horn countermelody that briefly emerges in bar 90, the interplay of D♯/ D♮ and the resulting modal-sounding harmonies in bars 93–98, as well as the surprisingly dissonant harmonisation of bars 99–100. Over arpeggiated chords of B major (harps) and a tonic pedal (strings), a solo horn makes a final reference to the choral melody (now with a chromatic E♯), echoed by flute (doubled by clarinet and glockenspiel). The extract ends on a bare 5th (B and F♯).

? Private study

1. Comment on the ways in which percussion instruments contribute to the overall musical effect of *NAM 47*.

2. Compare bars 68–76 with bars 37–49.

3. How successful is this extract in showing the potential of the synthesizer in combination with a large orchestra?

? Sample questions

In the exam there will be a total of three questions on this work, from which you must choose to answer **two**.

(a) The music of *NAM 47* accompanies a scene in which Titanic is about to steam out into the open sea. How does James Horner capture the atmosphere and epic quality of this moment?

(b) Comment in detail on the orchestration of *NAM 47*.

(c) Discuss the use of tonality in *NAM 47*, showing how it reveals Horner's very traditional approach to this aspect of music.

Continuity and change in scores for epic drama

Topic for examination in 2004 and 2005

You do not need to study this topic unless *Music for film and television* is the Area of Study that you undertook for AS Music and which you are now extending for A2.

Before starting work on this topic you need a thorough understanding of the material on *Music for film and television* in the AS Guide (pages 106–119). Remember that for A2 the topic draws on works from across the **entire** Area of Study, not just those in one of the two lists, A or B.

Epic drama

The term 'epic' originally referred to a long narrative poem about heroic deeds. An epic film is one whose subject matter explores universal truths, and which possesses a grandness of scale in terms of length, setting, cast, budget and music. In short, an epic film extends beyond the ordinary in terms of its size and ambition. Comedies such as *Passport to Pimlico* and television series such as *Inspector Morse* do not fit comfortably within such a definition so here we will concentrate on the four other works in this area of study. (Information on *NAM 42* and *NAM 46*, if required, can be found in the AS Guide as well as earlier in this book.)

On the Waterfront

NAM 43   CD4 Track 2
New York Philharmonic
Conducted by Leonard Bernstein

The screenplay of *On the Waterfront* deals with the struggle of the individual against a regime of corrupt practices. Bernstein's epic score highlights this fundamental conflict in clear musical terms. The melancholy, blues-like opening horn solo is unaccompanied – isolated from its surroundings – but is strong in its determined use of repeated ascending minor 3rds, and is aspirational in its ascent to a climax at the start of bar 4. Notice that Bernstein adds the comment 'with dignity' to the tempo direction. The continuation of this melody is thin in texture – initially supported by just one other voice, loyally following in canon, and then appearing distant (*lontano*) in the muted trumpets. In contrast, the seething and dangerous atmosphere of the New York docks is captured in the

Presto (again Bernstein adds a descriptive comment, *barbaro* – barbaric – to this tempo direction). The dissonant timpani parts are played with hard sticks, the piano is quiet but menacingly low, and the persistancy and harshness of the riff seem to reflect the mechanical, non-stop drudgery of an age in which dock work still involved intensive manual labour. While it is unwise to read too many specific images into the music, Bernstein's marking of the saxophone solo (bar 42) as 'crudely' leaves little doubt about the brash atmosphere he wishes to create. Only in the 'suspense motif' that appears in bars 106–107 and 110–111 does Bernstein fall back on a device that had become something of a cliché in film music, and even here Bernstein is careful to integrate it with its context.

Unlike many of the films of the time, *On the Waterfront* avoids the inclusion of popular song, something which can so easily make a film seem dated. Instead Bernstein draws on material from blues and bebop to a rhythmic style of Stravinskian intensity. The often dissonant, symphonic-jazz treatment was a challenge to cinema goers, but it reflects the harsh reality of the film and underscores its universal truths. For further details of this work, see page 131.

Jerry Goldsmith's style in *NAM 44* is similarly uncompromising in its use of a modern idiom to underpin the thrilling hunt sequence in *Planet of the Apes*. The film raises universal questions about the future of mankind and again its epic status is reflected in the use of a very large symphony orchestra, to which Goldsmith adds a range of special effects. These include electric harp and electric bass clarinet (both novel in 1968) but not electric guitars – perhaps because their association with contemporary pop music would tend to compromise the atmosphere of a film set 2000 years in the future on an apparently alien planet. Strings have more independent material in this extract, particularly from bar 74, although there is still a tendency to score much of the more prominent thematic material for wind or piano, and to use violins for special effects, such as the high sustained notes above the riff in bars 11–21.

Planet of the Apes

NAM 44   CD4 Track 3
Conducted by Jerry Goldsmith

This is not music with a memorable tune you can whistle, like that in *NAM 45* – it makes its impact through an energy that comes from its use of near-continuous quaver and semiquaver movement at a fast tempo throughout the first 74 bars (compare this with the much more episodic treatment of the music in *NAM 47*) and through the tight integration that comes from basing much of the material on a single idea – the piano motif first heard in bar 4.

The style is dissonant but Goldsmith is careful to include familiar tonal reference points – pedal points (on C, G and E♭) underpin most of the first 40 bars, and are used in later sections as well. And while cross-rhythms of increasing complexity add to the excitement in bars 42–58, these are separated by sections in which the driving ostinato patterns firmly re-establish a clear sense of pulse.

Although on one level *ET* is a children's fantasy, part of its success was due to the more universal questions it poses about the nature and innocence of childhood. This epic quality is reflected in John Williams' use of the traditional symphony orchestra – smaller than that seen in *NAM 43* or *NAM 44*, with no unusual or electric instruments and with only very modest use of percussion. Notice,

ET

NAM 45   CD4 Track 4
City of Prague Philharmonic
Conducted by Paul Bateman

for instance, how the orchestral (crash) cymbals play only two notes in the entire extract – at bar 55, for the most triumphant appearance of the flying theme, and again for its repeat eight bars later.

Unlike the previous two extracts, the warm sound of strings is to the fore throughout *NAM 45* and the music is based on a memorable melody that can serve as a motto theme for the entire film – the type of theme that audiences are likely to hum as they leave the cinema, and quite unlike the terse, motivic-based style used by Bernstein and Goldsmith. The use of this theme within the structure of the work, and some suggestions as to why it is so memorable, are given in the AS Guide.

Bars	Structure	
1–8	Introduction	8 bars
9–16	A (theme)	8 bars
17–24	A (repeated)	8 bars
25–33	B (transition)	9 bars
34–41	A (in dominant)	8 bars
42–54	B (transition)	13 bars
55–62	A (in tonic)	8 bars
63–68	A (repeated)	6 bars
69–87	Coda	19 bars

Williams focuses on the use of straightforward material presented in a familiar context. The quaver patterns in the Introduction are rhythmically much simpler than Bernstein's riff and their totally diatonic structure is far less complex than Goldsmith's ostinati. The tonality of *NAM 45* is also very clear-cut – the flying theme appears twice in the tonic (C major), once in the dominant (G major) and then twice more in the tonic (see *left*). The orchestration gives prominence to the melody which, on its main appearances, is presented in octaves by woodwind and most of the strings, the accompaniment for brass and piano being supportive and chordal. The harmonisation is essentially conventional, but added notes (such as D with the C-major triad in bar 9), major 7ths (such as the F♯ above the chord of G in bar 12) and occasional chromatic harmonies (such as $\flat VI^7 - A\flat^{maj7}$ – in bar 14) all add colour and excitement. The intention of the music is clearly to maximise the thrill of the heroic moment, achieved with great technical success in the film, when the child's bicycle soars up into the night sky under the control of ET – a musical realisation of the wonder and magic of childhood.

Titanic Although the film *Titanic* has been criticised for focusing too much on its romantic sub-plot, it is undoubtedly an epic – not only in its portrayal of the fate of the world's most famous liner, but also in the underlying truths its explores – over-confidence in technology leading to a disregard for safety, the tragic end for emigrants hoping to start a new life in America, the interaction between the poor and the fabulously wealthy when faced with death, and so on. The music in this extract, which focuses on the heroic start to the maiden voyage is discussed in detail earlier, starting on page 134.

Private study

Outline the ways in which *NAM 47* reflects both the majesty of Titantic's maiden voyage and the human interest of the story.

Sample questions

In the exam there will be two questions on this topic, from which you must choose to answer **one**.

(a) How does John William's approach to writing music for epic drama differ from that of Jerry Goldsmith?

(b) Write a commentary on *NAM 43* to show how Bernstein's music captures the mood of an epic drama.

Warning. Photocopying any part of this book without permission is illegal.

Popular music and jazz

> For examination in summer 2002 and 2003

The first part of this chapter deals with the two special focus works and topic set for examination in summer 2002 and 2003. If you are taking the exam in summer 2004 or 2005 turn to page 150.

Ray Davies, Waterloo Sunset

> **Special Focus Work 1 for 2002 and 2003**
> NAM 53   CD4 Track 12
> The Kinks

Before starting on this section you should work through (or revise) the information about the context and structure of this music given on page 128 of the AS Guide. Make sure that you understand all of the terminology used in that section.

'Really, I'm quite a traditionalist' said Ray Davies in an interview in 1969 for *Show Guide Magazine*. This modest statement from the lead singer and songwriter of the Kinks is surprising when one considers that this group, working under the shadow of the Beatles and the Rolling Stones, produced some of the first music that could be described as heavy metal as early as 1964, some of the first popular songs influenced by Indian music, and one of the earliest concept albums (*Arthur, or the decline and fall of the British Empire*) in 1969. Like most of the great artists in pop music, they never stood still and continually probed areas of the art form in which limitations accepted by others could be extended. This is true of recycling older traditions as well as creating new ones, and Roy Davies' statement about being a traditionalist does perhaps account for the success of *Waterloo Sunset* as one of the most memorable rock ballads of the 1960s. The simplicity of its graceful melody, its bittersweet lyrics and its elegant structure combine to produce one of the most perfectly formed ballads of its age. And simplicity is the key, as the critic Nik Cohen recognised in 1969:

> Davies has never been fashionable ... at all times he is entirely separate from the rest of pop ... and, as pop in general has got more complex, so he's got simpler, always more childlike, until his songs have become as pared as nursery rhymes.
> (*Awopbopaloobop Alopbamboom – Pop From the Beginning*)

The structure of the song is shown right. Its main ingredient is the five-note hook first sung to the words 'Dirty old river' (bars 8–9). This motif is repeated in descending sequence for 'must you keep rolling' and again, slightly varied, for 'flowing into the night'. This third appearance of the motif is extended to complete the four-bar phrase we have called 'A'. The downward direction of both motif and phrase echoes the imagery of the lyrics, but right from the start there is a dichotomy between such apparent melancholy and the use of the bright key of E major at a fairly fast tempo. We shall explore the effect of this combination later. Phrase A is then repeated to the second line of lyrics, the frequent repetitions of the hook nicely reflecting the words 'makes me feel dizzy'.

Bars	Form	
1–8	Intro	8 bars
9–24	Verse 1 (AABA)	16 bars
25–32	Middle eight ...	8 bars
33–34	and turnaround	2 bars
	Verse 2, middle eight and turnaround (ie a repeat of bars 9–34)	
35–50	Verse 3 (AABA)	24 bars
51–60	Coda	10 bars

Each of the three verses is in 16-bar popular song form – an AABA structure that rose to prominence in the music of Gershwin, Porter, Berlin and other song-writers of the 1920s and 1930s. In this very traditional form the third phrase (B) normally contrasts with the A phrase in melody and harmony. We can see this in bars 16–19 of

> **Warning.** Photocopying any part of this book without permission is illegal.

Waterloo Sunset – the hook line is dropped, the lyrics suddenly become defiantly positive ('But I don't need no friends'), the melodic line heads for an aspirational top G♯ on 'need' and the first use of chromatic harmony appears in bar 18. Finally, the verse ends with a return to phrase A, modified at the end, starting in bar 20.

The melody of phrase A uses a pentatonic scale (E–F♯–G♯–B–C♯) but the harmonisation makes the E-major tonality totally clear by using the three primary triads of that key (I, IV and V). Notice how the B section (known as the 'bridge' or 'release') explores the secondary triads of E major:

A	**A**	**B**	**A**
I–V^7–IV–IV	I–V^7–IV–IV	ii – VI – ii^7 – V^7	I–V^7–IV–IV
E–B^7–A–A	E–B^7–A–A	F♯m– C♯ – F♯m–B^7	E–B^7–A–A

This 16-bar verse is followed by two more structural features found in popular songs of the early-20th century. The first is a 'middle eight' (bars 25–32) which, following convention briefly modulates to a related key (the dominant, B major, in bars 25–27). Notice how the bass shadows the lead vocal by playing the same pitches (sounding an octave lower than written) but in a different rhythm. The second familiar feature is the two-bar extension in bars 33–34. This is known as a turnaround, as it prepares (by means of the extended V^7 chord) for the return of the main theme and tonic key at the start of each succeeding verse. All three verses use essentially the same music, with just slight differences in the backing tracks.

The simultaneous performance of different versions of the same melody, as in this shadowing of the voice by the bass, is known as heterophony.

The introduction is purely instrumental, and begins by defining the key of E major through four bars of dominant 7th below which the bass, in repeated straight quavers, descends stepwise from upper dominant to lower dominant. As this all resolves on to a tonic chord of E major in bar 5, the lead guitar plays through the opening A phrase of the song. The descending bass pattern below a B^7 chord is used again in bars 31–34, serving the same purpose of introducing the main A phrase and unifying this turnaround section with the introduction.

The coda reverses the order of events in the introduction. Here the instrumental version of phrase A comes first (starting in the second half of bar 51), accompanied by a more sustained descending bass pattern, and is followed by repeated dominant 7ths in the fade-out bars which match those of the opening (although now the bass remains on the dominant throughout).

With the exception of the two-bar turnaround, all the phrases are four-bars in length. Such intensely regular periodic phrasing can make a song sound predictably sectional, but this is disguised by the long pick-up (or anacrusis) of four quavers of the hook, which crosses the gap between sections, and by the guitar licks which fill those gaps in places such as bars 11, 15 and 23.

Lyrics

The lyrics centre on a person who views the world from his window as a series of images – the dirty old river, the confusing crowds, the dazzling lights, the lovers Terry and Julie meeting at Waterloo station each Friday (a reference to the actors Terence Stamp and Julie Christie who had just starred in the 1967 film of Hardy's *Far From the Madding Crowd*). He wants no part in the maddening crowd, he needs no friends and is content to gaze on the sunset. It seems a sad story – a recluse who views the world as an outsider. But the music is no melancholy modal ballad – its bright tempo and major key seem to tell a more positive tale. And that is one of the ways in which this perfect vignette works its magic – the suggestion in the music that perhaps it really is better inside than out, that perhaps there really is nothing better than gazing out of the window at the sunset, that perhaps pride in self is the thing that really matters.

This is very different from the 'boy meets girl, boy loses girl' content of so many pop songs of the day. The characteristically British notion of being happy with your lot in life, the very specific references to London, and the ironic juxtaposition of music and lyric all help explain why this song (like most by the Kinks) was not successful in America, but why it has appealed to generations of British listeners, more recently becoming a primary source of inspiration for the BritPop revival of the 1990s.

Damon Albarn, lead singer of Blur, recorded *Waterloo Sunset* (which he described as one of his favourite songs) as a duet with Ray Davies for the Channel 4 music show, the White Room in 1995. Their duet version is due to appear on a new Kinks tribute album to be released September 2001 – *The Songs of Ray Davies and the Kinks* (Praxis).

Private study

1. Explain the meaning of the terms hook, lick and turnaround and give examples of their use in *NAM 53*.

2. What do you notice about the rhythm of the hook?

3. Comment on the range of the lead vocal line.

4. Which of the following statements about the lead vocal is true?
   (i) It is entirely pentatonic
   (ii) It is entirely diatonic
   (iii) It is sometimes chromatic.

5. On the recording is *NAM 53* performed with swung quavers or straight quavers?

6. What do you notice about the rate of harmonic change in most of this song?

7. Comment on the role played by the backing vocals.

Lennon and McCartney, A Day in the Life

Before starting on this section you should work through (or revise) the information about the context and structure of this music given on pages 128–129 of the AS Guide. Make sure that you understand all of the terminology used on those pages.

The immediate precursors of *Sgt Pepper's Lonely Hearts Club Band* were the LPs *Rubber Soul* (1965) and *Revolver* (1966). In both of these the Beatles, encouraged by their producer George Martin, had begun increasingly to explore the full potential of the four-track recording techniques of the day, and to broaden their already wide stylistic range with songs such as *Norwegian Wood*, featuring the sitar, and *Eleanor Rigby*, sung to the accompaniment of a string octet. In late 1966 the group decided to abandon live performing on tours, since it had often become impossible for anyone to hear anything above the incessant screaming of adoring fans, and to work in future as a studio band.

Special Focus Work 2 for 2002 and 2003

NAM 54
This song is not included on the CDs that accompany the New Anthology.

The album

Warning. Photocopying any part of this book without permission is illegal.

Years later Paul McCartney confirmed that 'Pet Sounds was my inspiration for making Sgt Pepper ... the big influence'.

Complete track listing
Sgt Pepper [McCartney]
With a Little Help [McCartney]
Lucy in the Sky with Diamonds [Lennon]
Getting Better [McCartney]
Fixing a Hole [McCartney]
She's Leaving Home [McCartney]
Being for the Benefit of Mr Kite! [Lennon]
Within You Without You [Harrison]
When I'm Sixty-Four [McCartney]
Lovely Rita [McCartney]
Good Morning [Lennon]
Sgt Pepper (Reprise) [McCartney]
A Day in the Life [Lennon and McCartney]
Playout groove

Another song by George Harrison (*Only a Northern Song*) was recorded but dropped from the album – it was later used in the film *Yellow Submarine*. *Strawberry Fields* and *Penny Lane* were probably intended for the album, but were released as a single.

Undoubtedly another reason for the decision to concentrate on studio work was the critical acclaim received by the album *Pet Sounds*, from the leading American group the Beach Boys, released in May 1966. Over a year in the making, it was the first successful concept album in which all of the songs are related in style and purpose, and its success suggested that this type of major studio-based project could figure prominently in the future of pop music.

It seems that initially the Beatles planned a concept album around the theme of nostalgic childhood memories based on locations in Liverpool. A start was made with four songs recorded between November 1966 and February 1967: Lennon's *Strawberry Fields*, McCartney's *Penny Lane* (along with his earlier song, *When I'm Sixty-Four*) and *A Day in the Life*, which combined material from both composers. At this stage the nature of the project changed. Capitol Records, alarmed that the time-scale for the album was interfering with their wish to release new Beatles' records every few months, insisted that *Strawberry Fields* and *Penny Lane* be published immediately, as the two sides of a single. Thereafter the album developed in a different direction, using the old theatrical device of a performance within a performance. This is used to create an impression that it is not the Beatles we hear but Sgt Pepper's Lonely Hearts Club Band – an imaginery Edwardian concert band which presents a vaudeville of fantasies in styles old and new. The band's title is significant – they are a band creating an illusion for lonely people – but they themselves are lonely and it is the theme of loneliness, and how it is covered up, which links their songs.

This simple but effective device allowed the Beatles to create a concept album embracing a far broader range of musical styles than that found in the Beach Boys' *Pet Sounds*, in which the songs were linked by their musical similarity. It provides the opportunity to juxtapose music hall (*When I'm Sixty-Four*) and community songs (*With a Little Help From My Friends*) with surreal fairground music (*Being for the Benefit of Mr Kite!*) and the psychedelic imagery of songs such as *Lucy in the Sky with Diamonds*.

To create the illusion the album begins with tuning-up, audience noises and applause. To maintain the illusion, the separate tracks are closely spaced and sometimes overlap (a feature making it deliberately difficult for radio DJs to break up the concept by playing just isolated tracks). In addition, when the LP was released it sought to involve the listener by including Sergeant Pepper cutouts, a collage of portraits to decipher and a printed version of the complete lyrics. This last feature was most unusual at the time and reflects the fact that, unlike the words of most earlier pop songs, the lyrics are often ambiguous and open to interpretation. The illusion is seemingly brought to an end by a reprise of its opening number, now at a more urgent tempo and with its title line curtailed to produce poignently insistent repeats of 'Sergeant Pepper's lonely, Sergeant Pepper's lonely, ...'.

The reprise ends the performance by Sgt Pepper's Lonely Hearts Club Band, but it is not the end of the album. Our song, *A Day in the Life*, exists like an epilogue outside the context of the show. This at last is the Beatles performing. John Lennon's sardonic commentary on the news strikes an icy tone ... ('a lucky man who made the grade ... rather sad ... just had to laugh ... he blew his mind out in a car ... didn't notice the lights had changed'). Paul McCartney's interpolated middle section creates ambiguity – was the first half of the song as illusory as Sergeant Pepper himself? At first it might seem so – an alarm clock is heard ... 'Woke up, got out of bed'. But the ensuing account of humdrum existence quickly reverts to dreaming – he gets on a bus, goes to the upper deck, where smoking was allowed in those days, has a smoke (of what?) and 'goes into a dream'. Lennon's final stanza loses all sense of coherence ('Now they know how many holes it takes to fill the Albert Hall; I'd love to turn you on') and so does the concluding music. And so again there is a suspicion that everything thus far has still been part of the illusion. After the final colossal chord a locked playout groove presents sounds from the post-production party and an inaudibly high tone put there at Lennon's request, 'to annoy your dog'. So is this, at last, the return to reality?

Despite the worries about the length of the project, it was actually finished in a burst of creative energy, 16 songs (including the three not used in the final album) having been recorded in five months. The final mono mix of all the material was completed on 21 April 1967, matters such as the stereo mix (stereo still being relatively new in pop music at this time) and the order of tracks being left largely to George Martin. The album was officially released on 1 June 1967 (it actually appeared a few days early) and received considerable critical acclaim, although a few found it rather contrived. At the time the pop single was still the main way of marketing pop music and part of the signficance of *Sgt Pepper* was the role it played in establishing the importance of the album as a vehicle for more complex musical ideas in pop music. It was soon followed by concept albums from other groups, by double and even triple albums, by rock operas and by substantial progressive rock works that drew on elements of classical and avant-garde art music.

Sgt. Pepper is also significant for its approach to recording, in which the studio is no longer used as a way to capture the sound of a live performance, but as a tool in its own right – one of the consequences being that such studio music becomes difficult, if not impossible, to recreate in live performance. Above all, its significance is in its demonstration that pop music can be very much more than a transient three-minute song. As a coherent, entertaining and sometimes moving statement of the aspirations and counter-culture of its age, *Sgt Pepper* has remained one of the great works of popular music, returning to the top of the charts decades later with its release on CD in 1987 and again in 1995.

A Day in the Life begins as the final chord of the previous song fades away. It creeps in, almost unnoticed, with an acoustic guitar outlining the chord pattern (G–Bm–Em–Em^7–C) that will be used in the following verses, joined after two bars by piano and bass. When the drummer enters in bar 5 he is limited to a simple quaver rhythm on maracas. A key element is the dispassionate delivery of the lyrics. The singer's detachment is expressed technically through panning Lennon's voice hard to the right of the accompaniment in the stereo field. Musically it is expressed through motifs that sound more like repetitive thoughts than a melodic line – short, jumpy figures in

Just before the release of the album the BBC announced a ban on broadcasting *A Day in the Life* because it decided that the line 'I'd love to turn you on' was an encitement to drug-taking – an interpretation immediately denounced as false by Paul McCartney.

Form		
1–4	Intro	4 bars
5–14	Verse 1	10 bars
15–23	Verse 2	9 bars
24–34	Verse 3	11 bars
35–46	Transition	12 bars
47–57	Bridge	11 bars
58–67	Transition	10 bars
68–78	Verse 4	11 bars
79–89	Outro	11 bars

free rhythm, frequently coming back to the same intervals. The tonality is often ambiguous – the dominant chord (D major) is totally avoided in the verses, and the harmonic progressions often sound modal, especially with the use of F major, the chord on the flattened leading-note. In fact G major is never convincingly established as a key – the tonality eventually finds its resolution in E major.

Notice how the vocal line is slightly different in each verse, reflecting the essentially improvisatory nature of the singing. In verse 2 the tension almost imperceptibly begins to mount. The full drum kit enters on the critical words 'He blew his mind out in a car' and the previously ten-bar length of the verse is foreshortened to nine bars (neither verse being anywhere near as symmetric as the four-bar phrase lengths we saw in *Waterloo Sunset*). At the end of the verse a semitonal figure in semiquavers appears (bar 22) which will be of significance later – like so many of the melodic motifs in the song, it hovers around the note B – after which the vocal range is extended to reach a climactic top G. At the end of verse 3 the semitonal figure is inverted (the principal note is still B) and this is the idea taken up by the orchestra and transformed into an almost pitchless spiral of sound for the transition.

Mixolydian mode on E:
E–F♯–G♯–A–B–C♯–D–E.

The tempo is tightened for McCartney's bridge section, which is focused on the tonal area of E major although, as in Lennon's verses, there is a strong modal element, with prominent use of D♮, the characteristic flat seventh degree of the mixolydian mode on E (see *left*). The two sections are also complementary in other respects. Like Lennon, McCartney uses repetitive intervals (mainly 3rds) rather than stepwise melody, and assymetric structures made up of 2½-bar phrase lengths. And while Lennon's motifs mainly centre on the 4th between B and upper E, McCartney's focus on the 5th between B and lower E (thus reversing the normal role of the two singers, in which McCartney normally took the high notes).

In the second transition (bars 58–67) Lennon's vocalisation reflects the idea of a dream, and is underpinned by massive root-position harmonies that turn on its head the conventional circle of 5ths patterns – for here the 5ths rise instead of fall, twice outlining the pattern C–G–D–A–E with the full weight of orchestral bars.

The final verse is musically similar to verse 3 (although notice how 'the Albert Hall' is decorated with concerto-like piano chords). However, significantly it has left and right channels reversed – several commentators have remarked how this gives the effect that something has been fundamentally changed by the reminder of reality in the bridge. But the lyrics are now the most trivial of snippets from the newspaper, and they are dealt with in just the same deadpan tone as the report of the car accident in verse 1. The reappearance of the orchestral spiral links the coda to the earlier transition, but this time it leads to a dramatic silence followed by the brilliant light of E major, reverberating for 42 seconds before leading into the locked groove of the final track.

Further reading

The Beatles: Sgt Pepper's Lonely Hearts Club Band by Allan Moore. *Cambridge University Press* (1997). ISBN: 0-521-57484-6.

Private study

1. Write short notes to show the ways in which the music reflects the lyrics in *NAM 54*.

2. To what extent are the rather different styles of Lennon and McCartney successfully blended in *A Day in the Life*?

3. Why is *Sgt. Pepper's Lonely Hearts Club Band* regarded as such a significant milestone in the history of pop music?

Sample questions

In the exam there will be a total of three questions on these two works, from which you must choose to answer **two**.

(a) To what extent does *NAM 53* show Ray Davies to be very traditional in his approach to songwriting?

(b) Compare the structures of *NAM 53* and *NAM 54*.

(c) Discuss the composer's response to the lyrics in the music of **either** *Waterloo Sunset* **or** *A Day in the Life*.

Continuity and change in the handling of voices and instruments

Topic for examination in 2002 and 2003

You do not need to study this topic unless *Popular music and jazz* is the Area of Study that you undertook for AS Music and which you are now extending for A2.

Before starting work on this topic you need a thorough understanding of the material on *Popular music and jazz* in the AS Guide (pages 120–132). Remember that for A2 the topic draws on works from across the **entire** Area of Study, not just those in one of the two lists, A or B.

The instrumentation of *West End Blues* is typical of early jazz, consisting of a frontline of trumpet, clarinet and trombone, and a rhythm section of piano, banjo and drums (a cornet was often used rather than a trumpet in the very earliest jazz). Notice that on this original 1928 recording there is no string bass and the drummer uses only the novelty percussion device known as the *bock-a-da-bock*, perhaps because of the difficulty of recording drums and bass in these early days of recording.

West End Blues

NAM 48 CD4 Track 7
Louis Armstrong (trumpet and voice)
Jimmy Armstrong (clarinet)
Fred Robinson (trombone)
Earl Hines (piano)
Mancy Carr (banjo)
Zutty Singleton (drums)

The music was improvised, so there was no formal arrangement in the sense of a written-out score. Each player knew the chord pattern and understood the function of each instrument in the ensemble, and there was clearly a collective agreement about the main layout.

The use of different instrumental combinations from chorus to chorus produces a great deal of textural variety, although the main emphasis is on solo improvisation:

- solo trumpet (introduction) and solo piano (fourth chorus)
- soloist with rhythm-section accompaniment (second chorus)
- two soloists with rhythm-section accompaniment (third chorus)
- all three frontline players with rhythm-section accompaniment (first and fifth choruses).

Warning. Photocopying any part of this book without permission is illegal.

Details of the instrumental techniques used by the players, along with Armstrong's innovative use of scat singing in his vocal solo, are given in the AS Guide.

Black and Tan Fantasy

NAM 49   CD4 Track 8
Duke Ellington and his orchestra

Although recorded before *West End Blues*, the instrumentation of the *Black and Tan Fantasy* looks forward to the big-band jazz of the 1930s and 40s. The ten instruments, which now include saxophones, are divided into three sections (reeds, brass and rhythm) and the larger number of players makes collective improvisation impractical, thus requiring a written-out arrangement for at least the tutti sections. Within the arrangement, though, Ellington leaves space for improvised solos, and he had a reputation for the care with which he wrote material that would act as a showcase for the talents of his principal players – notice that *NAM 49* was written in collaboration with Ellington's lead trumpeter, Bubber Miley.

The gruff sounds of Ellington's jungle style contrast with the more transparent textures of *West End Blues*, but the basic format, in which the inner choruses each feature a solo supported by the rhythm section, is common to both pieces and to much other jazz from the 1920s. Even in the more fully scored saxophone solo the accompaniment is fairly static (compare bars 13–16 with the sustained harmonies in bars 55–58 of *NAM 48*).

The use of drums and bass makes the rhythm section sound more modern than that used in *NAM 48*, but the lack of definition of these parts on CD4 reflects the difficulty in recording these instruments at the time, mentioned earlier. The wide vibrato and almost constant use of portamento in the alto sax solo are characteristic of saxophone playing in the early-20th century. The use of effects by the brass, such as growling, plunger mutes and the trombone 'horse whinny', are features of Ellington's jungle style.

Four

NAM 50   CD4 Track 9
Miles Davis Quintet

NAM 50 is representative of the much more intimate style of jazz that became popular in the 1950s. Unlike the two previous jazz works, this extract is for the most part an accompanied solo. The introduction for drums lacks fidelity in comparison with a modern recording, but it does reveal how recording quality was starting to improve in the 1950s. After this, the extract is essentially a showcase for the Miles Davis' trumpet technique. This includes the use of effects such as half-valving, ghost notes and pitch bends, but its main impact derives from the very fast, virtuoso style of playing. The tenor saxophone doubles the trumpet at the lower octave in the first chorus, but has no independent material in *NAM 50*. The double bass maintains a busy line of its own with a wide-ranging walking-bass part, although it is never so busy that it detracts from the main soloist. After the opening solo the drummer concentrates on rapid but quiet patterns on the closed hi-hat cymbal, highlighting the many off-beat accents with a brief splash on open hi-hat or snare drum. The piano is used sparsely, just finding enough room for syncopated chordal stabs during the trumpet player's rests.

I'm Leavin' You

Warning. Photocopying any part of this book without permission is illegal.

The electric guitar first appeared in the late 1930s, and the bass guitar in 1951, both instruments being used initially to give more power to the rhythm section in the dance bands of the time. Both were quickly adopted by rhythm-and-blues bands in the 1950s, and together they have formed, along with the drum kit and sometimes a piano or other keyboard instrument, the foundation of most popular music ever since. The particular combination of lead guitar (usually a solid-bodied instrument) for solo work and rhythm guitar (often an amplified acoustic guitar) to concentrate on the harmonies was particularly favoured in the early days of rock 'n' roll. The full group of only four or five players delivers considerable power, even in a large venue, and so also obviously requires vocalists to use microphones, so that the voice can be amplified to balance the instrumental forces. Small instruments such as the harmonica (used here in the fourth chorus) are held close to the microphone so they too can be amplified.

NAM 51	CD4 Track 10
Howlin' Wolf (vocal, harmonica)	
Hosea Lee Kennard (piano)	
L. D. McGhee (guitar)	
Hubert Sumlin (guitar)	
S. P. Leary (drums)	

Howlin' Wolf's vocal style reflects the impassioned delivery of the urban blues style, and is much freer in rhythm and in its use of blue notes than contemporary rock 'n' roll. The many small differences in the melodic line of each verse reflect the fact that the music was essentially improvised and then notated, rather than being written down and then performed. The shuffle (or swing) rhythm of *NAM 51* is a fingerprint of the blues style, and the structure is typical of many blues-based pop songs of the period – six repetitions of a 12-bar blues pattern, with the singer replaced by a guitar solo (later joined by harmonica) in verse 4. The 'stop chorus' in verse 3 is a device to focus attention on the soloist by confining the accompaniment to mainly isolated beats. The fade-out ending is a technique that became increasingly popular in the 1950s, giving the impression that the music is slowly drifting away from the audience rather than coming to a definite end – although it was also popular because it solved the problem of finding a satisfactory conclusion for a song, something that can be particularly difficult in blues-based pieces.

Honey Don't

Rock 'n' roll combines elements of rhythm and blues with features of country-music rockabilly style, so it should not be surprising to find similarities between this song and *NAM 51*. It was written nearly four years before *I'm Leavin' You*, and its earlier date is reflected in its use of an acoustic double bass, rather than the electric bass guitar, which was still not widely available in 1955. The basic ensemble of solo vocalist, lead guitar, rhythm guitar, bass and drums is similar to *I'm Leaving' You* (although there is no piano in *NAM 52*) but the arrangement has less rhythmic freedom, being dominated by the even crotchets of its walking bass (often doubled and decorated by lead guitar), the regular strumming of the rhythm guitar, the firm back beat from drums and features such as the precise tutti interjections seen in bars 6–13. Two particular features to note are the occasional use of slap bass (indicated by x-headed notes) and the characteristic lead guitar technique of parallel 4ths in bars 30–33 and 74–80.

NAM 52	CD4 Track 11
Carl Perkins (vocal, guitar)	
James 'Buck' Perkins (rhythm guitar)	
Lloyd 'Clayton' Perkins (upright bass)	
W. S. Holland (drums)	

Waterloo Sunset

The Kinks employ the by now familiar combination of electric lead guitar, acoustic rhythm guitar, bass (a bass guitar, not a double bass) and drums. The wordless vocalisation of the backing vocals (sung by the instrumentalists) is a feature of much 1960s pop music. The scalic bass part contrasts strongly with the chord-based figures in the bass part of *NAM 53*. Further details of this song are discussed above, starting on page 139.

NAM 53	CD4 Track 12
The Kinks	

A Day in the Life

NAM 54
This song is not included on the CDs that accompany the New Anthology.

The accompaniment to *NAM 54* is largely chordal, and a piano therefore substitutes for the more usual lead guitar. The use of an orchestral backing, or at least a stage band with a string section, was common in lighter types of pop music, but it is the way the orchestra is used – really as a special effect – that was so novel in *A Day in the Life*. To create the long, gliding ascent each player was told to start on the lowest note of their instrument and then ascend by the smallest possible intervals to a top E, without attempting to synchronise with other players. The result was then double-tracked to thicken the sound. Also unusual in this song is the use of a different singer (not to mention a different composer!) for the middle section. The relationship between the two vocal parts, and other aspects of the vocal and instrumental writing were discussed earlier, in the section starting on page 141.

You can get it if you really want

NAM 55 CD4 Track 13
Desmond Dekker and the Aces

Carribean music often reveals the rich mix of influences that can be heard in *NAM 55*. The close-harmony vocals of the backing group are a legacy of 1950s doo-wop music, which remained particularly popular in Jamaica, the high trumpet riffs are a feature of music from the nearby island of Cuba and from Mexico on the American mainland, while the tight rhythmic style betrays Latin-American influences. Guitars have a much more subsidiary role in this song. The lead guitar is used essentially as a rhythmic instrument, its picked semiquaver patterns giving an almost calypso-like feel to the texture, while the second guitar provides background chordal support in partnership with the electric organ (an instrument often used in the Jamaican styles of ska, rock steady and reggae).

Much of the character of the song comes from its bass part. It is often low, prominent in the mix, and for most of the time plays the root of the harmony in simple on-the-beat patterns. Compare it with Paul McCartney's busy, scalic and often syncopated bass playing in *NAM 54*. The heavy, steady bass line of *NAM 55* lends it name to this style of Jamaican music – rock steady – and differentiates it from reggae in which the bass is usually syncopated and often silent on the first beat of the bar. The influence of reggae (which was just starting to appear around 1970) is thus not seen at all in the bass part, but it can be felt in the prominent back-beat of the drum part, The drums are supplemented by the fast tambourine pattern notated in bar 5, although this is so far back in the mix that it is often inaudible on CD4.

Tupelo Honey

NAM 56 CD4 Track 14
Van Morrison

NAM 56 has an improvisatory quality, and yet the texture seems too complex for true improvisation. The reason for this can be found in the way that arrangements of this sort were developed. As Mark Jordan, the keyboards player in this recording, explained in an article in *Rolling Stone* magazine, 22 June 1972:

> [Van Morrison] doesn't read or write music, so a lot of times you have to follow his fingers on the frets. Sometimes he'll have really dramatic lyrics but he needs to flesh out the melody. We'll throw out suggestions and he'll tell us when something's not working.

Essentially the arrangement was developed in a cooperative manner by the members of the band, in what was probably a similar way to the early jazz arrangement of *NAM 48*. Particular specialist contributions were credited on the original LP – for example, Bruce

Warning. Photocopying any part of this book without permission is illegal.

Royston was credited as arranger of the flute part. As Van Morrison himself said, 'I need to have guys who can take an arrangement and work on it'. A result of this empirical method of working was that details of the piece often changed in live performance (just as they do in jazz), although the version refined in the studio for this recording can reasonably be regarded as definitive – commentators at the time certainly felt that live performances of *Tupelo Honey* rarely captured the sweetness and innocence of the recorded version. The inclusion of a short flute solo is unusual, although the flute appears in a number of other Van Morrison songs and reflects the composer's roots in Irish folk music. The lead guitar is used as a melody instrument, largely in the upper part of its range, in much of the song. Initially this is in dialogue with the flute or voice, but from bar 21 it takes part in a complex web of counterpoint with high acoustic guitar, saxophone and bass. The high tessitura of the vocal and guitar parts, set against a low bass and with piano in the middle, gives the song its warm, rich texture. This is enhanced by its jazz-like freedom of rhythm and hypnotically repeating chord pattern – a mellow combination that produces, in the words of the *Penguin Encyclopedia of Popular Music*, 'an almost unbearable nostalgia, transmuted into art by talent'.

Since this is a homage to John Lennon, it is not surprising that it reflects some of the vocal and instrumental techniques of an earlier generation. This is particularly evident in features such as the piano introduction, the simple string overdub (starting in bar 13) and the lyrical melody of the chorus (bars 25–32). The bass-guitar part is entirely functional, being mainly confined to repetitions of the root note of the predominantly root-position harmony, and with none of the melodic interest seen in parts of *NAM 54* and throughout *NAM 56*. The use of distortion in the guitar solo is a technique that goes back to the 1960s, although its use in a slow ballad is more novel. Ultimately of course the basis of the song is a combination of voice, guitars, bass and drums – a line-up which illustrates a degree of continuity reaching back to the 1950s.

Private study

1. Compare the trumpet improvisations in *NAM 48, 49* and *50*, showing how each relates to the underlying harmonies.

2. Show how bass-guitar parts became increasingly sophisticated by comparing the bass parts in *NAM 51, 53* and *56*.

3. Discuss what you understand is meant by an arrangement in pop music and jazz.

Sample questions

In the exam there will be two questions on this topic, from which you must choose to answer **one**.

(a) Compare and contrast the style of the vocal parts in *NAM 55* with the vocal parts in *NAM 56*.

(b) Comment on the increasingly important role of the drum kit in popular music, choosing examples from three of the works you have studied.

Don't look back in anger

NAM 57	CD4 Track 15
Oasis	

Warning. Photocopying any part of this book without permission is illegal.

| For examination in summer 2004 and 2005 |

Popular music and jazz

This part of this chapter deals with the two special focus works and topic set for examination in summer 2004 and 2005. If you are taking the exam in summer 2002 or 2003 turn to page 139.

Joe 'King' Oliver, West End Blues

| Special Focus Work 1 for 2004 and 2005 |

NAM 48　　　　　　　　CD4 Track 7
Louis Armstrong (trumpet and voice) and his Hot Five:
Jimmy Armstrong (clarinet)
Fred Robinson (trombone)
Earl Hines (piano)
Mancy Carr (banjo)
Zutty Singleton (drums)

Before starting on this section you should work through (or revise) the information about the context and structure of this music given on pages 121–122 of the AS Guide. Make sure that you understand all of the terminology used in that section.

The instrumentation of *NAM 48* is typical of early jazz, although at first the cornet was often preferred to the trumpet. Bands often also included a double bass, absent in Armstrong's Hot Five recordings perhaps because it was so difficult to record in the early days of gramophone recording (he partially solved this problem by using a tuba on the bass line in other recordings of this period). In live performance drums would play a greater role than they do here, but again the limitations of recording often dictated that just quiet novelty effects (such as the *bock-a-da-bock*) had to be substituted.

West End Blues differs from the collective improvisation of New Orleans jazz in the way it gives prominence to solo playing. This is a fingerprint of the Chicago jazz style of the late 1920s and the greater use of solo improvisation enabled players to improvise away from the underlying chord pattern, giving jazz a freedom that became increasingly important in the years ahead. Such freedom is particularly evident in the unaccompanied introduction, where Armstrong's rhythm has a speech-like flexibility. This solo is justly famous for its daring bravura, but Armstrong's ambiguous handling of tonality is equally adventurous, first suggesting C minor, then E♭ minor and B♭ minor, before the band enters on an augmented triad on the dominant (B♭–D–F♯) in bar 6. And this chord is used not merely for its colourful chromatic effect but also because the F♯ is the first note of the theme, and so provides the smoothest of transitions to the opening chorus. It is only in bar 7, when the band so satisfyingly resolves this dominant discord on to tonic harmony, that it becomes clear we are to hear a blues in E♭ major.

The form of *West End Blues* consists of an introduction followed by five choruses of a slow 12-bar blues and a short coda. Within this structure there is considerable textural variety:

Form
Intro
Chorus 1　Theme (trumpet)
Chorus 2　Trombone solo
Chorus 3　Clarinet and vocal duet
Chorus 4　Piano solo
Chorus 5　Theme (trumpet)
Coda

- solo trumpet (introduction) and solo piano (Chorus 4)
- soloist with rhythm-section accompaniment (Chorus 2)
- two soloists with rhythm-section accompaniment (Chorus 3)
- all three frontline players with rhythm-section accompaniment (Choruses 1 and 5).

There is no written-out arrangement (remember that *NAM 48* is a transcription of what was improvised, not a score from which the music was played) but all players are thoroughly versed in the chord pattern of a 12-bar blues and there is collective agreement about what goes where as well as a spontaneity in developing the basic theme and accompanying harmonies.

| **Warning.** Photocopying any part of this book without permission is illegal. |

The example *below* shows the start of Joe Oliver's original song compared with the start of the five choruses in the performance by Louis Armstrong and his Hot Five. Armstrong begins his first chorus with a close paraphrase of the opening phrase of the song, although notice how he slides in an extra appearance of the distinctive initial motif at the end of bar two. This is probably a pre-arranged opening, since the clarinet follows the same pattern in 3rds with the trumpet. Armstrong then links this phrase with the next by a free improvisation, landing on the flat seventh in bar 10. The rest of the chorus moves ever further from the source, occasionally touching on a principal note or characteristic interval, but mainly becoming a free improvisation over the original blues harmony.

Chorus 2, in contrast, simplifies the original. Now the opening motif is reduced to just two notes – essentially the blue third (think of F♯ spelt as G♭) smeared into the major 3rd by the trombone. Again, the singer's rests in the original song are filled out by the soloist. Notice the chord substitutions in bars 20, 24 and 26.

Chorus 3 is a duet – a dialogue between the main melody in the low clarinet and the imitative responses sung by Armstrong in his innovative scat style. Notice how the opening motif is further exploited, now appearing twice per bar and in various transformations – the upward 3rd is melodically augmented to a 4th by the clarinet, the answer to which Armstrong decorates with an expressive appoggiatura in bar 32. The original motif is transposed and rhythmically varied by Armstrong in bar 34. The clarinettist then freely inverts the motif from the end of bar 34 onwards.

Chorus 4 is a free, virtuoso piano improvisation, with considerable elaboration of the chord pattern and with only the sketchiest of references to the original melody. Can you spot how the 12-bar blues pattern has been embellished by pianist Earl Hines?

Joe Oliver's original song can be be found in a number of standard collections such as *The Definitive Blues Collection* and *The Ultimate Jazz Fake Book*, both published by Hal Leonard/Music Sales.

Chorus 5 begins with the greatest possible simplification – the first phrase is reduced to just its distinctive three opening notes. Of course this belies what is to follow – the sparkling, cadenza-like treatment of the middle phrase, and the final piano phrase which vaporises into the tiny coda, based (as was so often the case in the early blues) on a decorated plagal cadence. The plagal nature of this cadence will seem clearer if you read it as $A\flat m^7 - E\flat^6$.

The supremacy of the soloist in this Chicago-style jazz is obvious in the three central choruses, but even in the tutti choruses (1 and 5) notice that Armstrong dominates the texture, the other frontline instruments supplying mostly sustained harmony notes, enlivened with the occasional short point of motivic interest.

Private study

1. (i) What is meant by the term 'the changes' in jazz?
   (ii) What are the changes in *West End Blues*?

2. On what type of chord does the band enter in bar 6?

3. The song *West End Blues* begins with the notes F♯–G–B♭.
   (i) Where is this motif **first** heard in *NAM 48*?
   (ii) How is this motif used in the rest of *NAM 48*?

4. Using examples from the introduction, explain the difference between swung and straight rhythm.

5. Which aspects of *West End Blues* suggest that there must have been some pre-planning of improvised material?

6. What do you notice about the rate of harmonic change in most of this piece?

Chester Burnett (Howlin' Wolf), I'm Leaving You

Special Focus Work 2 for 2004 and 2005
NAM 51   CD4 Track 10
Howlin' Wolf (vocal, harmonica)
Hosea Lee Kennard (piano)
L. D. McGhee (guitar)
Hubert Sumlin (guitar)
S. P. Leary (drums)

Information on the early history of the blues can be found on page 155.

Before starting on this section you should work through (or revise) the information about the context and structure of this music given on pages 125–126 of the AS Guide. Make sure that you understand all of the terminology used in that section.

The blues first became widely known in the 1920s, not only through its adoption by jazz bands in works such as *West End Blues*, but also through the recordings of early blues singers such as Ma Rainey and Bessie Smith, both of whom made their first records in 1923. However, the blues did not play a major part in the repertoire of the big bands of the 1930s and 1940s (with the exception of the Duke Ellington Orchestra). Instead the blues continued its own independent development, through the work of such artists as Muddy Waters, Howlin' Wolf, T-Bone Walker and B. B. King. By the early 1940s most blues musicians had moved towards the harder-edged sound of the urban blues, and it was with the adoption of louder instruments (electric guitars, saxophones and drum kits, with the vocalist needing amplification to balance), faster speeds and tighter rhythms (with an emphasised backbeat) that the blues was transformed into energetic dance music. Called 'race music' until the late 1940s, this later became known as rhythm and blues, and it significantly influenced the development of rock 'n' roll.

Warning. Photocopying any part of this book without permission is illegal.

Chester Burnett (stage name Howlin' Wolf) learnt the rural blues style during the 1920s and 1930s in the south of the USA, where he was a farmworker and part-time performer. It was not until 1951, at the age of 41, that he started to become widely known. Following a move to Chicago he adopted a rhythm and blues style and achieved a string of hits in the R & B charts during the 1950s. His songs draw on a wide variety of blues techniques – *Smokestack Lightnin'* (1956), for example, revives the historic format of a blues accompanied by just a single chord. Within 20 years *Smokestack Lightnin'* was in the repertoire of Eric Clapton and the Yardbirds, John Lee Hooker, the Animals, the Grateful Dead and many other others – giving some idea of Chester Burnett's enormous influence.

I'm Leavin' You was recorded in Chicago in late 1958. It consists of six choruses of a 12-bar blues in G, prefaced by a short introduction and rounded-off by a coda that fades out. The replacement of the singer by an instrumental in one of the middle choruses is typical of many rhythm and blues songs, and is a feature that was also adopted in early rock 'n' roll. The basic chord sequence is:

bars	3	4	5	6	7	8	9	10	11	12	13	14
chord	$G^{(7)}$	G	G	$G^{(7)}$	C^9	C^9	G^7	G^7	D^7	C^9	G^7	G^7
	$I^{(7)}$	I	I	$I^{(7)}$	IV^9	IV^9	I^7	I^7	V^7	IV^7	I^7	I^7

Form

Intro	1–2	
Chorus 1	3–14	Verse 1
Chorus 2	15–26	Verse 2
Chorus 3	27–38	Verse 3
Chorus 4	39–50	Instrumental
Chorus 5	15–26	(repeat)
Chorus 6	27–36	ending in 51–52
Coda	53–58	(fade out)

Although this is essentially the same 12-bar blues sequence used in *West End Blues*, Burnett prefers chord IV to chord V in the tenth bar of the pattern (bar number 12) – a very common variant. What is perhaps more striking is the much freer use of 7ths and 9ths in the accompaniment of *NAM 51*. In *West End Blues* such dissonances tend to arise more commonly through the clashes between solo lines and harmony, rather than in the accompaniment itself.

Further dissonance arises from the use of the blues scale, which contains all three blue notes of the key (indicated by asterisks in the example *right*) and the minor pentatonic scale, which is the same as the blues scale except that it has no flat fifth. These scales are freely used in the vocal and lead guitar parts, while the rhythm guitar and piano stick mainly to the major-key blues chords. Notice that both Howlin' Wolf and the lead guitar also freely mix major 3rds with their blue-note equivalents (eg B♭ and B♮ in bar 6).

Most of the vocal melody is based on the figure heard at the start – essentially a falling triad of G minor (D–B♭–G). In classic blues fashion this isn't transposed when the chord changes. So in bar 6 a similar G-minor figure is heard over a chord of C. Compare this with bar 11 of *NAM 48*, in which Armstrong similarly stays on a tonic minor chord of E♭ minor while the harmony moves to chord IV (A♭ major). Notice how Burnett's vocal line transcends the four-bar units of blues harmony – the first phrase is five bars long, and is followed by three two-bar phrases, plus a rest to complete the 12-bar period. The numerous small differences in the melody line of each verse are a clear indication that it is essentially improvised around a basic composed structure.

The tonal complexity of the melodic parts is underpinned by a simple bass part confined to the root of each chord. In the first verse

Shuffle rhythm

the accompaniment is based on a simple shuffle rhythm (see *left*). The alternation of 5ths and 6ths (and later 7ths) in the rhythm guitar part is a fingerprint of rhythm and blues. Drums also play a shuffle pattern, with accents on beats two and four – these heavy backbeats are another characteristic of rhythm and blues.

In verse 1 the lead guitar leaves a space of three bars for the initial vocal entry, and then improvises short licks in counterpoint with Howlin' Wolf. This is a relatively independent part, unlike the mutual dialogue between voice and clarinet in the third chorus of *West End Blues*. The piano starts with the shuffle pattern, but soon breaks out into passages of continuous triplets, based around the chord patterns.

The accompaniment in verses 2 and 3 offers contrast by starting with isolated chords ('stop time'). The continuous triplets in the fourth bar herald a busier texture in the rest of the chorus, with some high lead-guitar figuration from bar 19 onwards, and with cross-rhythms in bar 31. Notice how one of the band occasionally joins in with the vocal line at the lower octave – another indication of the essentially improvised nature of the recording.

The fourth chorus features a lead guitar solo, in which the typical heavy reverberation of the time is particularly evident. The diagonal lines between notes indicate the use of portamento (sliding between pitches). The band keep in the background for most of this chorus, Howlin' Wolf adds some simple vocalising in the first few bars, then switches to harmonica (mouth organ) for the rest of the chorus.

After the repeat of verses 2 and 3 the coda features the same descending blues scale from the lead guitar that was heard at the end of the instrumental, followed by a play-out based on the vocal motif from bar 7, accompanied by a short guitar riff.

Private study

1. Why could this be described as a strophic song?
2. In what ways is the rhythm-and-blues style of *NAM 51* different from the slow blues style of *NAM 48*?
3. Write out a blues scale in (i) C, and (ii) D.
4. Does the lead guitarist ever develop material from the vocal line, or are the two parts complementary merely because they both make use of the blues scale?

Sample questions

In the exam there will be a total of three questions on these two works, from which you must choose to answer **two**.

(a) Why is *West Side Blues* regarded as one of the first great jazz recordings?

(b) Explain what is meant by rhythm and blues, and outline the features of *NAM 51* that are typical of this style.

(c) Compare the approach to blues improvisation in *NAM 48* with the approach to blues improvisation seen in *NAM 51*.

Warning. Photocopying any part of this book without permission is illegal.

Continuity and change in blues and in rhythm and blues

> Topic for examination in 2004 and 2005

You do not need to study this topic unless *Popular music and jazz* is the Area of Study that you undertook for AS Music and which you are now extending for A2.

Before starting work on this topic you need a thorough understanding of the material on *Popular music and jazz* in the AS Guide (pages 120–132). Remember that for A2 the topic draws on works from across the **entire** Area of Study, not just those in one of the two lists, A or B.

The Blues

The blues emerged in the deep south of the USA in the early years of the 20th century. Its roots, though, stretch back much earlier to a long period in which music brought to America by slaves from west Africa merged with the traditions, particularly those of British folk music, that had arrived with the European settlers. The interaction was complex and documentation is scanty, for such music was not recorded or notated, and was rarely written about before the 20th century. It is wise to avoid simplistic descriptions about African rhythms and modes being combined with European instrumentation and harmony. For example, the characteristic blue notes of the blues mode (flat third, fifth and seventh) are found in the British folk music tradition as well as the west African. The folk song collector Cecil Sharp noticed that English folk-singers often sang the major 3rd 'so flat that it is hardly to be distinguished from the minor 3rd', and Percy Grainger commented on their use of an unstable 3rd and flat 7th. The almost blues-like ending of the English folksong *Dives and Lazarus* (see *right*) illustrates both these inflexions as well as a surprisingly syncopated ending.

A complete verse of this folksong, collected by Cecil Sharp in 1911, can be found in *Aural Matters* (Bowman and Terry), where it is recorded on track 67.

We tend to think of syncopated rhythm as a feature of much African music (which it undoubtedly is) but few of the complexities of African rhythm survived long in America – they tended to become absorbed by the metrical structure of western music. Thus additive rhythms such as the characteristic 5+7 and 7+5 divisions of a west-African 12-note pulse tended to settle into three groups of four (swing rhythm, in fact), and syncopation tended to become limited to mainly simple patterns, most of which were also common to the jigs and reels of country fiddle music, and later to ragtime.

The lyrics of a classic blues are based on a couplet in which the first line is repeated, the resultant AAB pattern fitting neatly over the 12-bar blues structure of three four-bar units. At first sight this seems quite unlike the various two-, four- and eight-line patterns of European song. However long before the blues emerged it is possible to see two- and four-line verse patterns being modified into AAB form in British folk music that found its way to America. The first of the two examples *right* shows the form of a well-known folksong as printed in Britain in 1611. The second example shows how it had evolved in the USA by the 1880s, with a three-part structure and a very blues-like repetition of its first line. The American version also includes a much abbreviated refrain ('uh-hmm, uh-hmm') sung after the first and third lines, sounding remarkably like the type of call-and-response pattern we associate with African music.

The Frogge he would a-wooing ride,
Humble dum, humble, dum,
Sword and a buckler by his side,
Tweedle, tweedle, twino.

Frog went a courtin' and he did ride,
Frog went a-courtin' and he did ride,
A sword and a pistol by his side.

Origins of the Popular Style: The Antecedents of Twentieth-Century Popular Music by Peter van der Merwe. *Clarendon Press (Oxford University Press)* 1989. ISBN: 0-19-816305-3 (paperback, 1992).

The interaction, in the southern states of America, between styles of music that originated in west Africa and Britain is of enormous importance because, through the blues, rhythm and blues, rock 'n' roll, and rock itself, it has been the source of constant renewal in many types of popular music and jazz during the last century. But it is a subject of great complexity that has occupied many scholars for many years. Perhaps the simplest explanation, offered by Dr Peter van der Merwe in *Origins of the Popular Style*, is as follows:

> The transformation of African idioms into the blues was very much a matter of *limitation*. The raw materials of the blues already existed in Africa, but mixed with an enormous wealth of other material. Gradually and unconsciously this other material was winnowed away, and what was left was the blues. Modes were simplified until they were stripped down to the bare tonic triad, a process that can be followed in detail in the case of British-derived tunes ... The wealth of African cadences was almost restricted to the characteristic dropping third. ... One can only guess what forces lay behind this tendency; but it seems reasonable to suppose that one of them was the catalytic influence of British folk styles.

It is thought that the direct antecedent of the blues is the 'holler' (sometimes known as 'field blues') sung by black farmworkers toiling on the land. Little is known about these, although it is reported that phrases were often echoed back in call-and-response patterns either vocally by other workers or by an instrument. The following example of a *Cornfield Holler* shows the free rhythm and plaintive vocalisation whose roots can be traced back to the Afro-Arab styles of west African vocal music. It also shows the same inflections of the scale that we associate with blue notes – flat third, fifth and seventh – as well as the reduction to what western ears would recognise as just one chord (C minor) and an emphasis on descending minor 3rds:

The process identified as limitation by van der Merwe is even more evident in Joe Turner (see *below*). Dating from the 1890s, if not earlier, it is almost certainly the first blues still known today, and was cited as such by many of the early blues singers. It was sung fast and, if harmonised, could be done so with just a chord of C major. Even this early, many later blues features are evident, including:

✦ a 12-bar structure with the first line of text repeated
✦ syncopation (but now expressed within a western 4/4 metre)
✦ blue 3rds (here notated as D♯) contrasting with major 3rds (E)
✦ cadential patterns based on falling thirds.

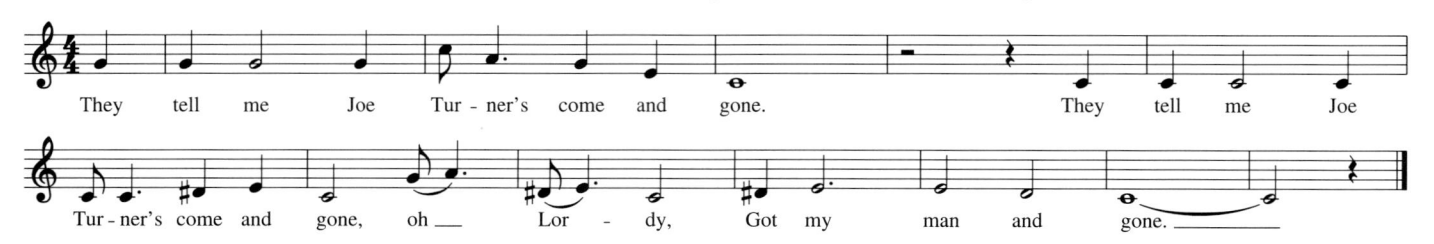

It was not until the 1920s that the blues became widely known, both through its adoption by jazz bands in works such as *West End Blues* and through some of the first recordings of blues singers such as Ma Rainey and Bessie Smith. The style of these songs is known as the classic blues, and it was at this time that the 12-bar chordal pattern became established. In its simplest form this is:

$$\text{I}-\text{I}-\text{I}-\text{I} \quad \text{IV}-\text{IV}-\text{I}-\text{I} \quad \text{V}-\text{V}-\text{I}-\text{I}$$

although a very common variant of the last strain is V – IV – I – I and many other permutations are possible. Its most distinctive features are:

- the use of IV (not V) as the primary move away from the tonic
- the absence of anything resembling an imperfect cadence
- the avoidance of the classical IV – V – I progression
- the use of a three-part, 12-bar structure rather than the balanced two- and four-part structures typical of European music.

The last of these features, far from resulting in a lop-sided form, sounds perfectly satisfying given this particular harmonic scheme, and has resulted in the blues' success over a long period in forming the basis of many different types of popular music and jazz.

We have commented in detail in the AS Guide on the influence of the blues in individual pieces, so here we will just summarise the main points about the most clearly blues-based works.

West End Blues

NAM 48 — CD4 Track 7
Louis Armstrong and his Hot Five

This is essentially an instrumental improvisation on the classic blues style. It uses five choruses of a standard 12-bar blues in E♭. The underlying harmony is mainly triadic, with occasional use of 7ths, but the improvised parts add a rich vocabulary of extra dissonance, including blue notes and 9ths (eg trumpet B♭ above A♭ major harmony in bar 11). Chord substitutions are already evident in this early work (eg ♭IV in bar 24). The salon music style of the piano chorus (bars 43–54) shows considerable adaptation of the blues chordal sequence. The rhythmic freedom of Armstrong's improvised lines reflects the free rhythm of blues singing.

Black and Tan Fantasy

NAM 49 — CD4 Track 8
Duke Ellington and his orchestra

This is based on six choruses of a 12-bar blues. The first is in the minor mode, the mainly undecorated harmonies emphasising the rough 'jungle' style. It is followed by a 16-bar sax solo that modulates to the tonic major and the blues pattern then resumes in bar 29. As in *NAM 48*, the underlying harmonies are mainly triadic, with occasional 7ths, the interest arising from the interaction of improvised lines against these chords. Chord substitutions become increasingly adventurous, starting with ii^7 (Cm^7) instead of V in the ninth bar of the sequence (bars 37 and 49) and including diminished sevenths (eg bar 58) and a cycle of 5ths (bar 59^3– 64). Notice that both the latter again occur during a piano chorus, where it is clearly easier for a single instrument to introduce such changes.

I'm Leaving You

NAM 51 — CD4 Track 10
Howlin' Wolf

See the section starting on page 152 for a discussion of how earlier blues styles were transformed into the urban blues, and then into rhythm and blues. This section also deals with the use of a 12-bar blues structure in the song and its use of the blues mode. Notice how, while the basic chord pattern of the 12-bar blues remains unchanged, by this time the majority of its chords are embellished with 7ths and 9ths.

Honey don't

NAM 52 — CD4 Track 11
Carl Perkins

The blues format is given several unusual adaptations in this song. Bars 6–29 contain two 12-bar blues sequences, but these 24 bars are divided into an eight-bar verse and 16-bar refrain, giving the song a more European feel than the more usual 12-bar structures of the blues:

	Verse							Refrain			
Bars 6–17:	E	E	C	C	E	E	C	C	B^7	B^7	E	E
Bars 18–29:| E	E	E	E	A	A	E	E	B^7	B^7	E	E
								Refrain			

The first of these patterns substitutes chord ♭VI (C major in the key of E major) for chord IV – giving the song more of a country-music feel, although this harmony actually supports the conventional blue third (G♮) of the key.

The guitar solo starting in bar 30 uses a clever contraction of the above chord scheme, cutting the first blues pattern down to eight bars and substituting B^7 for C in the eighth bar (bar 37) in order to then move straight into the second pattern:

Bars 30–37:   E   E   C   C   E   E   C   B^7
Bars 38–49:   E   E   E   E   A   A   E   E   B^7 B^7 E   E

A different type of contraction occurs in the second guitar break (bars 74–83), which reduces the first blues pattern to ten bars by omitting the eighth and tenth bars of the chord sequence.

The basic harmonic vocabulary of this song is typical of early rock 'n' roll, with a concentration on root-position triads (plus V7) in the chordal parts, and with the firm walking bass outlining these triads and adding to them 7ths and passing 6ths.

Private study

We have discussed only those works that are based directly on blues structures, but it is hard to escape the influence of the blues in almost any of the works in this area of study – the free rhythm of vocal solos, the colour given by blue notes in many types of music, and the tendency of much pop and jazz to avoid the tonic–dominant polarisation of classical music in preference for using the subdominant as a secondary tonal centre. These are all features which derive from the blues and ultimately from the folk music styles that preceded it. Identify the extent to which blues-related features appear in different styles of pop and jazz – whether in other items in the *New Anthology*, or in the music you listen to or compose.

Many ideas for practical work on the blues can be found in *Jazz Workshop: The Blues*, by Graham Collier. Published by Universal Edition (1988). ISBN: 900938-61-7.

Sample questions

In the exam there will be two questions on this topic, from which you must choose to answer **one**.

(a) Compare and contrast the influence of the blues in *NAM 49* with the influence of the blues in *NAM 52*.

(b) Discuss what is meant by blues harmony, using examples from at least three of the works you have studied.

(c) Explain why the blues has had such a long-lasting influence on the course of 20th-century popular music and jazz.

World music

> For examination in summer 2002 and 2003

The first part of this chapter deals with the two special focus works and topic set for examination in summer 2002 and 2003. If you are taking the exam in summer 2004 or 2005 turn to page 162.

Yellow Bird

> **Special Focus Work 1 for 2002 and 2003**
> *NAM 60* CD4 Track 18
> Red Stripe Ebony Steelband

Before starting on this section you should work through (or revise) the information about the context and structure of this music given on pages 134–135 of the AS Guide. Make sure that you understand all of the terminology used in that section.

The word calypso is thought to derive from the west African word *Kaiso* or *Kaito*, meaning 'Bravo!' – a cry of encouragement. To this day, when a good calypso is sung in Trinidad it is greeted by a shout of *Kaiso!* from the audience. The invention of new and topical words to traditional tunes is an important aspect of calypso and in the 19th-century this song form was used to spread news and political comment around the island of Trinidad. Calypsos can be slow and in the minor key, but the best-known types are in a major key, with triadic melodies that can be simply harmonised with the common chords I, IV and V. They are usually in a fast duple rhythm (*Yellow Bird* is effectively in 2/2 time, despite the 4/4 time signature given in *NAM 60*). The rhythm is frequently syncopated, a particular feature being the use of the pattern ♪♩♪, which is a characteristic of the Afro-Brazilian dance, the samba. All of these features can be seen in the following extract from a Trinidadian calypso, as well as in *NAM 60* itself:

A World Wide Web search on the word *Kaiso* will find much information about calypso, and reveal that it is still very much a living tradition.

[Musical notation: "Mur-der in the mar-ket, mur-der! Mur-der in the mar-ket, mur-der! Mur-der in the mar-ket, mur-der! Bet-sy Thom-as she kill Payne stone dead!"]

The version of *Yellow Bird* in the *New Anthology* is an instrumental arrangement for steel pans. As explained in the AS Guide, steel bands are a more recent Trinidadian tradition, although their origin can be traced back to the tamboo-bamboo bands of the late 19th century. Modern steel bands tend to play a wide repertoire of music, of which calypso is only a small, but important part.

The song and its arrangement are very straightforward, the piece making its impact with a tuneful melody (in just the right range to be sung or hummed) and the engaging tremolo tone of the long notes being rolled on the pans. European influence is evident in the harmonisation and phrase lengths. Essentially, the whole song is harmonised with the three primary chords of G major (I, IV and V) decorated by occasional 7ths and chromatic notes. There is no modulation (the C♯ in bars 1 and 5 is purely chromatic), although the use of F♮ (eg in bar 8) in the progression G^7–C enlivens the harmony with a brief transition to C major. The opening section (A) is a very regular 16 bars in length, while the B section in bars 17–25 has an extra bar of V^7 harmony (bar 24) to break-up the

> **Warning.** Photocopying any part of this book without permission is illegal.

periodic phrasing. Overall the form is AABAAB – notice the tiny descant that rises above the melody in bars 28–29 and 32–33, giving this repeat some variety.

Each part has its own clearly-defined function, which is maintained throughout the arrangement. The basses play chordal notes in a tango rhythm which never varies. The four-pan cello is a simple harmony part that moves in semibreves and minims. The double tenor plays a counter-rhythm in the first seven bars of the A sections, but semibreves elsewhere, and actual melody is invariably assigned to the upper instruments, sometimes in 3rds. A part for kit drums (not printed in *NAM 60*) underpins the homophonic texture of the entire piece.

> **Special Focus Work 2 for 2002 and 2003**
> *NAM 63*   CD4 Track 21
> Familia Valera Miranda

Se quema la chumbambá

At the time of going to press, Edexcel has announced that this work will be set as **an additional 'special focus' work** for World Music in 2002 and 2003 (this information was not included in the original exam specification). As always, be sure to ask your teacher to check the latest requirements issued by Edexcel. Information about *Se quema la chumbambá* can be found in the AS Guide.

Private study

1. What is similar about the harmonies of *NAM 60* and *NAM 63*?

2. To what extent does the music of the Carribean represent a fusion of musical cultures? Consider both *Yellow Bird* and *Se quema la chumbambá* in your answer.

3. Describe how syncopation is used in totally different ways in *NAM 60* and *NAM 63*.

Sample questions

In the exam there will be a total of three questions on these two works, from which you must choose to answer **two**.

(a) Why do you think *NAM 60* appeals to western audiences who have little or no experience of world music?

(b) Discuss the instrumentation of *NAM 60*, giving details of both the instruments themselves and the arrangement of *Yellow Bird*.

(c) Both *NAM 60* and *NAM 63* originate from Carribean islands. Outline their similarities and their differences.

Continuity and change in South American and European influences

> **Topic for examination in 2002 and 2003**
> You are advised to check the latest Edexcel specification to ensure that the requirements for this topic have not changed.

You do not need to study this topic unless *World music* is the Area of Study that you undertook for AS Music and which you are now extending for A2.

Before starting work on this topic you need a thorough understanding of the material on *World music* in the AS Guide (pages 133–143). Remember that for A2 the topic draws on works from across the **entire** Area of Study, not just those in one of the two lists, A or B.

European influence is most evident in the tonal structures of this work. The entire piece is in G major, defined by the use of frequent perfect cadences (D^7–G). Both the chromatic lower auxiliary note (C♯) and the chromatic passing note (F♮) are common features of European harmony, as is the use of melodic sequence (eg in bars 9–10). The structure is based on two main sections which are repeated in the order AABAAB. The chorus, or A section, consists of a 16-bar period constructed from four-bar phrases (each defined by a longer note in the melody at the start of its fourth bar). The verse, or B section, is essentially an eight-bar phrase that has been extended by one bar. This symmetry of structure is another clear European influence, as is the homophonic texture with its clear separation of melody, harmony, bass and rhythm parts.

The melody, which may originally have come from the nearby republic of Haiti rather than Trinidad itself, features the syncopated rhythm of the samba (♪♩ ♪). This is a dance of Afro-Brazilian origin and is thus clearly a South-American influence. The pattern played by the basses throughout the piece (♩. ♪ ♩ ♩) is the rhythm of the habanera, a dance from the Carribean island of Cuba and named after its capital city, Havana. It was popular throughout Spain and South America in the 19th-century. The instrumentation for steel pans gives the arrangement its Trinidadian colour, even though the band on CD4 are actually based in London's Notting Hill.

The music of Cuba developed from a combination of African and Spanish influences. In *NAM 63* the African influences are evident in the call-and-response patterns between solo and chorus, in the percussion instruments (maracas, bongo and claves are typical of South-American music, but ultimately hail from Africa) and in the persistent syncopation of alternate bars. The Spanish influence is particularly evident in the essentially strophic nature of the song, the use of the minor (and mainly harmonic minor) scale and the alternation of tonic and dominant-based harmonies.

The similarity in style between the newly-composed jig and the traditional reel provides a good example of the importance of continuity in the Celtic folk tradition. Details of both these works can be be found in the section starting on page 162.

Private study

Explain how traditional dance music is an important influence in *NAM 60*, *NAM 61* and *NAM 63*.

Sample questions

In the exam there will be two questions on this topic, from which you must choose to answer **one**.

(a) Compare and contrast the influence of European music on *NAM 60* with the influence of European music on *NAM 63*.

(b) Show how the music of the Caribbean combines both European and South American influences, drawing on examples from both *Yellow Bird* and *Se quema la chumbambá*.

(c) Which elements of *Yellow Bird* show European influence, and which do not?

Yellow Bird

NAM 60 — CD4 Track 18
Red Stripe Ebony Steelband

One of the most well-known examples of a habanera in western art music occurs in Bizet's opera *Carmen*.

Se quema la chumbambá

NAM 63 — CD4 Track 21
Familia Valera Miranda

Tom McElvogue's (jig) and New Irish Barndance (reel)

Warning. Photocopying any part of this book without permission is illegal.

> **For examination in summer 2004 and 2005**

World music

This part of this chapter deals with the two special focus works and topic set for examination in summer 2004 and 2005. If you are taking the exam in summer 2002 or 2003 turn to page 159.

Celtic Folk: Tom McElvogue's (jig) and New Irish Barndance (reel)

> **Special Focus Work 1 for 2004 and 2005**
> NAM 61   CD4 Track 19
> Niall Keegan (Irish flute)

Before starting on this section you should work through (or revise) the information about the context and structure of this music given on pages 136–137 of the AS Guide. Make sure that you understand all of the terminology used in that section.

Tom McElvogue's

The jig in bars 1–64 was composed by Tom McElvogue, a player of the Irish traditional flute who comes from Newcastle, England. It is in a style known as a double jig. This is the most common type of Irish jig, and is characterised by predominantly quaver movement in 6/8 time (the single jig, in contrast, is built mainly on ♩ ♪ patterns in compound time). In competitive dancing a jig is often played slowly to allow time for the complex footwork of Irish dance, but when played for listening (as on CD4) the tempo is usually fast.

Although *Tom McElvogue's* is a modern composition it uses the traditional form of an Irish double jig, which consists of eight-bar repeated sections in the pattern AABB (bars 1–32). This 32-bar structure is itself repeated in *NAM 61*, making the overall form AABBAABB. The repetitions are invariably decorated in different ways, but you should be able to spot that the A section always starts with a bar containing an upward leap of a 5th from low G to D (bars 1, 9, 33 and 41), while the B section always starts on a high G (bars 17, 25, 49 and 57). However to follow this you need to develop a feel for the eight-bar phrase lengths (or perhaps note on the score the sections shown in the box *left*) since the ear can be deceived by the many repetitions and variations of smaller motivic units that also occur within the jig. For instance, the motif of bar 1 is heard again in bar 3, while the whole of bars 1–2 are given a varied repeat to form bars 5–6 (see *left*). Furthermore, such small-scale internal repetition also binds together the material of the two main sections, so the third and fourth bars of each B section are actually a variation of bars 1–2 of the A section (eg compare bars 19–20 with bars 1–2, as shown *left*).

Form *(NB all repetitions are varied)*		
1–8	A	8 bars
9–16	A	8 bars
17–24	B	8 bars
25–32	B	8 bars
33–40	A	8 bars
41–48	A	8 bars
49–56	B	8 bars
57–65	B	8 bars *(the last note overlaps with the first note of Reel)*

The tonality of the jig is centred on the key of G major – each of its eight phrases ends with a cadential pattern in that key (V–I in the A sections and VII–I in the B sections). Between these cadences the leading note (F♯) is often altered to F♮ just before the cadential progression itself. Such inflection of the leading note is a fingerprint of much Irish music, and here it shows the modern composer associating himself with that tradition. It tends to give the music a modal tinge, but the cadences clearly indicate that this is not modal music. However, the flattened supertonic (A♭) that slips in as a passing note in bar 57 is neither modal nor a feature of traditional Irish music. This brief chromatic passage is a reminder that Niall Keegan is famed for the way in which he blends modern, often jazz-based, flute playing with traditional Irish styles.

The recording on CD4 comes from a 4-CD set called *From a Distant Shore* produced by Nimbus (NI 1752) which offers 74 pieces of Celtic folk music of different kinds for a current price of £19.99. Also of interest may be Garry Shannon, another flautist working in a modern idiom within the Irish tradition. His website at http://www.irish-flute.com/ provides more information and currently includes a fascinating and freely downloadable Real Audio file of his *Bach-Ward Jig* which shows how a Bach-like gigue might be interpreted in terms of traditional Irish flute playing.

The final note of the jig is also the first note of this traditional reel – a dance of Scottish origin that found its way to Ireland in the 17th century and is now one of the most popular Irish folk dances. It is characterised by accents on the first and third beats of 4/4 time, which are here represented by the dotted crotchets in the first bar of the melody. The most common structure is the same AABB form that we saw in the jig. Bars 65–68 form the A section (repeated in bars 69–72) while bars 73–76 forms the B section (repeated in bars 77–80). This entire AABB structure is then itself repeated, always with evermore elaborate decoration, in bars 81–96. As in the jig, there are many internal repetitions of motifs within these sections. (compare bar 67 with bar 65, shown *right*). Another similarity with the jig is a blurring of the distinction between the A and B sections caused by the use of common material. The first bar of B enshrines the figure from the first bar of A (see *right*) – the similarity is even more marked in bar 77, which begins on a low G. The easiest way to distinguish the two main melodies is to spot that melody A always continues with an alternation of the notes B and C, while melody B continues with an upward scale that starts on a low D.

A similar structure of repeated and decorated four-bar sections underpins the second half of the reel, but as the speed increases, and the elaboration and recycling of similar ideas (now often based on the octave G–G) becomes more intense, the dance structure is overtaken by a whirl of virtuoso ornamentation.

The key of the reel is G major, the same as that of the jig, and most of its motifs are based on chords I, IV and V of that key. Notice how every alternate bar begins on G in the first half of the reel, and in the second half every single bar (except bar 117), starts on this pitch, which acts almost like a pedal note, tying the tonality to G major. Again, there are indications of Keegan's modern approach to traditional music in the occasional chromatic decoration (eg bars 66, 75, 114 and 124–125).

Ornamentation is a key element in Irish traditional music. The amount and type distinguishes different regional styles of playing, and the spontaneity and dexterity of improvised decoration is a feature highly regarded by audiences. Notice that audible audience participation on CD4 effectively starts as a reaction of approval to the trills in bar 81. As stated at the start of *NAM 61*, there are many decorations in addition to those notated, but the main types heard in this performance include:

- the slide (bar 9)
- the mordent (bar 34)
- the acciaccatura (bar 60)
- the trill (bar 81)
- the treble (last three notes of bar 66)

The first four of these are also found in much western art music, but the fifth is one of the many types of ornament especially characteristic of Celtic folk music and consists of dividing a note into three repetitions of the same pitch. In addition to such specific ornaments, the constant decoration and variation of motifs is itself a type of ornamentation – for example, compare bar 65 with its more ornamented forms in bars 67, 71, 83, 85 and 87.

New Irish Barndance

Ornamentation

The performance on CD4 was recorded in front of a live audience at the Triskell Arts Centre in Cork, in February 1994. Notice how the flautist's foot-tapping is as much an expected part of the performance as the cries of encouragement from the audience.

Warning. Photocopying any part of this book without permission is illegal.

? Private study

1. Explain to an ordinary listener without specialist knowledge how to recognise the distinctive sound of the Irish traditional flute and its music.

2. Outline the differences and similarities between a jig and a reel.

3. In what way is the purpose of the score of *NAM 61* significantly different from the purpose of notation in western art music?

Rãg Bhairav

> **Special Focus Work 2 for 2004 and 2005**
>
> *NAM 58*   CD4 Track 16
> Ram Narayan (sarangi)
> Charanjit Lal Biyavat (tabla)

At the time of going to press, Edexcel has announced that this work will be set as **an additional 'special focus' work** for World Music in 2004 and 2005 (this information was not included in the original exam specification). As always, be sure to ask your teacher to check the latest requirements issued by Edexcel.

Before starting on this section you should work through (or revise) the information about the context and structure of this music given on pages 140–141 of the AS Guide. Make sure that you understand all of the terminology used in that section.

> All Indian words are transliterations and you may find alternative spellings in different books.

The classical music of northern India was originally perceived as an art form for the educated. Traditional performances were, and still are, similar to those of western chamber music, involving a small and knowledgeable audience in close proximity to the performers. In Indian music both audience and performers sit on the floor; most listeners understand the parameters set by the *rãg* and the *tãl*, and place great store in the way these are used in the improvisation. Each *rãg* is intended to express a particular mood and many are associated with set times of the day or seasons – *Rãg Bhairav* is intended for performance at dawn. These days, though, you could well hear *Rãg Bhairav* being sung or played in a film or being used as the basis for a popular Indian song.

The three main elements of *NAM 58*, explained in the AS Guide, are the *rãg*, the *tãl* and the drone (played by the *tampura*). The pitches used in the improvisation are known as the *thãt* – a term broadly equivalent to a scale or mode in western music. They are given at the head of the music, on the stave which shows the tuning of the sympathetic strings of the *sarangi*. The *rãg* itself is a melodic sequence using these pitches in a set order, which the musician constantly embellishes with microtonal inflections and portamenti. A good way to start exploring how this is done is to begin with the melodic figure at the start of stave 19. First see how many times you can spot this in different transformations in the rest of the piece (some clear examples are at the starts of staves 21, 23, 29, 31 and 33, but there are many more). Then listen to the first part of the piece, where the rhythm is more free and improvisatory, and see if you can spot how it was used there.

When following the score, remember that the flats at the start of each stave (A♭ and D♭) are not a key signature in the western sense but, like a key signature, they are there to remind you that these two pitches are flattened in this particular *thãt*.

Rāg Bhairav starts with a slow and improvisatory section known as the *ālāp*, to set the mood. After this there is a gradual build-up of intensity through the rest of the work. The music starts to develop a sense of pulse and becomes melodically denser in the central section (the *jhor*) after which the tabla enters, playing the *tāl*, for the concluding section (the *jhala*), which is the point at which the structured composition begins. Notice how the *sarangi* and the *tabla* come together on the first beat of the *tāl*, and how the pace builds up not only through an accelerating pulse but also through the use of shorter note-lengths in this final section. *NAM 58* is a complete piece, but very much a miniature one. In live performance each section would be considerably longer.

Private study

1. (i) What is a *tampura*?
   (ii) What is the role of the *tampura* in *NAM 58*?

2. What are the three main sections of the *rāg* called and what are the characteristics of each?

3. In what ways does this performance of *Rāg Bhairav* succeed in capturing the mood of a piece to be played at dawn?

Sample questions

In the exam there will be a total of three questions on these two works, from which you must choose to answer **two**.

(a) To what extent is it true to say that *NAM 61* makes its impact from the constant decoration and variation of short motifs rather than from any variation in mood, key or texture?

(b) Outline the characteristics of the Irish traditional flute and its music, referring to specific passages in *NAM 61*.

(c) Writing for an interested listener with no specialist knowlege of Indian music, explain the construction and main points of interest in *Rāg Bhairav*.

Continuity and change in instrumentation and vocal resources

You do not need to study this topic unless *World music* is the Area of Study that you undertook for AS Music and which you are now extending for A2.

Before starting work on this topic you need a thorough understanding of the material on *World music* in the AS Guide (pages 133–143). Remember that for A2 the topic draws on works from across the **entire** Area of Study, not just those in one of the two lists, A or B.

This is essentially a solo and often virtuoso work for the *sarangi*, a bowed string instrument with three main strings and a number of sympathetic strings tuned to the notes of the *rāg*. The traditional accompaniment of *tampura* drone and *tabla* rhythm is subservient to this solo, although the latter becomes increasingly important towards the end of the work. While the *tabla* part is governed by

Topic for examination in 2004 and 2005

At the time of going to press Edexcel had just announced a change in the wording of this topic, to that given here. You are advised to check the latest details with Edexcel to ensure that you are following the correct requirements for this topic.

Rāg Bhairav

NAM 58   CD4 Track 16
Ram Narayan (sarangi)
Charanjit Lal Biyavat (tabla)

the rhythmic cycle of the *tāl*, it is important to realise that this is nothing like the metrical drum parts found in most western music. Soloist and *tabla* come together on the *sam* (the first beat of the *tāl*, marked x in the score) but in between there is considerable scope for freedom between these two parts, a sense of firm pulse only emerging towards the end of the work.

Baris Melampahan

NAM 59   CD4 Track 17
Gong Kebyar de Sebatu

While *NAM 58* is mainly a solo work, *NAM 59* could hardly be more different. Not only is it an ensemble piece, but it is one in which the instrument itself is the ensemble. The instruments of a gamelan are made, tuned and kept together and its players regard themselves as performers of one common instrument. Once again, this is quite unlike western instrumental traditions in which individual players own their own instruments and bring them together for ensemble playing. This notion of sharing also extends to the music itself, the basis of which is the heterophonic performance of a common 'nuclear' melody.

Like several other pieces in this area of study, the role of each part is predetermined and largely unchanging. *Balungan* instruments play the main theme, the *Panususan* instruments simultaneously decorate it, gongs divide the sections, and drums and cymbals add contrast. In this piece the rhythmic cycle of the *gongan* is more obvious to western ears than the *tintal* cycle in *NAM 58* since the four-beat groups in the *ketag* tend to dominate the texture and give a western sense of pulse to the music.

Yellow Bird

NAM 60   CD4 Track 18
Red Stripe Ebony Steelband

The history and construction of the steel pan, and the functions of different sizes of pan, are outlined in the AS Guide. There are some parallels between the steelband and the gamelan, although no direct influences. Both are based on metallic sounds, both are normally made as a matching set of instruments and owned communally rather than by individual musicians, and for both the normal style of instrumentation is to assign a largely unchanging role to each instrument in the ensemble.

In *Yellow Bird* this last point can be seen in the clearly-defined function asssigned to each part and maintained throughout the arrangement. The basses play chordal notes in a tango (or habanera) rhythm which never varies. The four-pan cello is a simple harmony part that moves in semibreves and minims. The double tenor plays a counter-rhythm in the first seven bars (and again starting at bar 26) but semibreves elsewhere, and actual melody is invariably assigned to the upper instruments, sometimes in thirds. A part for kit drums (not printed in *NAM 60*) underpins the homophonic texture of the entire piece.

Tom McElvogue's (jig) and New Irish Barndance (reel)

NAM 61   CD4 Track 19
Niall Keegan (Irish flute)

Like *NAM 58* this work uses traditional forms for a virtuoso display of solo improvisation. There are similarities, too, in the way it is based on a limited set of melodic ideas which are subject to ever more elaborate variation, and in its use of accelerando to generate excitement towards the end of the piece. It is entirely monophonic music with no contrast in texture and the dance rhythms allow for only the briefest rests, demanding considerable stamina from the flautist in breath control. While there are no supporting players, as there are in *NAM 58*, notice how the musical style of this dance

Warning. Photocopying any part of this book without permission is illegal.

music demands a foot-tapped beat. Whereas a live performance of *Rag Bhairav* would traditionally be greeted by its audience with discreet nods and comments of approval (but not conventionally with applause), the performance of Irish traditional music such as this invites increasingly vocal audience participation as the playing becomes more exciting, culminating in spontaneous applause. In both pieces it is the skill of the instrumentalist in realising and elaborating a limited amount of material within the conventions of the style that is the focus of interest. Some notes on the distinctive features of the Irish traditional flute are included in the AS Guide.

Although the two pieces in *NAM 61* are a reel and a jig, the music is intended for listening, not dancing. Irish traditional dancers would demand a slower speed and constant tempo, with far less virtuoso decoration. Also the music would more likely be played not by a solo instrument but by a small ensemble, such as a *céilí* band, that might typically include fiddle, flute, button accordion, piano, double bass and percussion.

Unlike the stylised social dance music of *NAM 61*, the *agbekor* is a ritual war dance, originally performed before going into battle. The music of *NAM 62* is functional – it is the actual dance music, rather than the type of virtuoso improvisation around dance styles that we saw in the Irish flute pieces – and it is frequently performed as an accompaniment for ceremonial dance at cultural presentations.

Agbekor dance

NAM 62   CD4 Track 20
Mustapha Tettey Addy

Like *NAM 59* and *NAM 60*, the music is scored for an ensemble of mainly similar instruments. Those used here are all percussive: the *atsimevu* (or master drum), the *sogo* (a smaller drum) and the *gangkogui* (a double bell that can produce two distinct pitches). Details of these instruments are given in the AS Guide. Also like *NAM 59* and *NAM 60*, each of the parts has a fixed and unchanging role to play within the instrumentation.

The *gangkogui* acts as a time-keeper and reference point for the other parts by playing an ostinato – the one used here is a common rhythmic pattern in African drumming. The master drummer directs the performance, communicating cues to other players by striking the side of the drum and sometimes incorporating 'talking drum' effects, such as statements of praise to the tribal leader. The *sogo* plays its own rhythm against the basic pattern, and sometimes adds variations and improvisations.

The complexity (at least to western ears) of the polyrhythms and cross-rhythms seems in stark contrast to the homophony of *Yellow Bird*, or even the heterophony of *Baris Melampahan*, and yet the essentially co-operative nature of ensemble playing is as evident in the sophisticated interactions between the performers here as in works which have a much simpler metrical structure.

Although this is the only work in the area of study for a mixed ensemble of voices and instruments, it reveals the same style of instrumentation that we have seen in all of the other ensemble works. Each part has a fixed role and while that may be elaborated upon by improvisation (especially in the cuatro part), each essentially remains unchanged in function throughout the work. The harmonic foundation is supplied by the *cuatro* and double bass,

Se quema la chumbambá

NAM 63   CD4 Track 21
Familia Valera Miranda

Warning. Photocopying any part of this book without permission is illegal.

outlining alternate tonic and dominant-related chords throughout the piece. Percussive support is provided by the Latin-American bongo, claves and maracas, and within this group, each instrument again has its specific function. The claves provide the syncopated *son clave*, the most famous of the salsa rhythms. The maracas, in contrast, play simple on-the-beat rhythms against this. The bongos play mainly quaver patterns (although with much improvisation later) that emphasise the fourth beat. Finally, the voices are divided into *Prégon* (lead singer) and *Coro* (chorus) for the improvised call-and-response patterns.

Private study

The notion of 'continuity and change' may seem a little strange in the context of six pieces from such independent traditions as those represented by the works in this area of study. And yet there are common approaches, even if not direct links, in their use of voices and instruments. Make a list of all the points of similarity you have spotted, and then contrast this with a list of clear differences.

Sample questions

In the exam there will be two questions on this topic, from which you must choose to answer **one**.

(a) Compare and contrast the approach to improvisation on a solo instrument in *NAM 58* and *NAM 61*.

(b) What are the similarities and differences between the ensemble scoring of *NAM 59* and *NAM 60*?

(c) Contrast the use of instruments in *NAM 62* with the use of instruments in *NAM 59*.